James Robinson Newhall

Lin or Jewels of the Third plantation

James Robinson Newhall

Lin or Jewels of the Third plantation

ISBN/EAN: 9783337134464

Printed in Europe, USA, Canada, Australia, Japan

Cover: Foto ©Andreas Hilbeck / pixelio.de

More available books at **www.hansebooks.com**

OR,

JEWELS

OF THE

THIRD PLANTATION.

"I loue of worthies gone to tell ;
their virtues to discuss ;
For they that fought life's battels well,
ensamples are for vs."

BY OBADIAH OLDPATH.

LYNN:
THOMAS HERBERT AND JAMES M. MUNROE.
1862.

PREFACE.

> "The shunned Preface of a Book,
> Contains the Author's special say;
> And wary Readers there should look
> For lights to guide along the way."

A LEADING purpose of this volume is to illustrate, in a somewhat lively way, the character of the People, and the condition of Things, during a most interesting period of our history. Divers remarkable Personages and Occurrences, strangely overlooked by others, receive due attention. And such wayside reflections are interspersed as it is hoped may, at least here and there, prove good seed sown in good ground.

The Actors and Scenes are to a degree local. But we have endeavored to treat them in such a manner that they will, for that reason, be the more acceptable to the general reader.

We are aware that our style will appear rather episodical; and are also aware that it is a dangerous style to venture upon. But the plan seemed to demand that it should be adopted.

Slight circumstances often suggest important schemes. And it is becoming to acknowledge that a casual remark of the Ancient Bookseller of Nassau Street — whose dusty stall and obliging manners so often staid the Author's youthful steps, whose judgment of books was so penetrating that he discerned their value by their binding, whose modesty was so intense that he wrote the first person singular with a little i, and who descended from one of the brightest Jewels of the Third Plantation — proved so influential in inducing the present attempt, that it might, perhaps, be proper even to dedicate the work to him.

For many years of early life the Author procured his daily bread by laboring at the printer's case; and though for a long time other pursuits have engaged his attention, most agreeable recollections of the printing office have been entertained. Having a vacant hour, now and then, he was induced, after about a hundred pages had been set up by a printer, to procure a case of type, a composing-stick, and a few other implements

of the art, and, in a convenient back room, apply his own hand to the work. A famous marble slab, placed on a pine table, admirably filled the great office of "imposing stone." And as fair proofs were taken upon it, by a simple apparatus manufactured by his own ingenious hand, as gladden the weary eyes of many a proof reader in the well-appointed offices of the great cities. And when that consecrated slab shall have ended its usefulness in its present sphere, it will, perhaps, being set on end in a widely different place, continue to be useful, in a sadder way, as a lettered marble, or, indeed, as an imposing stone.

A good portion of the volume was never written; but with memoranda and sketches lying on the "upper case," the Author proceeded to compose types and sentences at the same time. Thus many leisure hours were agreeably occupied. And could he be assured that the Reader would, in the perusal of the volume, find a few of his leisure hours pass as pleasantly, he would certainly be well pleased, though at the same time acknowledging himself not so far etherealized but that a large sale of the book might add somewhat to the satisfaction.

It may be dangerous to make some of these statements, as they involve an admission of responsibility for mechanical arrangement, proof reading, and so on, even to spelling and punctuation. As to spelling, however, it may be remarked that the two great lexicographical lights of the age have so effectually succeeded in unsettling our orthography that it will require more than one generation to regain the uniformity that prevailed thirty years ago.

It is a blessed thing for some authors, that they can charge their blunders upon innocent printers and proof readers. And it may be eminently indiscreet in the present candidate for public favor to voluntarily bar himself from such a subterfuge.

CONTENTS.

PART FIRST.

"Roll back, thou mists of the dark brown years!
Unveil the paths our fathers trod!
We will lean upon their mossy tombs
And recount their noble deeds.
Then shall our souls be nerved
As by the bracing wind of the North!"

INTRODUCTORY REMARKS, ... 9
 Reflections and Reasons, 9 — Descriptive Passages, 12 — Defining the Position of the Third Plantation, and Clearing the Way, 14.

ZACHARIAH HART, ... 19
 His Birth and Early Experiences, 19 — Commencement of the Plantation, with Sketches of divers of the Worthies present, and Notable Occurrences that marked the Great Occasion, 23 — A Plea for Snakes, 31 — Description of the First Habitation, 33 — First Native Callers, 34 — Notices of some of Mr. Hart's worthy Descendants, 38 — Mrs. Hutchinson's Meeting at Lynn, 39 — Governor Vane, 42; his Picturesque Tour, 45 — Interspersed with Notices of Scenes of various complexion, in which Mr. Hart Exercised his peculiar Gifts, Sketches of Natural Scenery, Glances at the Civil Polity, Theological Views, and some of the strange Characteristics and Doings of the Settlers.

OBADIAH TURNER, ... 51
 Something about him and his curious Journal, 51 — Remarks on the Ancient Orthography, 54 and 91 — Old and New Style, 55 — The old Belief in the Corporeal Appearance of the Devil, in Ghosts, &c., 56 — Copious Extracts from the Journal, which embraces the whole period from 1630 to 1681; which extracts embody accounts of numerous Remarkable Occurrences and Discoveries, Tricks and Contrivances of Evil Spirits, and quaint Word-Portraits of Notable Characters, 57 — Indian Land Tenures, and some forgotten Facts

regarding the Indians, 91 — Abel Ballard's singular Experiences at Egg Rock and Nahant, 103 — Tragic Fate of Julia Anderson and her Lover, 109 — With observations on Mr. Turner's meritorious Acts and note-worthy Experiences, and sundry Historic Reminders.

THOMAS NEWHALL, ... 117
Romantic Accounts touching the Newhall Lineage, with Sketches of Saxon and Norman Characteristics, 117 — The Wiltshire Baron, and Arthur and Haroldine, 129 — Mr. Newhall's Experience with Bees, 148 — Extracts from his quaint Memoranda, 152 — His Theory of Compensations, 154 — Diversified by Sketches of his Peculiarities, his Home and Homestead, his Habits and Employments, and an occasional Historical and Philosophical Airing.

OLIVER PURCHIS, ... 157
His efforts as a Legislator, 157 — Stirring Incidents in Colonial History, 159 — Edward Randolph's unbecoming Conduct while on an Excursion to Nahant, 167 — His desperate Assault on Mr. Purchis, in his own house, 172 — Mr. Purchis on Horseback, preceded by a Trumpeter, 175 — His Mysterious Visitor, and the way in which he was saved from Arrest, 177 — With various Anecdotes, Personal Sketches, Speculations, and Deductions.

THOMAS DEXTER, ... 187
His Irascibility of Temper, and some instances of its exhibition, 187 — His great Projects for protecting Lynn Beach, 193 ; improving Egg Rock, 194 ; straightening Saugus River, 195 — Indian Account of the origin of said River, and the early Operations of the Great Sea-serpent, 195 — Mr. Dexter's Purchase of Nahant from Black Will, and what came of it, 197 — His Partnership with Thomas Laighton ; Mr. Laighton's extraordinary Maxim, and the results of an adherence to it, 200 — Their Store and Business, 202 — Mr. Laighton's disagreeable Experience that resulted in the loss of his Scalp, and the comical Expedient to which it led, 204 — With sundry Descriptive and Touching Passages.

PHILIP KERTLAND, ... 217
The first Shoemaker in Lynn, 217 — His disastrous Operation under the Laightonian Maxim, 220 — His Shop, 224 — His efforts to improve the Art, 225 — His Difficulty with a Lady Customer, and what it cost him, 226 — His extraordinary Physical Peculiarity, 226 — With Remarks on Trade, and various other Useful Topics.

PART SECOND.

"In the gray morn and purple eve,
  Spirit of Thought!
O lead me to those dim old rustic shrines
My fathers loved. Recall their lusty forms,
And let me ponder on their worthy acts;
Teach me to emulate their dignity,
And prosecute life's nobler aims!"

INTRODUCTORY REMARKS, ... 229
  Whys and Wherefores, 229.

THE OLD BURYING GROUND, ... 231

"Though storms and winds rule high in air,
And men's rough passions rave,
Calm rest the weary sleepers here,
Safe in the dreamless grave!"

Didactic and Descriptive Passages, 231 — Deborah Armitage, the pious herb seller, 239 — Verna Humphrey; Sunshine and Shadows of her Life, 247 — Rev. Mr. Whiting's Grave, 270 — Grave of Manasseh Guatolf, the apostate Jew, 271 — Obadiah Turner's Grave, 274 — The Reception Tomb, 275 — Elizabeth Melrose; the Strange Occurrence on the night after her Burial, 275 — Grave of Ephraim Newhall, a worthy Teacher of Youth, 278 — A Burial at Night, 278 — Meditations, 280 — Interspersed with Sketches of the interesting History of this ancient Burial Place, its Natural Beauties, &c.

THE OLD TUNNEL MEETING HOUSE, ... 283

"Hail, honored fane! Though not in thee
  Were gorgeous nave and aisle;
Yet was thy rude simplicity
  More loved than marble pile."

Account of the Dedication, with quaint description of the Dedication Dinner, from an old manuscript. 283 — Dedication Ball, 294 — Sage Reflections, 297 — Eeling Expedition of Mr. Shepard, the minister, in company with Samuel Walton, and the Mishaps that attended it, 303 — The Huguenots, 308 — M. Boudinot and Family, 310 — Great Military Parade, 312 — Instruction of Youth, 317 — Master Turnbody, 318 — Shrewdness of Wild Geese, 321 — Master Oldpath, 325 — Autumn Foliage, 328 — Indian Summer, 329 — Character of the early Teachers, 330 — Dr. Jotham Tyndale, 333; his Remarkable Cure of Aaron Rhodes, 336 — Interior of the Old Tunnel, 341 — Great Witchcraft of 1692, 342; Excitement at the Meeting House,

342; Mr. Oldpath endeavors to prevent Agitation, 343; Horseshoe nailed upon the corner-board of the Meeting House, 344; Wonderful Sights seen by Jediah Breed, 345; Ruth Chase's Discoveries, 347; Increase Carnes, and the mysterious Assault upon him, 349; Mr. Oldpath's judicious proceedings, 354; Attempts to Account for the "Delusion," 355 — Deacon Mudget, and his Lesson to the Singers, 359 — Nora Humphrey; her Indiscretion, and its terrible Punishment, 362 — Dame Ramsdell, and her claims to Distinction among Women, 369; her successful-through-tribulation Son Zephaniah, 370 — Something about the Sermons of those times, 373; Extracts from one, 375 — Francis Reddan, his Bravery and wonderful Escapes, 378; his daughter Cora, 381; her betrothal to Richard Lewis; 382; Mr. Reddan's dreadful Death, 383 — An exciting Occurrence at the Meeting House, on an evening in 1692, 383 — Daniel Graves, and his afflictive Death by lightning, 386; Startling Apparition of him, at the Meeting House, 387; its effect on a young Girl who was present, 387 — The Music at the Old Tunnel, 389 — Fugitive Hope, 390 — Remarks on Puritanism, and the Perseverance and Success of the Old Settlers, 391 — Interspersed with Sketches of Character, Descriptions, Deductions, Reflections, and Speculations, which, it is hoped, will interest the Reader if not magnify the Writer.

PART I.

NOTABLE PEOPLE
OF
OLDEN TIME.

"Roll back thou mists of the dark brown years!
Unveil the paths our fathers trod!
We will lean upon their mossy tombs
And recount their noble deeds!
Then shall our souls be nerved
As by the bracing wind of the North."

INTRODUCTORY REMARKS.

It is the duty of every man, while sojourning in this unsatisfying though rather interesting world, and beating about amid its perplexing and endearing vicissitudes, to endeavor something for the benefit of his miserable race. And every man intends to perform that duty at some time before his chance comes for escape hence. But how true it is that with most of us, that indefinite "some time" never arrives. Our healthful efforts are postponed till disabilities intervene or the better opportunities cease; and so we finally wither away, still unfruitful vines. Procrastination justly bears the evil name of thief. Yet with what sublime resignation men yield to her even in their highest concerns. Some, it is true, who pass through early and middle life in ways unapproved by themselves, and consequently void of real enjoyment, arouse, at the eleventh hour, and do much to retrieve their former delinquencies. But such instances are rare, and no more to be depended on than those death-bed repentances which our clerical admonishers so constantly warn us against trusting to. While one man makes a figure in the world after his head has begun to bleach, ten thousand pursue the old unprofitable course.

And, reflecting in this wise, the writer, having pen in hand, and not being able to recall any particularly satisfactory achievement of his past life, considered whether something might not be accomplished by making a Book. But then the mystic dread produced by that impatient ejaculation of the most patient of men — " Behold, my desire is . . . that mine adversary had written a book "— brought him shivering to a stand. Presently, however, coming to the conclusion that if in the attacks to which his temerity might expose him, no more formidable enginery than literary criticism were employed, annihilation, certainly, would not be the melancholy result, he bravely determined to proceed. Yet the labor is undertaken with unfeigned diffidence; for if a vicious sentiment should be promulgated, however unintentionally, the effects of the wrong might be felt long after his power to counter-work had ceased; though, being void of evil intent, he might reasonably hope to escape the future punishment denounced by the worthy old Catholic against depraved writers; namely, that they writhe in purgatory just so long as the mischievous effects of their writings are felt among mankind. A very wholesome adjustment; though one under which that dread abode will not be likely soon to want for population.

To keep in proper humor with an author, and most effectually secure the good he intends, the reader should, in the very first place, endeavor to bring himself to a realizing sense of the exact spirit in which the work originated; to explore the mind of the writer, so to speak, primarily as regards his object, and secondarily as regards his style. A writer is necessitated, much more than a speaker, to rely on the discernment and fairness of those whom he addresses, for he cannot resort to gestures, intonations, and the thousand little arts that a speaker can, to make clear his meaning and adorn his periods. We hope to be dealt justly with. Yea, more than that, generously. Most of us are great sticklers for justice when it falls on heads not our own. But when we ourselves are in danger, mercy is the cry. Men's ideas of justice, too, greatly vary. Few agree as to what it is; or they award to it an elasticity capable of suiting any purpose. It is quite instructive to the philosophical observer to see how often the claims of pure justice mongers are based on the most arrant selfishness. What, indeed, would become of the best of us, if strict justice were meted out? We bespeak, then, the generous consideration of the reader.

Some authors write to magnify themselves, and some to promote other selfish ends. Others write to instruct, and others to amuse. Hence the importance of the suggestion just made, that it be a first object to search the mind of the writer whose book is in hand. True, the search may sometimes lead into crooked ways and among mists. And the reader may possibly come from the exploration without finding any purpose at all. But such instances will be rare. Every book has some object, or it is not worthy of the dignity of being burnt by the hangman. As to the present volume, we trust there will be no necessity for complaint in this respect. It would be a matter of unbounded regret and mortification with the writer, should any reader deem the time occupied in perusing his production misspent; so much so, indeed, as to move him to endeavor some amends. But what amends? Pecuniary? People usually look that way first. And hence he might offer to acquit himself accordingly. But as no one would expect such unheard of generosity to extend beyond the profits of the work, and the profits depending on its merits, there might be some doubt as to the value of the offer.

We are to deal chiefly with scenes and characters of past time. And oftentimes more good may be derived from the contemplation of what pertains to former days, than from what relates to the present, though the latter may in itself possess the greater merit. "Whatever withdraws us from the power of our senses," says the sturdy old moralist, "whatever makes the past, the distant, or the future, predominate over the present, advances us in the dignity of thinking beings. That man is little to be envied whose patriotism would not gain force on the plains of Marathon, or whose piety would not grow warmer among the ruins of Ion." And by parity of reasoning we are forward to ask who can fail to be benefitted by considering the pregnant scenes and noble characters of New England's early days? Who would not receive inspiration from viewing the giant needle on Bunker Hill, the Pilgrim monument at Plymouth, when built, or even from wandering among our quaint old tomb stones?

In old Plymouth colony there commences a range of hills, varying in height, but never reaching an altitude rendering them eligible to the title of mountains, that extends eastward some sixty or seventy miles. These hills present great irregularities in shape, and diversity in soil and geological construction. They follow the line of the coast at distances varying from half a mile to six miles from the shore, and in many places bear strong evidence of once having been the boundary of the tide. Anciently they were well wooded; but as population extended, the axe in many places laid them bare to the genial influence of the sun, and orchards, gardens and arable fields took the place of the old vestments. And now, at intervals, the chain seems much broken, as most portions, likely for the present to repay the expense, have been reclaimed. Some sections, which nature left in the most wild and untamable condition, still appear in the primeval aspect.

In the vicinity of Quincy these hills present immense ledges of beautiful and durable granite, which afford an inexhaustible field for remunerative labor. Farther east tower stupendous cliffs of porphyry. The range sweeps up from Plymouth, through Norfolk and Middlesex, and terminates in Essex, near the Merrimack. Should one take a view from the cupola of the State House at Boston, or from the top of Bunker Hill Monument, he might trace for many miles the undulating course of this interesting chain. At intervals, along the whole line, are detached transverse sections, greater or less in extent, giving diversity to the landscape, and furnishing romantic nestling places for numerous little settlements. A principal spur traverses the whole length of Cape Ann, terminating at Rockport, where the billows of the Atlantic eternally beat against its granite butress.

The territory from the hills to the sea is in some places almost a perfect plain for miles in extent; in other places it is broken and abrupt. Some of the largest and most thrifty settlements of New England adorn and make busy this tract. Indeed, Boston itself is within the limit, as well as Roxbury, Cambridge, Charlestown, Lynn and Salem. Here and in the adjacent hill country were the first explorations of the pilgrim fathers; and here were many of the first English settlements. It was in the rear of Boston, that the apostle Eliot commenced his pious labors, perseveringly, through winter's cold and summer's heat, pursuing his intrepid course, achieving such noble conquests and gaining such enduring renown. In this vicinity, too, some of the most stirring of the opening scenes of the Revolution took place. And on those bright mornings of April and June, when our Pine Tree Flag unfurled at Lexington and Bunker Hill, the whole region resounded with the tramp of gathering patriots.

All along this vast range of hills are disclosed such magnificent marine and landscape views as it is believed are equalled nowhere else on the Atlantic coast.

The THIRD PLANTATION occupied a central portion of this charming coast territory, and was parent of the renowned City of LYNN, or "LIN," as it is spelled in the act bestowing the name; a place known and respected wherever shoes are worn and bay fish eaten. Several other ambitious towns are honored by the same parentage; but Lynn seems always to have ranked as the most eminent of the beautiful offspring of that memorable settlement; and hence the whole Plantation is occasionally distinguished by her euphonious name.

It was in 1629 that the good old Third Plantation was

commenced. And it is our purpose to follow these introductory remarks by some biographical sketches of the sturdy old settlers, they being eminently types of the times — interspersed by allusions and details of various complexion.

There is no kind of general reading more profitable than well digested biography. Every person possesses an instinctive propensity to imitate the actions of others; and it is on this account that evil communications corrupt. But it is also true that a channel is thus afforded through which the most beneficial results may flow. In reading the life of a great or good man, where the traits which led to his greatness or goodness are clearly and judiciously delineated, the most healthful inspiration is imparted.

"Plutarch's Lives" have probably moulded more great characters than any other collection extant, save the sacred writings. And how often do we find them spoken of by leading spirits of departed centuries, as well as those of modern times, as having furnished the models by which they endeavored to shape themselves. They have imparted energy to the regal arm; incorruptibility to the dauntless breast; inspiration to the patriot heart. Some of the loftiest principles of jurisprudence are in them developed, some of the noblest conceptions of genuine liberty enforced, some of the most exalted characteristics of true manhood presented. They were the companions of Alfred, of Elizabeth, of Shakspeare, of Cromwell, of Chatham, of Franklin and Bonaparte; yes, and of some of the stout-hearted wilderness battlers of whom we are presently to speak.

The history of every community may furnish characters for the skilful biographer to delineate with applause and profit. And such local biographies may perhaps in many instances prove most useful, because the circumstances and interests of the principals and those who should be the imitators are so nearly identical as to afford a more steady and comprehensible light.

But we approach our task with diffidence, considering how many biographers prove themselves unfit for the labors they undertake. The dispositions of some lead them to indiscriminately laud, of others to indiscriminately calumniate. Few have power to analyze character without bias, and perhaps fewer still the disposition. Yet, the biographer who conceals all the faults of his subject because he discovers much to applaud, or all his virtues because he discovers much to condemn, betrays his trust most sadly. And then again, many rampant authors have their own innate prejudices, whims and fancies to be provided for. And these are at times not a little troublesome. Little indeed do readers know of the throes of authors — of the ideas that spring up, kicking and ranting among the brains like unbroken colts, too ill-conditioned to prance before the critical and exacting world, and yet so impatient of restraint. If they knew they might pity and forgive.

And many readers fail properly to appreciate the labors of an author in a work like the one now in hand, from entertaining divers wrong notions touching the quality of the information. Some suspect if they happen to come across anything of which they have not before heard, that it must be false; forgetting that there may be some truths in the world with which they have never become acquainted — that many important historical facts have for ages slept in private records; where, having escaped the search of the antiquarian plodder, they have finally been stumbled upon, as it were, by the mere excursionist in history.

It has been remarked that much of the truth of history is stranger than fiction. It certainly is. And hence, worthy reader, we trust you will not question any of our statements because they detail strange or even absurd transactions. That would be to suppose men never do strange or absurd things. The moment that a relation should enter the territory of the impossible, however, it is right to reject it. And we are free to admit that errors will sometimes creep into the most dignified and solemn histories. Even the intelligent and conscientious Prescott, it has been discovered, was led to adopt many fictions for truth. It is not possible always to avoid this. And all that the best can safely promise, is to be faithful in the endeavor not to mislead.

An untruth, when it appears upon the page of a book, may be the instrument of much greater mischief than it could have occasioned as a mere spoken word; because in the book it is more enduring, more widely circulated, and comes before the world in more pretentious guise. Of this we are aware, and wish that every author would take due cognizance. Occasionally, it is true, an innocent fiction may prove an excellent illustration. In the Bible itself we sometimes find great truths illustrated by parable. And in this view a historical writer may take a little comfort; for while he cannot always know the truth of his statements, he can know their aptness to produce the desired impression.

The annals of that favored region which was the scene of much that we shall relate, are rife with brilliant characters which we are persuaded would, if faithfully exhibited, not only shed lustre upon her name, but exercise an influence powerful and good. Yet it is not our intention to undertake anything like extended biographies. All we propose is, to attempt a few sketches of certain early settlers — rather the bringing of them out as lights to show the condition of things during the interesting and eventful times when it pleased their Maker to direct their sojourn here. And the first of the ancient gentry with whom it is proposed to step upon the stage is ZACHARIAH HART, to whose name may be found on the records the prefix of Mister. The pseudo-aristocracy of the colony were very particular about titular distinctions. The simple appellation of Goodman was generally awarded to such as had not taken the freeman's oath, and the more dignified one of Mister to such as had. The rule, however, was not invariable. Of other titles something may be said hereafter.

ZACHARIAH HART.

" With brawnie arme and dauntless hearte,
he strode in godlie pryde ;
Nor ghosts, wolves, Indians, Devill's art,
could turne his steps asyde."

MR. HART was born in an ancient cathedral town, near the Scottish border, somewhere in the hitherward verge of the sixteenth century; it is believed in the year 1594. And as he had little or no religious training, he was liable, as he grew up, to be swayed by comparatively slight circumstances. He became a rigid puritan. And his principles were fixed, probably, by the fact that the hair of his head was of a rusty yellow, grew rather in tufts than broadcast, and was almost as stiff as the bristles on a swine's back.

It is well known that the good churchmen were careful in the dressing of their hair, taking much pride in the graceful curl and shining lock, while the dissenters dissented as strongly from all such vanities as from the grievous superstitions, as they deemed them, perpetuated by any of the fondly cherished ceremonials of the establishment. Slighter circumstances than swayed Mr. Hart in his choice of a religion, have swayed others in all ages.

He probably had a sort of underground apprehension that there was a natural impediment to his becoming a good, or at least a shining, churchman, and so the other party at once had his sympathies. And by the time he had attained one score and ten years, his principles were as well defined and stiff as the tufts that adorned his head. Of the common frailties of human nature he possessed a competence. But he also had conspicuous virtues. And in this brief sketch we shall probably be able to show that he was one of the most useful and meritorious of the little band who made the first christian lodgment on this heathen territory.

It is not worth while to spend time in details respecting the early life of our Subject, for that was passed much as the early lives of others. He was sent to a decent school, and now punished and now rewarded, as his merits determined or the caprice of his teacher dictated. And he left the school, improved by his instruction and discipline.

One thing, however, ought to be mentioned. While at school he lodged in an upper room, just beneath the window of which an outbuilding was reared. And over the roof of that architectural adjunct hung the unsuspicious branches of a fruit tree belonging to a neighbor.

Zachariah had not occupied the room long before the ripening fruit attracted a glance that he had to spare from his book. And that glance was the occasion of some reflection after his head was laid upon the pillow. In short, the luscious fruit was a temptation that could not be winked down; and he began to lay plans for the possession of a share. His plans and the fruit were ripe at about the same time. So by the light of the moon he lowered himself from his window, stole along the ridge-pole, and then commenced a slide towards the eaves. Unfortunately a shower had rendered the roofing exceedingly slippery, and do what he could it was impossible for him to arrest his progress downward.

As he gracefully sailed by the golden fruit that lay within reach, he cast upon it that mingled look of shame, contempt and contrition wherewith one is apt to view a tempter in whose snare he is fairly caught, and who looks impudently up, laughing at his calamity. After an interesting exploration among the branches of the tree, he landed upon a bed of rocks, and was presently found and taken up very much frightened and somewhat weakened by the loss of blood. There was a terrible wound on his forehead, but no bones were broken; and he was soon able again to take his place in the school. In after life he derived considerable benefit from this adventure.

After the healing of the wound a frightful scar was fortunately left. And this proved of much service to him, not only in a moral way, by reminding him how unexpectedly dangers may spring up in the path of the evil doer, but otherwise, by furnishing a mark that might indicate the performance of some perilous duty. And he was not backward in availing himself of the advantages of the providential bestowment. At one time it answered for a wound received in the Dutch war; at another, for one received in defending a fortification against the French. And it made him a hero here in New England, as being a badge gained in a desperate conflict with Indians soon after he landed. We are astonished that one in those days of simplicity should predicate such diverse theories on a single fact; though we should not wonder at any thing of the kind in these days; for men are now so given to lying that when one undertakes to tell the truth he becomes an object of suspicion, and people wonder what on earth his purpose can be, especially where no selfish end is apparent.

Among the manifold excuses that have been urged for Mr. Hart is the one that his false statements were made under a loss of self-possession; that is, we suppose, being suddenly asked the occasion of his scar, and unwilling to name the true cause, he would, in confused haste, attribute it to this or that imaginary agency.

That people do sometimes sin under a loss of self-possession is no doubt true. But no instance of any sin excepting that of profanity committed under such circumstances, at this moment occurs to us. We are told of a certain minister once living in this region, who would sometimes, under sudden excitement or alarm, swear in a way that would have done dirty honor to the armies in Flanders, but who, when the gale had passed, had no sort of recollection of his guilty utterances. And when the matter was pressed home upon him he would seek to change the issue and refer to the example of St. Peter, declaring that on the memorable occasion of his denying his Master, the swearing was added through inadvertence. We certainly think Peter's denial was bad enough without his vulgar addition, but do not learn that he ever sought to excuse himself on this singular ground. Still, there was ingenuity in the minister's position.

Mr. Hart's case is a little strengthened, too, by a statement in the journal of Obadiah Turner, which work will be more fully brought into notice hereafter. On the whole, anomalous as it may seem in one generally so steady and brave, there really is reason to apprehend that Mr. Hart did occasionally lose his self-possession to a degree that left him to do things of which he might well have been ashamed. In Mr. Turner's journal we find this statement:

"Zachariah Harte was wth ye firste companie y^t came to Lin. He worked wth greate brauerie in putting vp ye firste habitation. And there being no minister wth them, he did make a lustie praier at ye laying of ye corner stone wch for ye time was a stoute oake blocke. They do discourse mch of hjs skill and handiework and of hjs godlie exhortations on ye ocacion. But jt hath been given oute y^t he did use manie prophane words mch to ye scandall of those aboute. And vpon hjs being reprimanded therefor he did stoutlie denie ye same; whereat they greatlie wondered, there being so manie witnesses. But he further sayd y^t if jt so seemed to them, he could say y^t jt was onlie a wrong working of ye tongue, there being no euil speech in hjs hearte. But I thinke this strange talke."

Mr. Hart joined the pilgrims at Leyden and remained with them there a few years. Having thus cast his lot with the refugees, he scorned to desert them; and when they, as perils thickened, fled to these shores, with undaunted heart followed. In what particular vessel he came over, it does not appear. But we find him at Lynn, with the very first detachment of settlers.

It was a warm day in the early part of June, 1629, when the little band pitched their tent among the trees that overshadowed the beautiful plain stretching from the hills to the sea, and immediately set about erecting a habitation.

In speaking of this "goodlie companie," some historians have omitted to mention that Mr. Hart was one of them. But such a slight cannot extinguish him. He did more labor, sweat more, ate and drank more, and according to Mr. Turner, swore more on that eventful day, than any other individual present. But they all worked with the industry of bees and beavers and were right glad when evening drew on.

It should be borne in mind that on this great occasion there were several present who did not come with the intention of remaining. They were from Salem, it is presumed, and came by special appointment or invitation, to assist by their advice and skill in laying the corner stone, as it were, of the new settlement. Among these, as will afterwards appear, was the famous Roger Conant. The Captain of the day himself, was also one of these temporary sojourners. Now those historians who do not mention these, and what the number of them was is not readily ascertained, as among the first settlers, do right, for they were not settlers in a proper sense. Some appear to have remained a considerable time, and some to have left immediately. And furthermore, some who are reckoned as first settlers do not seem to have been here for the first few months. Indeed it was something like the signing of the declaration of independence; though purporting to have been begun and completed on the fourth of July, the fact is that many if not most of the signatures were affixed at different times subsequent to that date. The purpose of these remarks is to remind the reader that though there may be apparent conflicts between ourselves and others who have written on the subject, yet all may be right. We have no thought of being captious, making charges of ignorance, or casting reflections.

As the glorious sun sank behind the tall pines that threw their dense shade upon the little clearing that had been made, those sturdy pioneers looked with satisfaction upon the habitation they had erected. It was sufficient for temporary shelter, though not comely to the eye. On that day, for the first time, had the primary sounds of civilization, the noise of the saw, the axe and the hammer, been heard in these solitudes. But these sounds were now hushed.

The workmen had gathered together the tools with which they had been toiling, and washed in a neighboring rivulet. The little girl and her boy companion had returned from their rambles, with muddy feet and stained lips. And the whole company were gathered near the habitation in preparation for their evening meal.

The venerable leader of the band was seated upon a stately oaken stump. The refreshing breeze played on his manly brow and swayed his white locks. The mild lustre of his hazel eye, told of the undisturbed spirit within. Time had plowed deep furrows along his dingy cheeks, and having harrowed rather unskilfully, little ridges of warts were left, much resembling such as are sometimes seen upon the hard shell gourd. He sat in silence, evidently contemplating the results that might flow from that day of small things. And had he been permitted to extend his vision along the vista of years to this our day, how glorious must have appeared to him the end of that vista, though some dark spots intervened.

But the meditations of the worthy leader were suddenly interrupted by a little occurrence which will be best related in the words of the old writer to whom we are chiefly indebted for our account of the transactions of that important day:

"Y^e godlie and prudent Captain of ye ocacion did for a time sit on ye stumpe in pleasante moode. And ye others did strolle abovte as best sujted themselues their worke being done, save one or two who must needs always be at work at something. Presentlie all were hurried together in greate alarrum to witness ye strainge doing of ye goode olde man. Vttering a lustie screame he bounded from ye stumpe, and they coming vpp did discry him jumping aboute in ye oddest manner, snapping hjs fingers and throwing hjs arms arounde in such wise as to make all greatlie feare y^t he had been seized wth some sudden and direfull distraction, and would doe harme to all y^t got within hjs reache. And he did likewise puff and blow wth hjs mouthe and roll vpp hjs eyes in ye most distressfull way.

"All were greatlie moved and did loudlie beg of hjm to advertise them whereof he was afflicted in so sore a manner. And presentlie he pointing to hjs forehead, they did spy there a small red spot, and swelling. Then did they begin to thinke y^t what had happened vnto him was this, y^t some pestigious scorpion or flying devill had bitten him, and y^t he was crying oute in agonie of paine. Goodwife Norlan did seize a handfull of wett moss, and running vpp hold ye same vpon ye wounde, and y^t did mch abate ye paine. Then said he, y^t as he sat on ye stumpe he did spy vpon ye branche of a tree y^t stoode neare by, what to hjm seemed a large fruite, ye like of wch he had never before seen, being mch in size and shape like ye heade of a man, and hauing a grey rinde wch, as he deemed, betokened ripeness. There being so manie new and luscious fruits from time to time discovered in this faire land, none could know ye whole of them, and jt might be y^t a fruit of ye coccownut kinde might grow hereabout. And he said hjs eyes did mch rejoice at ye sight.

"Seizing a stone wch lay neare, he hurled ye same thereat, thinking to bring jt to ye ground, and thereby procure a daintie for ye svpper table. But not taking faire aime, he onlie hit ye branch whereon hung ye fruit. Y^e jarr was not enow to shake down ye same, bvt there issued from jt as from a nest, seeminglie in great rage, diverse little winged scorpions mch in size like ye large fenn flies on ye marish lands of olde Englande, bvt having more of a yellow color. And one of them bounding againste hjs forehead, did in an instant, as he declared, giue a moste terrible sting, whereof came ye horrible paine and agonie at wch he so cried out."

What the company then did about the newly discovered hornet's nest, as such it seems to have been — whether their curiosity overcame their prudence and they pelted it to pieces, suffering the penalty which the outraged insects knew so well how to inflict, or whether their fears overcame their curiosity and they let it alone — we are not informed.

The interruption was not of long continuance, and things were soon progressing as quietly as before. There is our worthy friend Zachariah Hart, busy again with his axe, chopping up fuel for the morrow's use. He is always at work and seemingly never tired. His short sword dangles with a sort of good natured defiance at his side. And having thrown by his slouched hat, the brassy light and swaying shadows fall upon his bristly locks giving them a picturesque tinge of yellow green.

And there, with his sinewy arms bared to the task of assisting in the preparation of the evening meal, is the renowned Roger Conant. Every reader of New England history knows well who he was. His image looms up at intervals in all the coast settlements. He came over in the very infancy of the Plymouth colony. And when Lyford and Oldham were expelled for their seditious proceedings and retired to Nantasket, he, being one of their adherents, packed up and followed. In 1625, he was appointed to oversee the fishing and planting station commenced at Cape Ann. Thither he removed. The next year, however, he broke up the establishment and with others "went west" — only about fifteen miles, to be sure, but perhaps enough to entitle him to the honor of having put in motion that westward tide of emigration which has continued to roll on with continually increasing volume, to this day. He immediately began a settlement at Naumkeag, which, under Hebraic inspiration, was soon called Salem; a name which Roger Williams, with pungent irony, used to render into Peace, in allusion to the almost ceaseless quarrels of the settlers there, as well as their severe treatment of himself. Conant, indeed, seems to have had as irresistible a passion to be present at the commencement of settlements, as his neighbor Endicott had to be at sein-drawings or pig-killings. So it is not at all remarkable that he was present at the auspicious birth of the Third Plantation. There he was — his athletic form towering above the group, his sharp eyes glistening beneath their shaggy brows, like black diamonds set in red putty — giving directions, explaining principles, and exhorting to christian faithfulness, in a voice that a juvenile hippopotamus might envy. Nor did he scorn any useful labor. His arms, that might have held asunder a struggling Heenan and Sayers, did not disdain to wield the axe or rear the knotty rafter.

Another interesting and useful personage present on the occasion was Mistress Huldah Collins, the portly dame who had been detailed for the supervision of the cooking department. Matters progressed with happy quietude during the day. But in the preparation of the evening repast, she had become a little hurried and also a little flurried, as cooks are liable to be at such times. So she must be pardoned if her shrill voice did now and then ring discordantly in the ears of Roger and Zachariah and the others who were enlisted as her aids. Her cap had been thrown aside, for the pretty frill had been burned off by a straying flame and her long gray hair streamed and twisted round in a manner more observable than becoming; a sample now and then finding its way into the utensil upon the fire. But all trials must come to an end.

She took the last little puffed cake from the frying pan that continued to tremble and spit over the embers, and directed Zachariah to give notice that all things were ready for the evening meal. In smoking state it was served upon the temporary board erected beneath the spreading branches of a huge pine. The spot was convenient on account of the shade, and convenient to receive the litter shaken down by divers squirrels and birds who entertained themselves in hopping about among the foliage and darting envious looks upon the preparations below. All being ready, by direction of the leader a blessing was craved by honest Roger. And then they proceeded, in decent order, to appropriately dispose of the frugal repast. No eye caught a glimpse of the hideous copper face that now and then peered upon them from a neighboring thicket, nor of the painted form that stealthily glided among the gray trunks in the valley below.

The meal ended, and it was now an hour of rest. The huge trunks that had that day fallen by their sturdy strokes, hewn blocks, boxes and chests, furnished them with lounges and seats. The young and the old, in groups, engaged in innocent sports or grave conversation. And the little band were happy; happy in the society and sympathy of each other; happy in their anticipations of the future; happy in having escaped the trials, temptations and persecutions of the lands they had left; and happy in having found so pleasant and peaceful a home.

The sun went down. The crescent of the new moon hung in marvellous beauty above the glowing horizon and the stars began to twinkle in the blue deeps above. The pilgrim band remained enjoying the virgin sweetness of that holy eventide. It was a season for meditation; a season and a scene in which the heart could not fail to be led to aspirations of the most exalted nature; a season and a scene in which a sense of the deceitfulness of all earth's promises, the nothingness of its objects of ambition, its hopes and its fears, must press upon the mind in glaring contrast with the transcendant worth of that spiritual discipline which alone can satisfy and save. And no people could have had a more stern realization of such truths.

The hour for repose drew near, and the venerable leader proposed the singing of a hymn. With one consent the sacred melody rang among the wilds to such purpose that there was a general rousing of the forest tenants of every nook within half a mile. And such startling responses were heard from rock, cave and hollow tree, that there can be little wonder that the pious old father imagined that the evil one was thus early marshalling his phalanx for an onset. This idea excited considerable alarm, but fortunately it was discovered that a Latin Bible and a horseshoe were in the camp. The idea so general among the early settlers that Satan had determined to destroy them by a regular corporeal descent is easily accounted for. Their fond conceits led them to fancy themselves the most pure upon earth, and hence the special objects of satanic jealousy and wrath. They did not seem once to realise that the old brimstone gentleman must have had many other spots in the wide world to keep an eye on, or might content himself with a general oversight of their progress, or, perhaps, despatch one of his trusty marshals to keep watch and ward. No, no, it could not be possible, in their view, but that he looked upon them, though few in numbers, as the most valiant and determined champions in the whole world of his adversaries.

The pious song was ended. Then they all arose with uncovered heads, the aged with holy aspirations and the young with damp resignation receiving the baptism of evening dew, and listened to a prayer, within the ample verge of which was comprehended a citation of all the wants and woes in mind, body or estate of each individual present; a thanksgiving for the mercies and benefits of the past day; and a petition for care and protection during the coming hours of repose. Nothing appeared to be forgotten; not even the accidental killing of a gray squirrel and the destruction of a four foot snake. But whether the latter was accidental or otherwise the prayer seemed to leave in doubt; the equivocation probably arising from the circumstance that the snake was forced to bid adieu to this happy life at the particular instance of the venerable leader himself.

And why is it, that snakes are so universally feared and detested? Many of them are among the most graceful and beautiful of the whole animal creation. Some are in a peculiar sense fascinating. And with very few exceptions they are timid and entirely harmless. It seems as if the universal horror of them among us could only arise from some fancied connection with that old serpent, the devil — though many who profess no fear of the devil are yet afraid of snakes. The horror lies in education, not in nature, for the Indians and many uncivilized people rather fancy them as companions. A question arises: Is it right to kill harmless snakes? The writer was once walking in the woods with a clergyman when a large glossy snake, beautifully marked with gay colors crossed the path. Our clerical friend by an instant blow with his cane disabled him. Following up the blow, by others, vigorously applied, the reptile soon lay writhing piteously. But during all this exercise the godly man was declaring that he had never been able to satisfy himself that it was right to kill harmless snakes. As lookers on, we could not avoid the reflection that it would be most satisfactory to the snake to have such violent proceedings suspended till the question in casuistry was settled. But the reptile ghost was soon yielded up and there the matter ended.

Most of the serpent kind undoubtedly possess great cunning and manage their little transactions with birds, toads, mice and such savory flesh with great shrewdness. And that they possess extraordinary domestic attachments seems not to admit of doubt. It is said that the male and female will sometimes even die for each other. The writer once had occasion to notice a really pathetic instance. A workman on his premises killed a large black snake, and was requested to let the body remain exposed, to ascertain if a companion would not soon appear. Watch was kept and in a few days a snake of the same kind and of similar size appeared. An unsuccessful effort was made to capture him; and after a few days more he was seen so frequently as to make it seem as if he had taken up his abode thereabout, resolutely determined to effect something. But he was finally found lying exposed near a frequented path, not far from the now decaying remains of the other, and manifesting no disposition to escape. He was easily despatched, making no attempt to avoid the fatal blows. The whole thing appeared so much as if he had come in search of his lost companion, had found her, and being satisfied that she was dead, was ready to throw his own life away, as to be really touching.

But to proceed. The prayer ended. It was from an honest and faithful heart. And though for these many years, near half a score of churches, or meeting houses, as the old puritans would prefer to call them, have stood almost within a stone's throw of that hallowed spot, never has an evening breath borne up a petition more heartfelt and effectual.

Of the habitation which was the product of that day's toil a word may be said. It was formed of the trunks of trees, interlaced with green branches, savory in their smell but dampening in their effects. And it unfortunately turned out, too, that not being acquainted with the botany of the region they had interwoven a considerable quantity of poisonous material, which presently laid up about half of the company. This untoward event was of course set down as another of Satan's contrivances to harrass and terrify them.

The structure was sufficiently capacious to accommodate a score or upwards with shelter, comfortable or otherwise, as each might determine for himself. The male and female departments were separated by a partition of branches and fern, diversified here and there by a more opaque patch of blanket or garment. No chimney or fireplace was necessary, as the cooking could well be done without, in nature's great kitchen; and there also, as to that matter, could the eating be done. And besides, this caravansary-like structure as has before appeared was designed only for temporary purposes. When at evening it was illuminated by the red light of numerous flaring pine knots it made quite a hospitable appearance; and was sufficiently attractive to draw the friendly attention of myriads of mosquitos. And during the night, also, sundry wild animals seemed to think it polite to make calls on the new comers. Among them was a gentlemanly bear, whose curiosity was so far excited that in addition to snuffing and rubbing his nose against the posts, he undertook to ascertain the strength of the erection by the strength of his claws, not once appearing to dream that Roger Conant was there, that he had a gun, and that the gun was loaded and liable to go off. He was greatly astonished when the weapon was discharged directly in his face, and more astonished still when he found himself flayed and hanging from a walnut tree limb, with Zachariah Hart, bloody knife in hand, viewing him by the light of a lantern and with grinning satisfaction declaring his weakness for fat bear steak. This certainly did not seem to be doing the handsome thing by one of the first neighbors who had the politeness to call. But those imperiled old pioneers were not in a situation to yield much to considerations of mere courtesy.

The night was balmy and brilliant. And different indeed were the surroundings from which our little colony were to receive their first impressions from those which encompassed their forlorn brethren when first landing at Plymouth. There, the wintry winds howled and the drifting snows danced eddies, while the leafless old branches creaked a surly welcome. Here, the summer breeze gambolled among the sweet fern and blushing flowers, while the unfettered mountain rill and the gay bird warbled their compliments.

Such is a brief history of the first day of this now famous City of Lynn; so famous that even a railroad locomotive bears its name. We look down the shadowy vista of antiquity, and behold the lusty host who came with battle axes and trumpets to lay the foundation stones of Babylon; upon the bearded band, with broad phylacteries, who toiled in uprooting the olive trees that Jerusalem might be built; upon the strong armed adventurers who labored in cementing the basement walls of Rome. But nowhere can we find a nobler band than those who toiled and sweat on the momentous occasion just noticed. Their limbs were nerved by the beautiful sunshine of early summer, and their hearts inspired by the more beautiful sunshine of christian hope.

Zachariah Hart, the subject of the present biographical sketch was one of the most active and consequential personages among that pioneer band, though not the leader, as has before appeared. He was at this time a man of middle age, in form extremely well developed, and endowed with great physical strength and courage. His well tried powers soon pointed him out as the most suitable person in the settlement to conduct the wolf and bear hunting expeditions. Indeed, he stood foremost in all perilous enterprises; and the Indians soon came to stand more in fear of him than of any other man with a white face; not to say that his was very white, for all the lower parts remained an unreclaimed jungle of hair, while above, appeared a sunburnt region resembling a mixture of Spanish brown and beach sand.

We spoke of his activity. But that was not his greatest virtue. He was persevering, unmurmuring; and, under every discouragement, kept his spirits up; not in the way that some of his neighbors did, by pouring spirits down, but by constant and useful occupation. How many unfortunate ones there are, who, conceiving themselves born to ill luck, sit down disheartened, and pass their days in repining indolence. Ten to one, they never deserved success. And no one ought to complain of evil fortune if he never did any thing to deserve good fortune. What a useful example did Mr. Hart present for the contemplation of such grumblers.

But our Subject was by no means a perfect man. We feel bound to state this, as by setting him up too high, we might discourage those who would perceive the hopelessness of emulating unattainable virtues. He had one leading vice; and that being patent, it may be inferred that otherwise he was comparatively guiltless, for it is seldom that more than one great vice inhabits a human heart at the same time. Metaphorically speaking, the hounds of the nether world are not accustomed to hunt in couples. The grievous vice to which we allude, was the inordinate love of tobacco, or "ye vile weed tabakka" as it was called in his day. His indulgence of this evil habit was bad for the morals of those around him; and the drouling evidence of it, which sometimes appeared when he was earnestly wrestling with his perplexing duties, was bad for their stomachs.

Of the learning of Mr. Hart, enough has already been said. And of his piety it may be remarked that it was of that rigid, dogmatical and uncompromising character, that rendered him unfit to undertake a missionary enterprise, or to lead in a community of intelligent minds.

Before Mr. Batchellor, the first minister, came, Mr. Hart exercised his gifts as preacher and exhorter, to quite as great an extent as was acceptable, in an informal way. And a Mormon prophet would not have been more egotistical or denunciatory than he. But on the appearance of Mr. Batchellor he gracefully retired, leaving the sacred field to be occupied by one more learned and disciplined, indeed, but yet hardly better endowed in view of the virtues of patience and humility.

The services that Mr. Hart rendered the infant settlement were very great and worthy of remembrance. On two occasions, in severe winter weather, when provisions were scanty and supplies not to be obtained from any of the neighboring settlements, he traveled on foot to the Plymouth colony and successfully negotiated for what was needed.

He was once chief actor, or equal actor with his four footed antagonist, at a cave near Sadler's Rock, in a scene much like that at Pomfret from which old Putnam gained such laurels. But he did not, like the hero of Pomfret, come unscathed from the conflict. A magnificent wound adorned his breast, which as it healed, left a noble scar. This good fortune took some of the lustre from the old scar on the forehead.

Mr. Hart died at the good old age of three score and twelve years. He was the father of a family of four, two hopeful sons and as many aspiring daughters. And they, in turn, became fathers and mothers. Several of his descendants were of some account in the world.

Among them were brave Harts, for two took the field in the great King Philip war, and four in the Revolution: bewitching Harts, for one dame was imprisoned, in 1692, for practicing witchcraft on Mr. Shepard's maid, and another turned the head of a lieutenant governor by not returning his love: learned Harts, for two were lawyers, two doctors, four schoolmasters and two traveling lecturers: great Harts, for one weighed four hundred pounds, and another was seven feet tall.

John Hart, one of the signers of the declaration of independence, seems to have been a descendant of Zachariah, he having proceeded from a scion that was at an early period lopped from the Third Plantation stock and planted in New Jersey.

Another descendant, a century or so since, by a fortunate matrimonial alliance, became connected with a titled and wealthy old English family. That family seems now on its last legs, and those somewhat attenuated, there being but a solitary individual remaining, and he nearly four score years of age. So it may not be long before those of the Hart line, hereabout, may have an opportunity to devote a portion of their spare change to feeing agents and attornies to look after shares in a large estate in the old country that goes begging for heirs. And it is hoped that they may be more successful than such phantom chasers usually are.

Edm. Hart, architect of the Constitution—we mean the frigate, not the political constitution—was a Lynn man, though we are not sure that he was of the Zachariah lineage. He certainly did honor to the place of his birth as well as to himself, by his skill and faithfulness. And it must be concluded that he did not swindle government much, through the contract, for he lived in those unsophisticated days when it was not customary for every one to look upon government as a fat goose made ready for all to pick; particularly as he died in moderate circumstances.

Another descendant was Alpheus Hart, who had an extensive orchard just about where the central rail road station now is. He made great quantities of cider for the Boston and Salem markets; and when he got a little muddled, in trying the quality, was for stirring up mischief generally. He was several times put in the stocks, near the meeting house, and otherwise kindly dealt with, but apparently to little purpose. But finally, all of a sudden, a new fountain seemed to spring up in him. He came out a warm politician; bought a new suit of clothes; left off drinking; removed to Reading; and ultimately became a shining light in the General Court. Thus presenting a most astonishing metamorphosis. Politics generally ruins; here it saved. Perhaps, however, the salvation is to be attributed to something else, and that it should be said he was saved in spite of his politics.

Another descendant of Mr. Hart attained a high position at Boston, some scores of years since, but came down with such a jerk that his spine was dislocated. And that was the end of him. Indeed, the family history of Mr. Hart is not very flattering; but yet it is no doubt true that they have turned out quite as good as the average of families. And there is a sort of negative comfort in that.

We have spoken of the unyielding nature of Mr. Hart's religious principles. But there was one occasion on which he was in imminent hazard of deviating. And that was when the celebrated Mrs. Hutchinson held her meeting at Lynn, in 1636; of which it will probably be in our way to give some account on a subsequent page. It may be, however, that he was ensnared more by her personal charms than her doctrines.

And speaking of Mrs. Hutchinson leads us to allude to the inconsistencies of which so much has been said, as strongly marking the character of the puritan settlers. If they claimed that their object in coming here was to enjoy liberty of conscience, they certainly did not seem to think the same liberty desirable for others. On that ground alone can their treatment of this lady and her adherents, as well as their violent proceedings against the Quakers, Baptists and others, be explained. This was a curious kind of religious liberty; and in what way it was an illustration of the godly principle better than the English or even the Romish church afforded, it would puzzle one to determine. But, for reasons that may presently appear, the reader is reminded that there were substantial differences in several important respects between the Plymouth and Massachusetts settlers. And no doubt many individual immigrants of character, themselves misunderstood the real objects of the patentees.

The first members of the Bay Colony, as a general thing, were superior to those of the Plymouth. The settlement of Massachusetts was commenced under a well-ordered emigration, in which not a few of the leading people of the mother country were interested. And the purpose was to found an orderly and prosperous commonwealth, as well as to secure an asylum from persecution.

Some of the first who came here were persons of dignity and influence at home, eminent for political sagacity and learning as well as for piety. And not a few were ambitious in a worldly way. The immigrants were liberally provided with things necessary for their comfort and prosperity. Some of them were not Puritans but Episcopalians, and hence did not come to avoid persecution for their religion; a fact which has been made strange use of by some historians. But the number of churchmen was not by any means sufficient to change the character of the settlements from that of genuine puritanism,— puritanism characterized by the most rigid demands, as we have seen.

The earliest settlers of Plymouth, on the other hand, were of more equal condition and religious character; a forlorn band, destitute and depressed, fleeing from evils against which they had little power to contend, and seeking an asylum where they might pass their lives in peace, pondering upon the great matters of revealed truth, and repressing all aspirations of the worldly heart after temporal greatness and renown. And no shade of suspicion has been cast upon the purity of their puritanism.

We cannot follow Mrs. Hutchinson through her career, brief though it was, of exaltation and adversity, to its calamitous termination. Her teachings created a ferment that threatened to tear asunder the very frame of government. But it seems as if the mischief might have been easily avoided. Had the authorities proceeded in a different manner, and as the authorities of this day would proceed, little trouble, one would think, could have ensued. The Come-outers, as they were called, who created some disturbance here in Essex county about the year 1840, were dealt with in that sensible way that caused them soon to disappear. And what we say in regard to the mistake in the way of proceeding against this woman may perhaps apply with equal force to the proceedings against the Quakers and Baptists.

The mistake made by the old puritan authorities seems to have been in proceeding against Mrs. Hutchinson as a teacher of false doctrine; in denouncing her opinions as heresies and herself as a heretic; instead of directly charging her with breaking a positive law, if she were guilty of so doing, and requiring her to answer, like any other law breaker, before the established courts. By charging her with being a disseminater of erroneous doctrine, they opened the great questions of right of conscience and religious liberty. And they also opened the door for an examination of the doctrine taught, as well as a channel through which might flow in upon her the sympathy of enlightened minds, for there were those around her, imbued with the spirit of true religious liberty. In this case, the course pursued by the authorities was certainly the most troublesome one for themselves; for she was unquestionably a woman of strong and subtile mind, fervid and chaste eloquence, charitable and pure life.

Governor Vane — of whose visit to Lynn we shall have something to say, a few pages hence — as well as other eminent men, earnestly sympathised with Mrs. Hutchinson. His views of true liberty appear to have been in some respects in advance of the views of those around him, and he had nerve enough to withstand almost any pressure. And had he remained longer in the country he might have averted the terrible fate that finally overtook that persecuted woman.

We have spoken of the superiority of some of the early immigrants under the Massachusetts patent — eminent people, whose footprints on the virgin soil of New England can never be effaced. Vane was one of these. And by giving a few glimpses of his character and course we shall shed light upon some features of the past.

Sir Henry Vane, though perhaps we should omit the Sir, as he was not knighted till after his return to England, it will be recollected, was the fourth Governor under the first charter — or we might say the fifth, for Matthew Cradock was chosen by the Company in England, though he never came over — having been elected in 1636; at which time he was but twenty-four years of age, and had been in the country but about a year. And though he remained here for a short time only, he will be remembered as long as interest in our history shall be felt. In him, however, were united great contrarieties of character. And his official life here was turbulent and on the whole anything but satisfactory. His subsequent career in England has furnished the theme for many a puzzling as well as glowing passage in the history of his time. Hume, Clarendon, Hallam, Burnet, Macintosh and others give sketches of his character and opinions of his writings, and it is quite amusing to observe their differences. In their attempts to analyse his character they seem to be engaged in a most embarrassing task, and rather ready, each, to seize upon this or that prominent point and thence take a general view.

Milton, in a poetic panegyric, calls Vane the eldest son of Religion. But the sayings of Milton are certainly of little value, when his temper and peculiar principles come in play. His passions seem to have led to a bewilderment in controversy; while in poetry, all mankind admit he was sublime. Macintosh pronounces Vane scarcely inferior to Bacon in mental endowment.

Vane belonged to one of the most distinguished families in the kingdom, was highly educated, and had travelled in the continental countries before coming to America. He had also been early called into association with leading personages. King Charles himself was occasionally entertained in feudal pomp at Raby Castle, the home of the Vanes.

While yet a mere stripling, as it were, Vane became firmly set in puritan principles. This created much grief, and the celebrated Archbishop Laud was appointed to the task of endeavoring to lead back his straying feet to the fold of the establishment. But all efforts to reclaim him were unsuccessful. His father was a member of the privy council, and felt much distressed at the estrangement of his son. And when the young man announced his determination to join the puritans in America, all but coercive measures were looked to for his detention. But the king rather approved of his design, probably thinking that he might be less troublesome here than at home, and parental desire succumbed to regal.

Hither he came; but, as before intimated, remained a short time only; sufficiently long, however, to create a great ferment among the political and religious elements. After his return to England his restless soul continued to work among the loftier interests of mankind. But we cannot follow his course there. It is sufficient to remark that he became a member of Parliment as early as 1640, and held various high official positions, sometimes with honor to himself and profit to the people; and sometimes to the injury of both. Brilliant and yet perplexing passages appear all along his course till its termination on the scaffold, in June 1662. He had taken an active part in the affairs of the Commonwealth, though opposed to Cromwell, who uttered many bitter things against him, induced, probably, by the circumstance that he would not aid in schemes for the personal aggrandizement of the Protector. And he was beheaded for treason to the monarchy. No doubt he was a republican, and desired to establish a republic. And hence, in the settlement of accounts at the Restoration his head was required. At least the vacillating monarch seemed to think so.

One of the most deeply regretted occurrences of Vane's life appears to have been the strange affair of the "red velvet cabinet." Its startling effect on the fortunes of the Earl of Strafford, and the grievous estrangement it produced between him and his noble father, are well known to the reader of English history. View it as we may it was a deep stain upon his honor. True, Parliament undertook to purge it of dishonor by a vote. But funny things are sometimes done by vote. A Roman council once voted Jupiter's satellites out of heaven. And the French Convention voted the Almighty out of the universe.

Some worthy writers have spoken of Vane's conduct as fanatical and ruinous in its tendency; of his principles as variable and often dangerous; of his writings as confused and contradictory. But he must have been a man of commanding talents, or he could not have sustained himself in such positions as he occupied. It is, without doubt, however, well that he did not long remain in the colony; for his persevering wilfulness certainly would have stirred up dangerous if not fatal disturbances.

Soon after he was elected Governor, Vane made a tour to the eastern towns. On the ninth of July he entered Lynn. Everybody turned out, and a great parade took place. Finding an account in the journal of Obadiah Turner we cannot do better than adopt it:

"Y^e morning being faire Govn^r Vane and hjs companie appeared betimes wthin ye towne, all on horse backe, & making some show of armes, as swords, musquettes, and halberds. Likewise behinde them walked some Indjans, stepping verie proudlie, gaylie painted, and haveing many coloured eagle feathers vpon their heads and scarlitt & yellow cloths about their bodies. And in their hands they carried tommyhawkes and speares, and some long pipes. A lustie trumpeter did goe before ye Govn^r whose blasts did ringe in ye woodes wth such a mightie ringe as seemed enow to shake down ye walls of anie Indjan Jericho. His trumpett was of shining brass and he was begirt wth a red sash and had a cap of bear skin so mighty in size, y^t seeminglie he was more head than bodie. Y^e trumpett advertised all ye people y^t ye Govn^r was with vs, and there was presentlie mch running to behold him.

"At ye house of Goodman Dexter they did halt to recruit somewhat, by meate and drinke. And thither did manie assemble to make their dutiful obeisance. Y^e Govn^r was very gratious, tho grave & thotfull, and gaue mch godlie counsell wch was well receaved. Zachariah Harte was there, all ye time, making hjmself verie common, as he would faine act ye parte of usher. And he must needes shake hands over and over with ye Govn^r and secretaire bidding them welcome againe and againe. He would have all ye men and women make their respects. Likewise he seized ye children & took them in his armes to ye Govn^r that hee might speake to them and chuck them vnder ye chinn.

"Y^e staie of ye Govn^r was so prolonged y^t most had time to appeare. And seeminglie hee was much pleased wth hjs entertainment, making manie inqviries regarding our affaires; in a particular manner touching our gospel priviledges, our husbandrie, our fisheries, and our defences against ye sauvages and other potent adversaries, roareing devills and all y^t would distress God his people. And he did discourse pleasantlie of our future increase, saying y^t this bee a most goodlie inheritance, wth noble woodes and fields and waters wth aboundance of savorie fish; and needing nothing save stoute heartes and strong hands to make ye place one of great prosperitie, wch jt must in time surelie come to bee. And God bee praised y^t jt is soe.

"Thomas Newhall hee did make some discovrse to ye Govn^r, informing of our dutifull love to him and hopes of mch good from hjs godlie life and experiences. And hee made known to ye Govn^r y^t tho wee did not make discharge of ordnance on his comeing, as ye people of Salem would likelie doe on hjs entering theire towne, jt was not from haveing a mind against soe doeing, but because wee had not ye meanes wherewith to acquit ourselves of y^t honor, ye people of Salem haveing ye daie before sent over for ye big gunn wch we had borrowed from them.

"When ye Govn^r and his companie would proceed they were detained somewhat at ye river crossing by reason of a parte of ye bridge haveing of a sudden broke downe. So wee must needes gather hastilie wth our axes and other tooles to repaire ye damage, they patientlie waiting ye while. While ye worke was going brisklie on, Zachariah Harte hee fell into ye riuer and wee were some putt to jt to get him oute. And when wee had him oute ye bonie tayl of a horse shoe crab was sticking through his nose. But no other disaster happened on ye occacion, and presentlie they were all safelie ouer.

"Att Mr Newhall his house they did againe halt, and ye Govn^r and secretaire going in did hold some private discourse wth ye grave men of ye towne, wch being ended he would saie something more on ye greate matters of religion, and it be given oute y^t he hath some views not soe well liking to manie godlie people, vpon ye keeping of ye Lord his day; for they saie he doth boldlie declare y^t there be no warrant of scripture for ye observance thereof; saying y^t all must be blind who doe not see y^t what wee call ye Lord his daie is but a festivall established by ye popish church in remembrance of ye resurrection, and not meant for a Sabbath; and saying, too, y^t ye great archbishop Laud declared vnto hjm y^t soe likewise was hjs beliefe. He thot contrariwise till being putt vpon examination, when he did come to ye same mind wth ye bishop. But our Govn^r being yet young and some giuen to change he may presently come oute from svch oppinions. Some other godlie people hereabout have laid holde of ye same notion, and where these things will end I know not; ye more because they who thvs thinke be of ye learned and wise. But wee be in God his hand & I trust no evill will come vppon vs.

"Wee finde ye Govn^r trulie a man of partes and faire presence, wth learning and gravitie. He hath bin in ye greate school of Geneva. But I must saie y^t he doth mch loue to doe things in his own waie, & dispiseth covnsel; wch I greatlie feare will presentlie lead to trouble and strife.

"When they had againe taken meate and drinke, ye Govn^r mch admiring ye sauce of craunberries made by

Dame Newhall, spreading it thick vppon his bread, they departed. And as they moued along wee did make readie & blast divers rockes, wch by theire loude reports did well answer for ordnance.

"In ye afternoone wee did heare ye noise of ye Salem cannon wch certified vs y^t ye Govn^r and ye others had reached y^t plantation. So ended ye great ocacion of Govn^r Vane his comeing."

To return to Mr. Hart. He does not appear to have accumulated any great amount of this world's goods, but he always lived comfortably. Perhaps he read his Bible enough to learn the danger of wealth.

If we take a survey of the community we shall find it the same now that it was in Mr. Hart's rude times, the same as it always is, in regard to men's characteristics. Some live within their means; some up to their means; some up to their expectations, and some up to their hopes. The first are comfortable and secure; the second on dangerous ground; and the others on ground that is quite sure occasionally to upheave disastrously. Mr. Hart belonged to the prudent class. He left a comely homestead, several fair acres, a share or two in some fishing boats and lobster nets, a cow, pigs, poultry and a famous bear trap of his own invention.

But we cannot ask the reader to tarry longer in company with Mr. Hart; though if he never finds himself in worse company he will be remarkably fortunate. We must dismiss the patriarch by simply adding that he lived to see this community, in the fostering of whose infancy his best energies had been spent, and for whose prosperity his most fervent prayers had been offered, in a flourishing and happy condition. And when he laid down to his everlasting rest there were kindred to weep and associates to hold him in grateful remembrance. There was not, perhaps, an individual in the settlement whose loss would have been more keenly felt, for there was not another who could so readily turn his hand to every sort of useful labor, or who had better judgment in directing his industry. The wintry storms did not protect the hale old trees of the forest from his sturdy strokes; nor did the melting suns of summer, so enervating to the early comers, drive him from the field. And he had a liberal share of that courage, perseverance and shrewdness from which our boasted Yankee character is derived.

Mr. Hart was not a learned man. But there were enough learned ones without him. And the success of the Plantation was in a great measure owing to the happy intermingling of classes. Had all directed their attention chiefly to intellectual pursuits, things would soon have come to nought. And, on the other hand, had they all been mere workers, without some trained intellects to counsel and direct, poverty and servility would have characterized these days.

We repeat that Mr. Hart was not a learned man. But the learning of the schools does not always make men better. True, it enables them to do more good. But it also enables them to do more evil. It adds to the happiness of some; to the misery of others. The common schools of our day are much lauded. But what is there taught in them save that which is calculated to promote mere temporal success? Is not moral training most sadly neglected? And is this in accordance with early New England ways? Is it not indisputably true that the people of this day are inclined to place intellectual culture above moral? And, lastly, is that the right thing?

OBADIAH TURNER.

" With honest hearte and pleasantlie,
the chronicler hath writ;
And he was there to heare and see;
soe who than he more fit."

THE next of our worthies of earlier date to be brought into notice is the one whose name is placed above, and to whom we have already more than once alluded. He appears to have been one of the most energetic, fair minded and hopeful of the personages present at the laying of the foundation stones of this now towering community. Of his personal history, however, we know but little, excepting what is derived from a journal which he appears to have written up with much care and diligence. This journal is now of great value both from its comprehensiveness and reliability. In it, we find recorded, in quaint language, many of the common events of life as they transpired among our forefathers. It may be spoken of as a series of graphic pictures, illustrating the every day life of the early settlers and the circumstances by which they were surrounded. And Mr. Turner has agreeably interspersed his details of facts with sage remarks, keen thrusts and frolicksome delineations. He evidently had a mind wakeful to objects of humor, and the usual attendant, a vein of sentimentality. He also possessed sound judgment and a clear perception of the duties devolving upon those who attempt to lay foundations upon which are to rest the liberties and rights of others.

The journal of Mr. Turner fell into the hands of the writer by one of those fortunate turns that sometimes happen to a man, to wit, the turning over of a barrel of old papers. And said turn took place while ransacking the garret of an aged relative. A large deposit was found of collections made by an ancestor, who seems to have been very industrious in collecting and preserving whatever related to colonial days earlier than his own. We might perhaps say that most of the historical learning of a local character developed in these pages, was derived from this source. In some instances, however, labor was required to shape it for convenient use. Mr. Turner was in most cases very methodical and clear; yet there were occasions when his pen produced such involutions as are not easily unraveled. But we cannot speak so well as this even of most of the other manuscripts. Mr. Turner appears to have been quite liberal in his views; so much so, indeed, as to justify the suspicion that he leaned somewhat towards episcopacy. But yet he was by no means free from the notions of the good puritans regarding the corporeal onsets of the Devil and the necessity of keeping constantly on the alert to avoid falling into the snares and traps set all about by satanic hands.

In the journal of Mr. Turner we find few of those improbable stories of perils and natural wonders, that most of the early writers on New England affairs loved to indulge in. They certainly endeavored to make the most of wonders; seeming to emulate the old Spaniards in their accounts of Mexico and Peru. It is strange that historians fall into such errors; thus bringing discredit upon themselves and suspicion upon others. It were better for one even to omit telling improbable truths than to be so careless of damaging his character for veracity. It is refreshing, therefore, to have in hand such a work as that in question. And we bless the author's memory for the valuable legacy to posterity.

Mr. Turner was a native of the north of England, and was born, it appears, in the year 1606. He seems to have come here, not because of any oppression in his own country, but, like many others, to seek his fortune or gratify a love of adventure. And he appears, soon after his arrival, to have given up all thought of returning to his native land. He was a young man at the time of his advent here and lived to the good old age of between three and a half and four score years. His journal, though in its latter pages somewhat imperfect as to dates, and bearing evidence of a trembling hand and waning light, is brought down to the year 1681. It commences in 1630; thus covering a full half century.

The reader will not understand that we have quoted in full or invariably preserved the original order. Many of the most interesting passages have been entirely omitted, for the reason that in other parts of this volume the same subject might be in hand, and it is an object to avoid unnecessary repetition. We mention this, lest it might be imagined that Mr. Turner had omitted even allusion to persons and events which it will elsewhere be found appeared to us worthy of being brought prominently into view. It is really wonderful how few things of importance, escaped the notice of the worthy and wakeful journalist. Indeed he often notes, with gratifying minuteness, matters which at the time must have appeared to be of little moment.

In the orthography we have made a few changes for the reason that the original spelling would, in those instances, have perplexed the reader. And occasionally a slight change in the syntax has been ventured on. But beyond these, we have endeavored to be faithful to the text. And these last remarks will apply to extracts which we have introduced from other ancient records and memoranda, and will explain what otherwise might appear a remarkable similarity of style; a similarity by the way, which will much aid the reader. In writing, different individuals seem to have pursued systems almost peculiar to themselves, in some respects. In the matter of abbreviations, for instance, from the earliest times, some wrote &, y^e, y^t, wch, wth, y^o, for *and, the, that, which, with, you,* in all cases; others spelled the words in full, or used the abbreviations indiscriminately. Some seldom or never abbreviated; others had a passion for abbreviating, and acquitted themselves in a most grotesque manner. The y^e and y^t grew out of a peculiar way of forming the letters in *the* and *that,* as any one may see by examining old records. Some letters were used interchangeably, as i and j, u and v. In short, orthography does not seem to have been deemed a matter of much importance. The writers, in many cases, appear to have simply endeavored to express themselves in the shortest intelligible way, regardless of uniformity or appearance. As remarked on page 14, the name of Lynn, in the act giving that name, is spelled Lin; the n has a line over it, denoting that it should be doubled.. Mr. Turner, it may be remarked, seems to have been in some particulars quite fond of a short hand way of writing.

And here it may be proper to say a word regarding dates. Some historians have not been sufficiently careful in stating them, where they were material. The Julian mode of computation having been in use in the old colony times, mistakes are liable to occur. The Gregorian or present style was not adopted either in Old or New England till 1752. The old style made the civil and legal year commence with Lady Day or Annunciation, the 25th of March. The new style changed it to the 1st of January. The correction of the calendar was made in 1582, by Gregory XIII., and the new style was forthwith adopted in all Catholic countries. We do not imagine that protestant England was apprehensive that any popish poison lurked in the new style, but yet she was singularly tardy in adopting it. However, the change was long expected here and in England, and hence the double dating so frequently found in old records and on old grave stones: thus, Feb. 12, $\frac{1682}{1683}$, or 1682-3; the month being in 1682 according to the old style and in 1683 according to the new. The same act of the British Parliament (1751) which provided that the next ensuing first day of January should be the first day of the new year, also provided that the second day of September should be called the fourteenth; thus dropping eleven days. Every fourth year was also ordained to be a leap year, with certain modifications that cannot much affect the reckoning of people for a thousand years to come. The causes which existed for the change of style are of course familiar to the reader. In the earliest times of New England, too, the months were frequently indicated by numbers instead of names, much in the style of the Quakers of the present day, as 3d month (May); 12th month (February), &c.

Mr. Turner was possessed of a considerable estate, and carried on farming to some extent. He married a lady from Salem, and reared a family of children. But it is likely that his sons had a propensity to rove, or to live bachelor lives, for it does not appear that at any time his was a prevailing name among us. He must have been quite popular with the people, for he was perpetually in the discharge of some responsible duty. Though a man of piety, we should not conceive him to have been one of the strict religionists of the time. In short, as far as we can gather, he possessed a most genial mind, and was inclined to the indulgence of pleasantry and all innocent amusements; in these and some other respects resembling another great philosopher, born just one century after his nativity.

But it would be quite impossible to enter much at large into a history of the life of Mr. Turner, even though the materials were all at hand. And, moreover, it is apprehended that a few pages from his journal would be more acceptable than anything else that could be offered.

Allusion has been made to Mr. Turner's belief, in common with the world in general at that time, regarding the occasional corporeal appearance of his satanic majesty. Now some may smile and greatly wonder at this. But yet, has this and the concomitant belief in ghosts ever been shown to be false? The question has been discussed for ages, and a vast majority of the christian world, to say nothing of the heathen, are unquestionably, at this moment, to be ranked as believers. It is yet an unsettled question; and no one has a right to treat it as settled. Neither you nor I, reader, have perhaps had proof satisfactory to our minds. But it does not follow that others have not. And it is a little presuming in us to laugh at such men as Sir Matthew Hale, Addison, Blackstone and Dr. Johnson, because they believed that such appearances might take place; or at the many great lights in divinity who declare that the Bible fully sustains the affirmative. All know the difficulty of proving a negative. But in this case innumerable witnesses appear in the affirmative, whose testimony has not been invalidated. Some of the instances are certainly strange enough, and to a reasonable mind seem somewhat shaky; as, for example, that in the experience of Martin Luther, the redoubtable reformer, who, while denouncing such vengeance against all liars, declared that the Devil came into his sleeping room at night and wantonly disturbed his rest by cracking hazel nuts upon the bed post. Luther conceived himself to be such a shining light in the world of truth and piety that the evil one took especial pains to extinguish him. The puritan fathers thought very much the same of themselves. And many individuals at this period fancy themselves of much more importance in this world and consideration in the other than they really are. And it is generally about as easy to be at peace with an east wind as with such people, however willing one may be to accede to all moderate assumptions.

We will now, for the benefit and gratification of the reader, present a few extracts from the aforenamed journal of Mr. Turner:

1630. Iulie ye 28: On ye last 4th day some of vs did goe afar into ye wildernesse towards ye river on ye west, and thence about by ye hills on ye north. And this wee did y^t wee might discover what ye land and productions of this our heritage be. Wee found vallies of mightie trees of such kinds as Old England is a stranger to. And wee made sore our feet by ye climing of hills among rocks and thornie brambles and vines. Great store of wild berries were on everie hand. Among them were manie black shining berries as big as ye pills of apothecaries; and these berries be of sweete, milde taste and grow in clusters on low bushes with light green leaues wthovt thornes. Wee did pluck some and found them savory to eat in fire cakes; and did think them apt for puddings. Then there were found other large black shining berries growing on creeping vines, of most luscious taste. And wee did eat till our mouths were black as ye chimney back.

As wee journied wee did sometimes see skulking abovt among ye trees, what wee conjectured to be Indjans or Devils; jt being patent y^t ye great foe of all God his people hath alreadie begun to harrass and plague this godlie companie. But wee doe some expect to have over from Nehumkeage a big ordnance whereby to defend ourselves from ye one, and some godlie bookes and catechisms to fortifie against ye other. And God being on our side wee feare not what Indjans or Devils can doe.

In a vallie wee found a small store of corn growing wch we did conjecture belonged to ye sauvages. And a little way off we did see some fruites growing whereof wee knew not ye name or vse but did surmise y^t they were all for food. But wee saw none watching thereabouts and no habitations.

Of wilde animals wee spied but few. But wee heard terrible roareings as if there were bears or unicornes away off in ye wilderness; or may be they were wild asses or roaring Devils seeking to devour God his people.

Wee did see some reptiles and serpents. And two y^t we saw had rattils in their tailes, wherewith they made a strange whirring noise mch like ye noise of ye rattils of ye night watch in London only not so mightie a rattil.

Of birdes wee saw great store. Some eagles and hawkes and manie of wch wee knew not ye names. But wee are of a truth in a paradise of those moving things y^t be good for foode. In ye woodes, in ye pondes and on ye sea shore, wee have multitudes of fowle, fish and game, most savory to ye appetite and healthy for ye stomach. Y^e Israelites fared less daintilie than wee; wherefor praised bee God.

It was somewhat within ye night when we came in sight of home. In coming over ye hillock nigh ye doore of our habitation I descried a daintie white rabbit, as jt seemed, wch I deemed would make a savory dish for breakfast on ye morrow. Giving chase, I was soone almost vpon him, when lo, he whisked vp a bushy tail over his hinder parts, and then threw jt towards me wth a mightie rush; and jt shed upon me a liquor of such stinke y^t nothing but ye opening of ye bottomless pit can equal. My eyes were blinded and my breath seemed stopped foreuer. When I recovered, ye smell remained vpon me, insomuch y^t they would fain drive me from ye house, saying y^t they could not abide wthin while I remained. And I still carry jt about wth me, in a yet terrible degree. I am persuaded y^t this is another device of Satan; y^t four footed beast being an impe let to do ye Devil his baptism by sprinkling.

1631. Ap^{rl} ye 2: Last third day such of vs as coulde, turned out to help goodman Iohnstone to begin ye building of his new house. Wee had goode hope y^t by this time our towne might become some famous and be faire in comlie habitations. But wee have been much put to jt to get materialls of ye right sorte wherewith to build. In Salem they now haue some bigge sawes, wherewith to make boardes. But few come to us, as the way hither is harde to travell by reason of ye stumpes and rockes y^t be in it. And likewise ye people there mch want their own bordes. So wee must do as wee best can wth our axes and adzes and smaller sawes, and what few bordes wee can from time to time make out to haul hither. Wee haue stones in plentie, but no mortar wherein to lay them. And wee haue aboundance of clay y^t might bee used in ye making of brickes, but none of us haue ye skill to rightlie molde and sett vp ye killen; and if wee had, ye mortar would bee wanting.

1632. Ap^{rl} ye 28: Wee had great discourse in generall meeting, on 6th day about ye planting of trees. Some few payr and appill trees haue already been sett oute. { It is undenyable y^t ye making of cyder is goode to keepe ye peeple from getting drounke on stronge liqvors and fire waters.} Wee can now procure, at small charge, from other plantations sch trees as in a few yeares will supply our wantes. And it seemeth high time y^t orchards should be set and growing vp even as our children be growing vp. God hath done mch in bringing us to this goodlie land, and we should do something for them y^t will come after us here. Itt being ye dutie of each generation to keep ye tyde of blessings rolling on to benefit ye next. Wee haue some wilde fruites in ye woodes it is true, but not manie and they not well liking.

Ian^{ry} ye 12: Y^e winter still continueth mightie colde, insomuch y^t ye sea be froze far into ye offing. Wee can goe to Nahauntus on ye ice. Our houses be halfe buried in snow. And we have to strapp boardes to our feete whereby wee may walke on ye snow, wch wee call snow shoes. Y^e women goe oute but little, being forced to follow ye Bible commandment to bee stayers at home; save y^t they go out to meeting. But praised be God, wee haue plentie of fire woode all arounde, so wee can keepe warme when wthin doores. But ye brute beastes suffer as well as wee from ye colde, for they bee mch put to jt to get foode. Y^e famishing wolves howle piteouslie about our habitations in ye nighte; and jt would fare harde, I think, wth one who should fall among them.

1633. Novr ye 1: Y^e Gen^{rl} Courte did last month make order to regulate ye wages of divers kinds of workemen and labourers. For master joyners, masons, sawers, carpenters, and them of other like trades, and mowers, it is ordained y^t not aboue 2 shillings a day, they findeing theire owne victualls, shall bee paid; and if they haue victualls founde, then not aboue 14 pence a day. And ye penaltie for takeing or giueing above y^t, is five shillings. Workemen y^t bee not masters, to haue such pay as two discreet people of ye labourer his own choosing, together wth ye constable, shall say. And itt is further ordered y^t they shall worke ye whole day, saveing onlie such time as may be needfull wherein to take their dyet and reste. {But, methinks, all such things should be left for men to agree vppon betwixt themselves. Some bee worth much more than others, by reason of their judgment, prudence and industrie.}

Y^e Courte too must needes keep makeing lawes to regulate ye price of corne and other produce raised. Then there being a great cropp or a poore cropp, they must presentlie undo what they haue done. Better lett ye people bee a law to themselves in such things. My neighboure Edward Tomlins hath built a famous mill vppon ye fresh brooke y^t runneth from ye greate ponde, nigh where ye same floweth into ye river Saugus. He hath thereby done a noble thing to supplie our needes, there being but one other mill in ye whole collonie and y^t not able to do ye halfe y^t is to bee done. But Mr Tomlins is now somewhat exercised by ye doeings of ye Courte, and saith y^t ye olde mortars wherein wee have bin forced to crack our corne had better not bee given to ye Indjans nor made into fire woode as yet, for ye foolish Courte may make such hard lawes vppon hjs mill, y^t hee may bee forced to give vpp ye same.

1634. May ye 5: This day have I helped my neighboure Masters in planting flaxe. Y^e garments brought wth vs soone beginning to weare oute, wee caste aboute to finde y^t wherewith to renew our clothing. And wee did try what might be done wth flaxe, wch wee are now shure groweth well here. With this we are well

pleased and hope soone to be prouided wth plentie of
stronge and comelie cloth; for there be them among
vs who haue skill in curing ye materiall and preparing
jt for ye spinning wheel and weaving frame. And our
women can do ye spinning and weaving. And wee
doe hope soone to haue plentie of sheepe too, for wool
as well as for meate.

At this time there is not mch braverie in dress
among vs, save that ye new comers from ye old countrie do sometimes proudlie appear.

Wee be yett a small place, and this is, as jt were,
ye beginning of things; but wee haue them among vs
who be able to turne hand to almost everie thing
necessary to be done for our comforte, and to make
vs lustie growers; so wee do hope soone to haue within ourselves all y^t can be found in any of these our
loyal plantations. And praised be God.

Iulie ye 10: Yester even I did have much pleasant
discourse wth William Woode, conccarneing this our
Thirde Bay Plantation, while sitting on ye oak logg by
my back doore; for he hath given oute y^t he shall
presentlie depart for Old England, there to sojourn a
briefe space. He hath bin here from ye beginning of
ye settlement, and hath writ enow to make a faire
booke, aboute affaires wthin ye pattent. And I did
mch urge him to printe ye booke while in England.
He hath trauelled mch amongst ye settlements and by
chearfull wordes and other wise helpes stopped manie
y^t would haue gon from vs, some to Virginia, some to
Plymouth and some elsewhere. And ye book, mch of
wch he hath read to me, speaking to our praise and to
ye praise of ye land, I doubt not, being printed at home,
will doe greatlie for vs, as there be manie who want
but to be shure of our being well planted firste and
they will send over mch to our comforte and helpe.
But some things he hath putt down y^t methinks will
not looke well in printe and I would faine haue had
him drop them: as hjs discourse about lions at Cape
Anne. Quoth I, I doe not beleave y^t anie such beaste
ever was founde there. He, being a little heady, did

warmlie replie, y^t then they were Devills, for nothing
but one or ye other could make such terrible roareings
as have been hearde thereaboute. And soe, said he,
I will have jt one or ye other. Well, well, quoth I,
Master Woode, if so you will, jt must be, tho I would
faine haue all discourse about revenous beastes and
Devills left out. If jt be thot at home y^t our lande
doth abounde in such, but few will be founde readie to
come hither. Lions they cannot be for ye bookes of
trauell have jt y^t such beastes live onlie in burning
desert lands. Devills they may be, for such be found
everiewhere. And as manie would rather face Devills
than lions, jt were better to call them Devills if one
or ye other it must be. And blessed be God wee
have ye holie Bible for protection against them.

1635. Ap^{rl} ye 20: There hath bin for some days
an uproare about ye destruction of ye salt workes.
Thomas Dexter and some others deeming y^t salt might
bee made to advantage here, not onlie to meet our
own needs, but also of a surplus to supply others at
a proffit to ourselves and cheape to them, went about
setting up neare ye foote of ye hill y^t overlookes y^e
beach a kettle or two and ye needed pans. Y^e work
went bravelie on. But on six day morning jt was
found y^t during ye night some Indjans, as they say,
came down and pitched ye kettles into ye sea and destroyed ye pans. But I am persuaded y^t not Indjans
but Devills did ye dirty worke, and y^t jt is onlie another attempt of Satan to drive God his people hence.
But wee will not goe, salt or no salt. I am ye more
moved vnto thjs belief, because Indjans be not stronge
of limbe, and a verie Samson might haue found ye mischief harde worke. Manie fish being now taken salt is
mch needed in ye curing thereof. And wee hope to
see other pans and kettles set vp. In Plymouth colonie we bee told salt is mch wanting. And ye workes
at Cape Anne have been burnt vp.

Septm^r ye 10: Y^e traine bande exercised to day on
ye common fielde. Wee have good store of firelocks,

and ammunition in aboundance. And wee deem ourselves able wth God his helpe to beate back a potent adversarie. Sometimes ye sauvages do threaten to fall vppon vs in greate numbers and destroy vs. But wee haue stout heartes, and do not feare but wee can helpe ourselves. Nevertheless wee must be vigillant and reddy. Wee haue a blocke house beside ye great ponde wch wee may fortifye and make a saife place for ye women and children to flee to when ye foe cometh; and thinke wee can holde out against ye worst till we may get succor from abroad.

Mr Batchellor, ye minister, made a loude prayer at ye training and exhorted to braverie in defence of ye faire lande wherewith God hath made vs rich, saying y^t such be our christian dutie; and bringing from ye holie scripture manie shining ensamples for our edification and encouragement. Some doe stumble at ye teachings of Mister Batchellor, saying he be an angell in hjs publick walke, but a devil in hjs own household. But who is there y^t is not better in hjs sayings than in hjs works.

Y^e musicke of ye fife and drum was mightie enspiriting. And ye conke shell trumpet was meet to terrify ye sauvage hearte.

Iohn Markes he got drunke at ye training and was pvt into ye stockes by ye big oake tree on ye common fielde.

1636. Decm^r ye 7: Y^e minister, Stephen Batchellor, left vs this yeare and as I haue hearde would goe to Ipswitch. He was ye firste minister here and did come among vs some above two yeare after wee did begin this oure plantation. Before his coming wee must needes doe our own preaching, exhorting and catechizing; save that sometimes wee could procure help from abroade; and some of vs used to go hence, when ye weather allowed, to heare preaching elsewhere. Mister Batchellor had mch zeal in preaching and exhorting; and some stranger Indjans once passing by ye meeting place were mch terrified saying y^t ye white man his council was open and y^t they hearde ye war yells. He was three score and ten yeares olde, as I learn, when first he came. Hjs hair is thin and gray, but hjs eyes be black and fierie. He hath an unseemlie wen on ye side of hjs nose wch presseth y^t member in an unshapelie way. He needeth no staff to stay hjs steps but is quick a-foot and sure. In person he is tall and leane, and when he speaketh earnestlie doth mch exercise hjs bodie. Some scandal hath appeared against him, partlie on ye score of chastitie and partlie on ye score of temper. He hath a strong will and liketh mch y^t people doe his bidding; or, as we say, he is heady. Hjs indignation is easilie roused, wch I doe not thinke seemlie in a minister. One happening to say to him a provoking worde at ye general meeting, got a blow for his paines. But mch must be forgiven where mch hath been suffered. Y^e godlie virtue of patience is not given to all in like measure. Some tempers grow harde and soure under ye same treatment where others keep tender and sweete. Few among vs haue been so badlie dealt wth in ye olde countrie as he. He began a minister in ye establishment and when he came out wth ye puritans he had mch evil usage to endure from ye bishops. He was mch put upon both before he went to Holland and after his return to London. He hath mch learning in ye Hebrew and Greek, is an easie preacher for words and doth easilie work himself into a holie frenzie. He hath baptised ye firste children born among vs, one being his owne.

1637. Augt ye 1: Mch hath been said of wonderful things being from time to time founde in divers of these parts. My neyboure Hawkes he being wth others at worke in ye greate easte field, did digg from a hillock toward ye shore two skelettons of stoute men swaddled and encoffined in a manner never known to ye Indjans, as they declare. And wth ye same they did finde divers implements of mettal, as a speare head of brasse, and some tubes seeminglie meant for ye deposite of medicine y^t they would alwaies haue wth them. It is judged y^t these be ye remains, not of Indjans, ye sauvages all declaring jt such they cannot be but of

5

some antient white people who must have come here for discoverie or by shipwrecke manie yeares before ye plantation began. And ye sauvages doe tell of theire old people hauing hearde from their fathers y^t a wonderful canoe did in antient times appeare in ye offing; and being driven by greate stresse of weather, was forced wthin ye greate Birds Egg Rocke, there goeing to pieces. Strange people wth white faces, they say were in ye shipp, and some reached ye shore alive. Presentlie they built a habitation on ye headlande, wherein they dwelt all ye summer, planting, fishing and hunting for their sustenance. But none ever hearde of what became of ye strangers.

Some declare y^t they have seene at Nahauntus sundry wonderfull tracks in ye solid rocke, as of some beaste like unto a great oxe. And I did goe thither wth some fishermen to looke for ye same, but we could finde nothing. Yet manie of faire credit doe stronglie affirme y^t they have seen them.

We doe have to be sparing of credit to ye Indjan tales. Y^e sauvages mch like to amaze us and excite our feares. But manie besides Indjans doe love to tell of wonderfull things in this wonderfull place. And we be sometimes puzzled to know what to beleave.

1638. Iune ye 19: Some going down to Nahauntus on thirde day laste, did see two ravenous wolves; being ye same, I think, y^t tore in pieces goodman Lakeman hjs cow. But they could not shoot them, for they were too quick into ye woodes there.

Vpon ye beach y^t lieth most southward they picked vp manie great clams, from wch a savorie dish was made. They also cacht great store of fish, wch, building a fire by ye rockes they cookt, and thereof with artichokes, and some bread, they made a right heartie meale.

Ioel Tomlins, he getting a little drounke, must needs show off his agility by dancing and balancing himself in dangerous places. And soe jt fell out y^t he fell over ye rockes into ye water, and they thot jt was all over with him. But one poising himself, was able to catch him by ye hair of his heade as he floated atop of ye wave, and so pulled him out againe. I doe thinke y^t people who get drounke, and there bee too manie sch hereabouts, should not goe a fishing on ye rockes of Nahauntus.

Upon ye beach they spied great multitudes of birdes of manie kindes, they being there to pick vp ye wormes and little fishes. They haue long bills wch they thrust into ye little holes in ye sand and pull up ye fat wormes wth great relish. They lay eggs in ye sand and ye heate of ye sun being vpon them they speedilie hatch, and ye little birdes betake themselves to feeding. Y^e beach birds be verrie shy and quick a-wing, but our sportsmen, nevertheless, do bring down great plentie for our own vse, and if need be to supply other plantations.

Itt hath bin writ in a booke y^t oysters be unwholesome to eate in everie moneth y^t hath not an R in jt. And soe some of our people will have jt y^t all shell fish, as lobsters, crabbs, clamms and ye like be not fit for foode betwixt Ap^rl and Septm^r. I know not that they bee poison att such times, but they bee not soe fat and luscious.

1639. Marche ye 28: There appeared in ye heavens a mightie sign wch may be ye forerunner of some direfull calamitie, as sickness, earthquake or other evill commotion. It seemed like unto a broade sheet of white light, in shape mch like ye tail of a fish, hanging in ye weste for some hours wthin ye night, from sunsetting. It did then fade away by little and little and disappeare. Some felt greate feare and ran to ye minister. But he did quietly tell them to feare not, for God is wth vs. And he bid them remember y^t ye Israeljtes did see cause to reioice in ye pillar of fire. And are not wee better than Israeljtes? He did goe out and studie ye wonder, till he almost froze in ye colde blast from ye northweste, and would have it y^t it was noe signe of anie thing wonderfull to come, and no more awfull than ye winde, or ye sunshine, onlie not so common.

1640. Iulie ye 19 : An Indjan boy did cunninglie creepe into my backe roome on yesternight and therefrom steale my axe. Y^e sauvages be mch given to thieving. Wee do haue to watch constantly when they be aboute, and complain to ye chiefs, wch doth little goode. And they sometimes boaste of what wonders they will do bie and bie when other nations come to helpe them. Hereaboutes there be but few sauvages, and they desperate poore, soe poore in sooth that they cannot afforde themselves naimes. And soe wee giue names vnto them, whereof they seeme mightie proude. One wee call Kettle Iohn, another Lobster Bill, another Soreface Ioe and soe on, they being fonde of hauing a meaning in theire names. They doe boaste of having been a greate nation in yeares gone by, but say that a dreadfull sicknesse carried manie off and soe mch weakened them as a nation. Y^e landes they holde in common and doe not worke to any advantage, haueing no tooles to boaste of. And as they hunt and fish mostly for theire foode they do not deeme theire lands of mch value, and seem glad to sell at a small price. A jewsharpe will do wonders wth them in a bargaine for lande. All ye old Sagamore his hill that overlookes ye beache and contains manie acres, was bought for a hatchett, a red jackett and two jewsharpes. And most of ye Indjan titles have been bought in, some for an iron kittle, some for a few iron nailes, and some for cast off clothes; in every bargaine, a jewsharpe or two being added, they being fonde of ye musicke therof. They have no great appetite in eating and live at a cheape rate. If they can get nothing else, a few clams pickt vp on ye sea shore, or a few eares of corn roasted in ye ashes contents a whole familie for a meal.

1641. Septem^r ye 5 : Some being on ye greate beache gathering of clams and seaweede wch had been cast thereon by ye mightie storm did spy a most wonderful serpent a shorte way off from ye shore. He was as big rounde in ye thickest parte as a wine pipe; and they do affirme that he was fifteen fathom or more in length. A most wonderful tale. But ye witnesses be credible, and jt would be of no account to them to tell an untrue tale. Wee have likewise hearde y^t at Cape Ann ye people have seene a monster like vnto this, wch did there come out of ye sea and coile himself vpon ye land mch to ye terror of them y^t did see him. And ye Indjans doe say y^t they have manie times seene a wonderful big serpent lying on ye water, and reaching from Nahauntus to ye greate rocke wch we call Birdes Egg Rocke; wch is much above belief for y^t would be nigh vpon a mile. Y^e Indjans, as said, be given to declaring wonderful things, and jt pleaseth them to make ye white peeple stare. But making all discounte, I doe believe y^t a wonderful monster in forme of a serpent doth visit these waters. And my praier to God is, y^t jt be not y^t olde serpent spoken of in holie scripture y^t tempted our greate mother Eve and whose poison hath run downe even vnto vs, so greatlie to our discomforte and ruin.

Decr ye 1: Wee do bless God y^t soe much good health hath bin our lot; for our feares were greate y^t coming from a land soe different in heate and colde, and being putt vpon new foode, sore plagues and paines might fall to our lott. True, wee have bin some exercised by sickness, and sometimes direfull pestilence hath ravaged vs. But for ye most parte it hath bin contrariwise. This is a goodlie lande for herbes and rootes wherewith to make medicines. And ye Indjans have mch skill in preparing ye same. There be manie doctors among them who gather greate bundles of ye herbes and rootes and store them vpp in their wigwams for winter use. And they mch love to show their skill vppon ye white people, being kind, and readie to goe miles for ye meanes, if they have them not at hand, wherewth to abate our pains. An olde Sagamoure did declare to me y^t he never knew of a sore or paine or sicknesse for which he could not find a cure somewhere in ye swamps, woodes, or pondes, vnless ye same was ye worke of some witchcraft; in wch case charmes must bee turned to. And charmes he had as well as herbes.

1643. Octr ye 1: This morning ye watch did begin ye blowing of their hornes, wch is to be in this wise: One to starte from ye hill near ye roade to Nahauntus and walk westerlie; ye other to starte from ye forke of ye roades at ye west end of ye common landes and walk easterlie. Y^e two to meet at ye halfe way poste, both stoutlie blowing their horns all ye way. They to starte one hour before ye rising of ye sun, and to walke some hastilie, and returne back without stopping. And whatsoever houses they find without a light or some token of stirring therein they are to reporte. And at nine of ye clocke at night they are to doe likewise onlie reporting all such houses as have lights or other tokens of ye people not being a-bed. And this is ye regulations to make ye people industrious and keepers of good hours.

1644. May ye 2: Ioel Breede is chose hunter for ye year. Hee is to destroy all four footed plagues, likewise crows and venomous serpents y^t he can, giving to ye dutie one half of everie day. And he is to haue his boarde for his paines, and to take it round among ye families.

1645. Ap^rl ye 7: Iohn Newhall was set in ye stockes by ye meeting house, for stealing of pumpkins from ye widdow Humfrey. Some boyes did pelt him wth rotton egges. And an Indjan did throw vpon him some blacke stuff of mightie stinke.

1646. Iune ye 3: Allen Bridges hath bin chose to wake ye sleepers in meeting. And being mch proude of his place, must needs have a fox taile fixed to ye end of a long staff wherewith he may brush ye faces of them y^t will have napps in time of discourse; likewise a sharpe thorne wherewith he may prick such as be most sounde. On ye laste Lord his day, as hee strutted about ye meeting house, hee did spy Mr Tomlins sleeping with much comforte, hjs head kept steadie by being in ye corner, and hjs hand grasping ye rail. And soe spying, Allen did quicklie thrust his staff behind Dame

Ballard and give hjm a grievous prick vpon ye hand. Wherevppon Mʳ Tomlins did spring vpp mch aboue ye floore and with terrible force strike wth hjs hand against ye wall, and also, to ye great wonder of all, prophainlie exclaim, in a loude voice, cuss ye woodchuck; he dreaming, as it seemed, yt a woodchuck had seized and bit his hand. But on comeing to know where hee was and ye great scandall hee had comitted, he seemed mch abashed, but did not speake. And I think hee will not soone againe go to sleepe in meeting. Ye women may sometimes sleepe and none know it, by reason of their enormous bonnets. Mʳ Whiting doth pleasantlie say yt from ye pulpitt hee doth seem to be preaching to stacks of straw wth men sitting here and there among them.

1647. Augt ye 8: There hath suddenlie come among vs a companie of strange people, wch bee neither Indjan nor Christian. And wee know not what to liken them vnto. Some will have it yt they bee Egyptjans or Jypsjes, wandering thieves, jugglers and beggars, so long a pest in ye old countries, and in England till Edward ye Fourth made hard lawes against them. But if they bee of that heathen people how came they hither and what doe they seeke in this wilderness where is little to steal and mch justice to give them stripes. If they bee Egyptjans jt is patent yt ye devill hath sent them hither to do his bidding and harrass God his people. Where ye most godliness is to bee founde there ye devil maketh his strongest effort. But how such people could get here none can tell. Being wth their olde captaine I did ask him by signs, for they speake in vnknown tongues, whither they came. Whereuppon he did point southward, not meaning towards Plymouth, but far beyond. And he would haue me understand yt they did not come over sea. Never hearing yt any such people were in ye Dutch settlements or Virginia, I surmised yt hee did mean yt they came from ye Spanish settlements, thousands of leagues awaie.

This strange companie hath made their camp in a

valley a little within ye woodes. And there they live in no better plight than ye Indjans; eating all manner of unclean meats, as frogs and rats, and deeming daintie foode such cattle and pigges as have died of murrain, if they can begg them of us. They come often into ye settlement, and sometimes travel, mostlie by night, to other townes. They doe use palmistry and other devilish arts and witchcrafts. And we are much exercised to watch against their pilferings. Neither doe wee let our children goe mch in their waie, for jt hath been sayd y^t these people sometimes steal little folk and rear them in all their heathen waies. And I doe surmise y^t a maid wth them may be of this sort. Her years may be eighteen or thereaboute, and she hath such a faire complexion with blooming cheeks as are not like unto ye other maids with them. She doth not besmear her hair like ye others, but jt falleth vpon her shoulders, clean and glossie. Her eyes may be likened unto pretious diamonds being so lustrous. And her teeth being without staining from druggs are white as snow. She hath a merrie looke and gay laugh and is withal neate in her clothes and always cleane in face and hands. She sometimes cometh into ye town wth ye olde captaine, having her head decked wth flowers and is bewitching to ye younge men, stepping soo daintilie and looking soe comelie. But shee hath their evil waies, and will make delicate signs to some youth y^t she would bestow favors vppon them. But praised bee God all here bee so brot vpp in his holie ordinances y^t ye bodie being under subjection, temptation doth not overcome.

They doe sometimes make merrie at their lodges, wth great outcries and laughter. And vppon ye holie Sabbath they doe dance and riot. And they would fain entice our young men and maids to come and haue their fortunes told, bringing pay therefor in fish, Indjan loafs, artichokes and other meats, and in strong drinks of which they bee mighty fond, and will spend daies in drounkenness when ye meanes bee at hand.

Their men do sometimes goe from door to door about ye towne with tools wherewth to mend pans and kettles and doe ye worke of cobblers. But thanks bee to ye Lord, we have good shoemakers here enow for all our needes, and would helpe our owne. The women make divers ointments and medicines for burns, cuts and other hurts, and gather herbs which they bring to our doors for sale.

Wee little like to haue these pestigeous people among vs, and will presently drive them hence if they do not goe of themselves, for they bee all theiving, unchaste and disordalie uagabonds, wandering vpp and down and prowling about by night and daie. When nothing of greater value comes in their waie, little bits of iron, fish hooks and even broken pottery do not come amiss. And the Indjans much complain of the stealing of their jewsharpes.

Hearing a great outcrie among my poultry yester even, & hastening oute by ye backe doore, I descried one leaping over ye stone wall, to gain ye bushes. Y^e wall falling, he fell likewise, but not being hurte, he was presently againe on his feet; and I then comeing vpp to ye wall seized him by ye skirte of his outer garment; but he being on ye other side, and seeing hjs advantage gave me a lustie pluck, bringing me sprawling across ye wall. Some stones being thereby knocked down, and falling against me did disable me from further pursuit. Going back to ye poultry house, I was much distresst to finde my proudest Chester cock wth his head twisted from his bodie, and sundry pullets in ye same plight.

Coming down ye roade by ye rivver Saugust on ye last second daie, I did descry them all, men, women and children, in stark naked plight bathing together in ye rivver, shouting, throwing water vppon one another, and challenging to swimming races, and doing many like indecent feats. But I presentlie turned my eyes from beholding soo great a scandall, tho I could not stop my ears to their wild outcries and prophanitie as it seemed. Such things were never before heard of in these parts, no, not even among ye Indjans. But I haue heard tell of there being like shamefull doings among ye Spanish in Mexico and other places to y^e

D

southward, whence, some will have jt y^t these came. But we must presentlie put a stopp to these things or ye plagues will be vppon vs.

Their Captain, as wee call him, is of manie years. He is of noble presence, wth thin white hair and beard, and a scar vppon his forehead. He hath a voice loude and commanding; but his manners bee not discourteous. He seemeth to feel ye care of a father for hjs charge; doth comfort them in sickness, plead for them in difficulties and fight for them in danger. And well may they love him and obey hjs commands. They do all seem to wish no better life than their wandering one. And I am fain to believe y^t ignorance is ye mother of mch of their evil doings. Mr Whiting hath wrestled in praier for them and would give them mch good discourse but for ye difficulties of ye language. And he saith trulie y^t ye soule of one of these outcaste children is as pretious wth God as ye Christian his soule, for He is no respecter of persons. And doe wee not all know y^t Christ his blood can wash ye one soule white and clean as ye other. And praised be God his great name for this. But yet, take these vagrant people as they bee, in temporal wise, they be such companie as wee doe not crave to have among vs and will presentlie rid ourselves of them by ye best means in our power. So all declared, in general meeting.

September ye 3: Praised be God ye vagrant Egyptjans or whatever they be, haue departed from among vs. In ye last seventh day night they marched awaie, taking y^t holie time, methinks, for feare of pursuit and punishment for their evil deeds while sojourning here. But wee were mch too glad to be rid of them to parley or seek our own. Manie have lost by their thieving waies; one a hoe, another a hatchet another a cod line; and few of vs doe not miss some moveable thing. Farmer Newhall his plow hath disappeared, tho what on earth such people could want of a plow wee doe not know. He would have followed and sought ye implement, but wee did persuade him from jt lest they should return, and helped to make vpp for his loss, which is indeed a sore one, for there bee not manie plows among vs, and he was alwaies ready to loan to a neighbor.

1650. Iulio ye 14: Some youngsters being in ye woodes on ye last Lord his day did wickedlie play at cardes on a flat rock. And while ye game was going on, they say there did appeare vpon ye solid rock, in ye middest of them, a foote printe, plaine as a foote printe could be made vpon ye sand of ye beache; whereupon they were greatlie terrified, as well they might be. Y^e goode peeple say y^t jt be ye devill his foote printe. But it seemeth strange y^t ye devill should desire to drive them off from doing hjs own worke or to disturbe ye breakers of ye Lord his daie, or other euil doers. But by whomsoever ye miracle was wrought, methinks it was meant as a solemn warning to Sabbath breakers and card players. And my praier to God is y^t jt may be rightlie heeded.

1651. Augt ye 4: Yester even wee did return, mch tired, from ye West Precinct. At ye Iron Workes wee founde all ye men wth smutty faces and bare armes working lustilie.

Y^e setting vp of ye forge here, wch was done some six years agoe, is a mightie helpe to vs y^t want iron worke some times. They do make here all kindes of affaires wanted by our farmers, such as chaines, plow irons, sythes, boltes and ye like. And their axes and trammels be strong and well shaped. There be no other iron workes hereabouts, and soe mch work cometh in from abroad. Some of ye workmen be exceeding skilfull and ye fame of ye workes be verrie great. Y^e Courte, I am told, think so well of hauing ye workes here among vs, y^t they be readie to doe all things lawfull for them to doe to encourage ye undertaking. Tho ye oare found hereabouts be not of ye first qualitie, they yet finde it sufficient to pay for ye digging and smelting.

Y^e workes be mostlie owned by certain rich men in Old England, and monie is not wanting for ye supply of all things necessarie. And jt be a great comfort to us in this new countrie, where mch labour and money is needed, to know y^t soe manie men at home, yea and women too, of substance and high favour, do take a livelie interest in our goode, and be so reddie to lend a helping hand. But some of ye richest and wisest men here haue something to doe with these workes, wch showeth y^t they think them of worth. God prosper them.

Y^e workemen be mostlie from Old England, and mch skilled in ye work. Y^e headmen be of substance and godlie lives. But some of ye workemen be young, and fond of frolicking, and sometimes doe frolicke to such purpose y^t they get before ye magistrates. And jt be said, mch to their discredit y^t one or two hath done naughtie workes with ye maidens living thereabouts.

There hath been talk of some iron workes in ye Plymouth colonie. But if any be there ye fame thereof is not soe great as these. And ye people of that colonie do sometimes send hither for articles made.

Y^e Iron Workes be in a delightfull place, beside ye river Saugust. Manie tall pines grow neare by; also oakes and walnuts. And it is pleasante to see ye smoke of ye workes curling up among ye trees.

Y^e Indjans sometimes come about ye workes, and will haue sharpe arrow heads made. But ye workmen haue been warned againste supplying them, for such weapons may if neede come be turned against themselves. One should not make a gun wherewith himselfe is like to be shot.

Y^e overseer of ye workes did show vs greate courtesie. He would haue vs view ye premises, and heare ye storie of their greate doings. And he entertayned us wth a noble dinner; giving vs fresh meat in plentie and fish. And to crown all wee had a most daintie pudding, wherein were cherries of most delightfull taste. And wee had fruite and savorie dishes of berries, some black and some red, wth plentie of sweetening spread vpon them. A good tankard of well kept cyder furnished drink for vs. He hath a wife of great comelinesse and pleasantrie, haueing no soure lookes nor angry wordes. She hath two children verie faire and smarte. And being of goode learning she delighteth to instruct and catechize ye little folk of ye precinct.

Y^e minister, Mr Whiting, doth sometimes come hither to preach in ye big barne, and soe ye infirme and lazie y^t cannot or will not go elsewhere haue preaching at hand.

Y^e enterprise of ye Iron Workes we haue much at hearte. It hath our labors and our praiers and must needs prosper if God be wth vs in jt; and methinks he is, for wee are his peeple and he seeth our need.

Augt ye 25: Gooddie Baker was ducked in ye great ponde by ye east roade for being a common scolde and ye using of unchaste and prophane wordes. She was deckt in a petticoate of yellow cloth wth a high red cap on her head, and a crow feather stuck a-top thereof. And being strapped to ye stoole wth leathern strappes, she was let down under ye water three times. She did sneeze and shake her head each time as she came vp, much as a dog doth when he hath been plunged into ye sea. Twas not till she had been brot vp ye laste time y^t she sued for mercie or would saie one word as if sorrie. There was a multitude present. Some hissed and some taunted her about her evil sayings, but, as jt appeared, not greatlie to her discomforte. Y^e duckinge, methinks, will do her good for she is thereby punished for her evil speech and washed withall, wch she seemed mch to neede.

1652. Decem^r ye 12: In selling some corne this daye there was payed unto me a shillinge of ye new stampe wch ye minte at Boston hath sent out. Y^e Courte hath ordered ye making of these, likewise sixpences. But I question if ye collonie hath a right to do sch a great thing, tho I be not one y^t will refuse ye taking of them on account of ye unlawfull making of ye same. Our needes in ye matter of small silver pieces hath been verrie greate. We have, jt is true, a little Spanish money but not enow to supplie our needes; and most of our trade hath been by barter. Y^e superintendent

of ye iron workes informed me y^t ye die for ye pieces
was made at hjs workes, and y^t hjs wife did draw y^e
famous design y^t appears thereon. These be ye first
pieces made in ye land. And we do hope y^t ye mint
may be kept in motion. It will be a long time before
our needes be supplied. And as we be a growing
people, and our trade greatlie encreases, we shall never
be overstocked for monie.

1653. Apr'l ye 14: Mch debate was held at ye last
publick meeting concerning ye buryal place. I did make
motion to haue a faire wall raised around ye same and
some unseemlie heaps of stone and gatherings of thornie
brambles removed. But most would haue jt y^t we
neede do nothing; y^t ye cost would be great and no
gaine come thereby to ye dead or living; saying too
y^t when ye bodie is buried jt be dust given backe to
duste; and ye golden chain being broken at ye grave,
there should end all our care; and y^t jt be but superstition to make show and pomp aboute ye dead as doe
manie Churchmen and Catholics. Surelie we doe bless
God y^t there be a resurrection of our better part from
ye foule clay. But still ye hearte will sometimes haue
its way above reason, and love best to think of ye dear
ones lying in pleasant places. I do hope y^t if these
things be not done by this generation, ye time will
come when others will doe ye same; for ye ground
may be made verie faire wth ye ponde and manie noble
trees.

1654. Iune ye 20: Mch grief hath fallen on Mr Whiting and his familie. Y^e Indjan maid Ruth, whom they
did so mch love, on ye last Lord his daie did run awaie
and again join herself to her heathen people of ye wilderness. It be now eight years or thereabout since
ye godlie minister took her a gift from her Indjan
mother to bring her vpp in ye nurture and admonition
of ye Lord. And she hath been these manie years as
one of hjs own children, eating of hjs own bread and
drinking of his own cupp, receiving godlie instruction
at meeting and under his roofe and learning at hjs

schoole. And she did trulie seem like a fresh blooming wilde flower, wch we so loved to liken her unto. And she had too a loving hearte as well as bright mind, cleaving wth mch tenderness vnto ye good man whom she did call father, weeping at his paines and rejoicing at his pleasures. But she hath gon. And tho she hath done a great seeming wrong, yet may it somewhat abate when well considered. It is hard to overcome our first love. Y^e hearte will sometimes turn back while ye eyes look forward. She hath gone to her forest home, awaie from our christian habitations, their comforts and blessings, from our protection and godlie instructions. In ye wigwam, her learning will stand her in poore stead against cold and hunger, and she will tear vpp her braive red scarf to adorn her dark lover his speare. But sunshine hath once broken into her soule and blessed bee God, all ye mists of heathenism cannot smother jt out again. And I did say to Master Whiting, seeminglie mch to his comfort, y^t she maie yet be a meanes of grace to manie a poore red man. God grant it — and likewise mch happiness to her both here and hereafter.

1655. Augt ye 7 : Some have bin mch exercised touching ye heavenlie signs wch have of late appeared; as a noble shipp wth sailes spread, lifted high in aire, saileing bravelie against ye wind, and so out beneath a beautjfull rainbow; ye trees, yea and rocks of Nahauntus lifted high in air; ye islands wch be half a score of miles in ye offing seeminglie brot nigh to ye shore, insomuch y^t we could well descry cattill and sheep grazing thereon. Tho these be wonderfull things, yet they be so ravishing y^t we may well say that they can not betoken evill to come, but contrarywise, good. And blessed be God they have turned to ye good of some; as Obed Oliver, his speech, wch had before bin mch distempered wth prophanitie, hath now become of better qualitie. And Gooddie Welch hath turned from her unchaste ways, and craved ye sacrament of Mr Whiting. We do well remember ye phantom shipp that sailed into ye harbour of New Haven half a score of years agone, and did weep over jt as bearing tidings of yᵉ loss of Captaine Turner, wth yᵉ other noble men. But that shadow fell to pieces as betokening a wreck; not so yᵉ appearance here.

1656. Decemʳ yᵉ 15: Yᵉ reverend teacher, Mʳ Cobbett did leave vs this year haueing been with vs about a score of yeares. He hath greatlie helped Mʳ Whiting in hjs laboures and they lived together in yᵉ most friendlie and christian way; he doeing mch in catechizing and instructing yᵉ children. He hath good learning, having once been an Episcopal minister in Lincolnshire. And he hath mch witt and curious knowledg. He knowing mch of public affaires, hath composed some poetry on matters of government, wch made some stir among yᵉ people, some scolding and some laughing. He is mch thot of abroad, we hear.

In person, Mʳ Cobbett is rather short and a little stoopeing. He hath thick lipps and eyes seeminglie full of mirth. He loveth mch to take long walks, in yᵉ woodes and on yᵉ beaches; and he goeth with one hand ahind hjs back and wth hjs eyes toward yᵉ ground, as if in great studie, and I think he be in studie, as one being neare him may see him sometimes smile, sometimes frowne and sometimes talk vnto himself. Hjs haire is dark and verrie thin and he sometimes weareth a little black capp, at yᵉ meetinges mch to yᵉ amusement of yᵉ young folk.

But in walk and conversation Master Cobbett is a right godlie man; and in temper loving peace and goode will, wch maketh amends for all other things that be wanting. He is a good friend to all yᵉ children and they love mch to meet him. He laboreth to make them good and apt to learn. And he saith yᵗ by soe doing he is preparing yᵉ foundation stones for a great nation. He hath been installed at yᵉ church in Ipswitch, I hear.

1657. March yᵉ 27: This day hath been yᵉ funerall of Goodman Burrill. We had plentie of wine and cyder and stronge liquors, and sugar wherewith to sweeten ye same. Several did drinke more than was meete and bring great scandal vpon ye occasion. Widdow Hamsteade did do in y^t way and make prophane and indecent speeches, much to ye mortification of ye friends. Uerilie I think it not meet to offer strong drinks at such times. A little wine for ye women and near friends, and cyder for ye men is enow. But ye giving of gloves and rings if they can be afforded can be in no wise harmeful. A famous pair of gloves did fall to me on this occasion. It was dark night before ye bodie was in ye grave, and a cold rain set in wch wth ye snow upon ye ground hath made ye trauelling verrie plashie and bad, and ye rain continueth to this hour.

I think y^t ye Bible should be read and praiers always made at ye burial of ye dead. No matter if they of ye Church of England do ye same. Must we dispise a good thing because they do approve jt? Y^e custom, I am glad is growing among vs. Christian feeling and good sense methinks will finally master ye preiudices y^t still linger among vs. And I dare prophesie y^t ye time will come when none, even here in this puritan land, will be carried to ye grave withoute praiers. And wth ye same faith I dare prophesie likewise y^t ye time will come when strong drinks will not be had at funeralls, even among ye puritans.

Iune ye 8th: Lord protect us. My neighbour Purchiss hath run in to stir up hue and crie on a terrible deed of blood y^t he saith they report hath iust been committed, by olde Rattlesnake, ye Naticke Indjan, hee having killed Goodman Anderson, his daughter, and likewise her betrothed, who hath lately come hither, they being with ye party of young people in ye woodes to-day. I yet doubt y^t so dreadful a thing hath been done, tho we do well know y^t Mr Anderson hath wrathfull enemies amongst ye savages.

1658. Decem^r ye 14: This year there hath been a great and terrible earthquake; such a one as was never before known hereabouts. Y^e houses shook and dishes did fall down from y⁰ shelves. Some being out did feel y⁰ ground rock. Y⁰ sea roared wth a dismal roareing, as if a mightie storme was coming on. And some being near y⁰ shore said y⁰ tide was turned before y⁰ time. Some chimnies were shook down, but not mch michief done of wch I have heard. In y⁰ morning y⁰ air was so yellow, like vnto brasse, and thicke, y⁰ we did fear some great evil to come. But y⁰ most mightie worke done by y⁰ earthquake, hereaboutes, was y⁰ splitting of a great rock in y⁰ woods. It hath by some been called y⁰ Dungeon Rocke, because there appeared to be beneath y⁰ same a dungeon cave. And jt hath been said y⁰ Thomas Veal, a crooked, grizzley and ill looking shoemaker did live in y⁰ cave and do his shoemaking there. Some of vs did use to purchase his works of him; for tho not neat and comelie to looke vpon, yet they were strong and tight; iust what we want where there be so many stumps and briars and so much mud and plash at times. On y⁰ splitting of y⁰ rock by y⁰ earthquake as some think y⁰ old man was shut vp alive in y⁰ cave; and no great loss to y⁰ world as they will have jt; he not beeing thot well of. Some say he was once a pirate robber and did bury treasure hereabout. But it seemeth strange if jt be so, y⁰ he should live so poorlie and work so hard. He did often come among vs to trade hjs shoes for provisions, and hath been known, but not often, to haue some small pieces of Spanish monie. It hath been further sayed y⁰ he was one of a number of pirate robbers y⁰ lived hidden in a glen by y⁰ river towardes y⁰ Iron Workes.

1660. Octo⁰ y⁰ 30: We hear y⁰ M⁰ Burton hath been to y⁰ Courte to complaine of Winnie Johnstone for y⁰ keeping of Christmas wch jt is said is not lawful here. But God forbid y⁰ it should be unlawful to keep y⁰ holie birthday of y⁰ Savioure of mankind. We did hope y⁰ sch things might not be in this pleasant lande, where there be manie who tho no churchmen yet be willing to acknowledge sound doctrine, tho churchmen yea even popish catholicks doe y⁰ same. And y⁰ minister, Mister Whiting, thinketh such things grievous, he being of large minde and good heart, and yet far enow from ye establishment. But ye first minister, Master Batcheldor, was stout to beat down everie sproute of ye episcopacie in this puritan soil.

1663. Decem^r ye 10: Mch distress hath been in ye churches about ye Quakers who be now rampant in ye land. Y^e laws and ye magistrates be hard vpon them. Women as well as men haue been stript and whipped at ye carts taile for manie miles from town to town. And some haue been brought to ye gallows. Y^e more peeple be put vpon for their belief ye more do they set theire faces against changing their ways. (And besides, ones religion is a matter betwixt him and his God.) He should be let alone so long as he injureth not and intereferth not wth others; wch keeping to themselves I am sorrie to say seemeth not always to haue been ye case wth ye Quakers. Yet do I think y^t our laws and our magistrates haue been mch too hard vpon them, and vpon others that do not think alike wth vs. Surelie wee, of all people, ought to know how pretious libertie of conscience is, for manie of vs here haue suffered enow for its sake. (And I do say y^t a church y^t cannot stand of its own strength ought to fall.) And I doe say further, y^t when one strippeth naked and goeth about uttering lamentations and outcries against ye evil ways of ye people, they themselves are in evil ways and should be dealt with by ye civil power, be they Quakers or what nots. And so I end my says about ye matter.

1671. Marche ye 30: Y^e past year hath been one mightie in stormes. A great and terrible snow fell in ye middle of Ianuarie, insomuch y^t houses were buried to ye chimnies. Y^e poore cattle suffered grievously, being wthout food and drink for days, none being able to get unto them. One getting out of his chamber window thinking to go to a neighbor his house, did sink down in ye snow till nothing of him appeared, and he came nigh being stifled. But ye window being left open, his wife did hear a small cry, and hastylie throwing out ye table top, did get thereon and help him to recover himself. Presentlie after there came a day of melting, and then a mightie cold, wch froze ye snow hard enow to bear ye stoutest man. And we did travel forth, sometimes greeting our neighbours at their chamber windows, and were able to grasp ye tops of ye trees.

Again, of a Lord his day in ye middle of Maie, there did come such a storm of thunder and lightning as was never before known among vs. It began iust within ye night wth a high wind and some hail, wch did break and beat down all ye grain and other things planted y^t were grown above ground. Y^e thunder and lightning were terrible to witness. Farmer Harte his barn was struck and set on fire, and his famous brindle cow killed. A great rock by ye back road was likewise struck and ye noise of ye explocion was awfull indeed.

In Iulie a direfull whirlwind did pass thro ye settlement. Its path was about two poles in width, and its violence exceeding great. Trees, fences, yea, houses, all y^t stood in its way were cleared like chaff. Goodman Collins his house standing in its way was cut off and ye part carried manie poles and dashed into ye pond, a heap of ruins. Widow Bridges her house was taken up bodilie and turned over first vpon its top and then down ye bank into ye creek, and twas a mercie y^t she was not in jt, she having just before gone out to pick vp some chipps. My own well curb was taken vp by ye wind and carried thro ye air over ye tops of houses and trees, and dashed to pieces on ye ground a long walk away. Gooddy Billin being out wth her apron thrown over her head, ye wind took both her apron and her capp of goat hair and lodged them in ye top of ye great beach tree near ye minister his house. And after ye blow was over they in ye house were some mirthful, saying y^t ye wind was so strong as to blow ye haire off her heade. After ye terrible whirlwind was past, wch was not manie minutes, some did go out to see ye road y^t it had cut and to wonder at ye great destruction. A number of beastes and birds, a few killed and others so lamed y^t they could not get away were pickt up; and some did live daintilie for one day certaine.

1679. Iune ye 20: It is now fiftie years since this now famous towne was first begun. Wee have grown from ye small beginning of about a score of poore pilgrims dropt as it were in ye sauvage wilderness, to be a people well to doe and manie in number. And all this by God his blessing for which his name be praised.

Wee have good houses and gardens and large fields well cleared and sufficient for growing all wee need and more for exchange for such from abroad as we desire; for it is always wth a people y^t their cravings increase wth their means. Wee have horses and cattle and piggs and fowles in aboundance. And have we not enow wth all these. So let vs thank God for his undeserved bountie and purge our hearts from all uncleanness.

Wee haue butchers to supply vs wth flesh meat and fishermen to supply vs wth fish both fresh and salted, likewise clams and other meat from ye sea. And we have smiths, carpenters, and brick layers; shoemakers, weavers and manie other handicraftsmen to make and mend for our comfort. Who, then, are better provided than we. And for ye same, we doe againe and wthout ceaseing thank God. But above all doe we bless his holie name for our gospell priviledges, for our aboundance of good preaching and diligent catechising; likewise for the faire schooles wherein our children are taught.

Wee prospered under Charles ye firste; we prospered under Cromwell and ye Commonwealth; and wee yet prosper under Charles ye second. But wch was ye greatest prosperitie I do not rightlie know. Wee had most libertie under Cromwell, and were not soe often called to account for our doings; being moreover allowed to doe most for ourselves by way of gouernment. And had ye gouernment wch he established bin continued I doubt not y^t we, when strong enough to protect ourselves would haue been made independent.

But yᵉ monarchie being now againe established, and yᵗ being yᵉ most costlie kind of gouernment, I fear yᵗ we shall be held whether we will or no, in hopes yᵗ our trade and growing riches may turne out to be a help to yᶜ crown. But haue wee not, as they say, cut our own fodder. Haue we not cleared our own fields, caught our owne fish wth our owne bait, and fought our owne battles wth yᵉ Indjans as witness yᵉ great Pequot war fortie yeares agone and yᵉ war wth King Philip of late. And are we not rightlie some proud of our doings. But after all I doe think yᵗ yᵉ destinie of a people is under God, wth themselves. Wth intelligence, energie, frugalitie and industrie they will prosper, tho they be set downe in a barren land. And we have taken much paines to haue good schooles to make vs intelligent; to haue good exhortations to perseverence, economie and activitie; and good lawes to make vs industrious. Shall wee not then, continue to prosper whatever they doe aboute vs over yᵉ water. If they do illy by vs while wee be weak, when wee get strong enough wee will surelie haue a reckoning wth them. So yᵉ wheels being now in motion on yᵉ right roade let vs keep moveing.

Decemʳ yᵉ 12: Yester even died yᵉ dear & reverend Mʳ Whiting. He hath laboured among vs this fortie yeare and vpwards, and was mch beloved both here and abroad. Hjs godlie temper was seen in yᵉ sweet smile yᵗ he alwaies wore. Hjs learning was great. In yᵉ Hebrewe jt hath been said none on this side of yᵒ water could come vp to him. He greatlie labored for yᵉ children, and for manie yeares would haue as manie as he could come to hjs house on everie Lord his day after yᵉ publique worship was over, and be catechized and instructed by him in Bible truths. And on week daies he also instructed yᵉ children, such as would, in Latin and other learning of yᵉ schooles. He was not fond of disputations and wordie wranglings about doctrine, but laid down hjs poynts plainlie and then firmlie defended them by yᵉ scriptures, not taking yᵉ time, as yᵉ manner of some is, to tell how others look vpon yᵉ same and then to tell how false was ye eye wth wch they looked. He writ some things y^t came out in print and all testified to their being sound in doctrine, liberal in sentiment, and plain and practicall.

Mr Whiting was a good liver saying y^t he did not find y^t mortifying ye flesh meant pinching ye stomach. Hjs wife was a right comelie dame and belonged to a great familie, being Chief Iustice Saint John his daughter. She was a godlie woman and did mch to chear and help her husband. By her learning she was able to giue mch instruction to ye damsels of ye parish, and they did all love her as she were a tender mother. She died some above two yeares agone; and he did greatlie mourn for her.

Mr Whiting had a noble garden wherein were delicious fruits and manie good things for kitchen vse. He had a score of appill trees, from wch he made delicious cyder. And jt hath been said y^t an Indjan once coming to hjs house, and Mistress Whiting giving him a drink of ye cyder, he did set down ye pot and smaking hjs lipps say y^t Adam and Eve were rightlie damned for eating ye appills in ye garden of Eden; they should haue made them into cyder.

Mr Whiting was of a quiet temper and not mch giuen to extasies, but yet he would sometimes take a merrie part in pleasant companie. Once coming among a gay partie of young people he kist all ye maides and said y^t he felt all ye better for jt. And I think they too felt all ye better for jt, for they did hug their armes around hjs neck and kiss him back again right warmlie; they all soe loved him.

For ye few past yeares Mr Whiting hath been mch exercised by sickness. His paynes haue at times been soe greate y^t he must needes cry out. But he bore all wth godlie patience and had kind wordes for them y^t were by him.

He was a man of middle size, dark skin and straight fine hair. Hjs hands were white and soft mch like some fine ladys. In preaching he did not mch exercise hjs bodie. But hjs clear voice and pleasant way were as potent to hold fast ye thoughts of old and young.

He had great care in his dress while preaching, saying y^t hjs hearers should not be made to haue their eyes vpon an unseemlie object, lest ye good instruction might be swallowed vp in disgust. And for a reason like vnto y^t he would also haue hjs discourses in milde and winning wordes. { In generall ye sermon would be an hour and a half long and ye long praier another half houre, wch wth ye reading of ye scriptures and ye singing would make ye whole above two hours; ye hour glass upon ye pulpitt telling ye time. } He did not love sleepers in meeting time and would sometimes stop short in ye exercises, calling pleasantlie to some one to come and wake ye sleepers. {And once of a warm summer afternoon he did take hjs hat from ye peg in ye beam and put it on saying he would goe home and feed hjs fowles and come back again, when may be, their sleep would be ended, and they readie to hear ye remainder of his discourse. } And at another time he did exclaim y^t he wished for ye Church of England service, wch by making them rise and sit often, would keep them awake. And this wishing for ye Episcopal service one may be sure was competent to keep some eyes open for a month to come. }

Y^e towne was called Lin in compliment to Mr Whiting who came here from Lin in old Norfolke. Before, wee were called Saugust, wch wee did not mch like, some nicknameing vs Saw-dust. Most thot ye name a good one, tho some would have it y^t it was too short. But to such wee said, then spell it Lynne. Y^e change was made fortie yeare and more agone : [1637] : and none now find fault.

Mr Whiting his funerall js appointed to be on third day next. And ye whole towne is alreadie in an uproar wth preparations. Wee must entertain manie from abroad and greate store of meate and drink will be needful.

1680. Decr ye 19 : When ye great and terrible comet of ye present yeare appeared wth jts fiery tayl reaching nigh half way acrost ye heavens and allmost as bright as ye moone, wee did greatlie feare y^t some dire calamitie was soon to break vpon vs. For manie days after it departed, a wonderfull fogg or smoke did fall vpon vs everie day. It had a strong smell of brimstone and was not wet like other foggs; and it seemed to come wth ye wind, blow wch way jt would. Wee did at first think jt to be ye smoke of great fires in ye woods; but jt could not be y^t; nor could jt be a fogg from ye sea; and we knew not what it was. Sometimes in ye middest of ye night jt made ye aire so light y^t we could read thereby. But no great evill hath yet come vppon vs, save ye storme about ye time of ye equinox. Our Plantation hath prospered wth great prosperitie. And God grant y^t these wonders be not ye forerunners of calamities yet to come. Hjs name be praised.

1681. Octr ye 17: Another parish meeting hath been held wherein ye village orators made mch discourse about ye new Meeting House to be built next year. Somewhat hath alreadie been done in ye way of getting out ye fraime. It will be a famous house and one of wch wee may be a little proud. Y^e time hath been when our neighbours of ye other townes haue spoken scornfullie of our poore plaice of worshipp; but everie tide will turne. Mr Shepard, ye new minister, had a hand in ye plan as I hear. Y^e plan hath been vp in ye old meeting house porch for some Lord his days mch like a marriage notis. And everie one seeing jt hath some better notion of his owne for this or that part. And one might know y^t sch would be ye case. I being on ye comitte did counsell ye others to go on & ask opinions of none save ye builders. To make publique requeste for opinions, and then not follow what we get sows evill seeds among vs. But when one gets advice wthout asking, no blame is vpon him if he doe not follow it. Some declare y^t ye top part will look like vnto a huge tunnell standing wth ye bottom vp. But then some be always thinking of tunnells or tankards or what runs thro them down their throates. Y^e women seem well pleased to haue a new house. And ye young folk promise greate helps on their parte.

Y^e spot whereon ye building is to stand, being on y^e

open comon land is easie to be got to from all parts.
True, there be but few habitations thereabout, and ẙe̊
bleak winds of winter will blow harde vpon it. But a
few old forest trees yet stand thereby and ẙe̊ green hil-
locks are pleasant to stand vpon and look over to ẙe̊
water. On ẙe̊ whole wee count jt a verie fair plaice.
And my prophesie is ẙt̊ new comers will soon set down
there and build houses; and before ẙe̊ new house
grows old manie others will be there to keep it companie.

Y̊e̊ new minister, M̊r̊ Shepard, we find sound in doctrine and strong in speech; but wonderful grave and
solemn, wch, after M̊r̊ Whiting, seemeth like clouds
after sunshine. Wee doubt not hjs pietie; but pietie
recomended by gloom cometh wth but a poore recom-
end. However, he is mch of a stranger wth vs as yet.
He dresseth in black cloathes and weareth black gloves
in ẙe̊ pulpit, wch he must needes cut off at ẙe̊ finger
ends, ẙe̊ wch is done to enable hjm to turne over ẙe̊
book leaves. His age wee think about thirtie and
three. He is middling tall in person and hath strong
and well shaped limbs. He walketh mch, and with a
brisque step; and seemeth fond of taking long solitary
walkes on ẙe̊ beaches and in ẙe̊ woodes. He hath declared himself not over fond of musick and said ẙt̊ if jt
were done away wth in ẙe̊ meetings more time would
be left for ẙe̊ preaching, wch setteth not well wth
some; for there be those who would even loue to haue
ẙe̊ good old chaunts of ẙe̊ church. (And to me jt seemeth ẙt̊ preachers are apt to think more of their preaching than some others doe.) Preaching and ẙe̊ worshipp
of God in psalms and hymns are both good. I dont say
wch is most to be desired, but thinke part of both sets
best.

And now we are admonished to close the journal of
the good old settler. His honesty of heart and quaint-
ness of style must have possessed such a charm, that
no reader, we are persuaded, can have passed over
unheeded any passage. Many of the brighter and

darker phases of early colonial times have been given, as well as faithful glimpses of the every day life of a community of genuine old Yankee fathers.

In the introductory observations we said something about the orthography of the journalist. Very little change has been made by us; no change excepting where it seemed necessary, to avoid perplexity to the reader. One of the most curious things in all the writing and much of the printing of that period is the variety of ways in which the same word is often spelled. We are led to believe that there could have been no acknowledged standard. During the latter years embraced in the journal, however, a considerable degree of uniformity had been attained in printing. But in writing, the free and independent use of the alphabet was still persisted in.

There is an old printing office tradition, by the way, to the effect that in the early days of the art the means for spacing the lines were so imperfect that the compositor was allowed to add or omit in any word such letters as might be convenient, provided the right sounds were expressed. And by tracing the progress of the art, it seems as if some such custom must have prevailed, and that it fell into disuse as the necessities for it were obviated.

Having concluded our extracts, it may be proper to introduce a few remarks and details illustrative of certain matters called to mind as we proceeded.

Our journalist, under date of 1640, has something to say regarding the Indians, their habits and occupations, their poverty and weakness. And his allusion to land tenures, leads us to think that as many readers may not have taken an opportunity to examine the interesting subject, a few plain observations on that and kindred matters may not be unacceptable.

One of the most interesting and important topics in the whole range of American history is that relating to the dispossession of the Indian tribes and the occupation of their lands by the European settlers. Our forefathers have been visited with unmeasured opprobrium for their course of alleged injustice and oppression. And a great deal of sympathy has been excited for the forlorn race who were deemed wrongful sufferers under inexcusable aggression. But by taking a more extended view, the case may appear different; not, however, that there were not constantly transpiring individual cases of great enormity.

Those who imagine that the colonists made an indiscriminate seizure of the Indian lands, in all cases where their power was sufficient, greatly err. And those who imagine that the royal charters afforded the grantees authority for so doing, also greatly err. These charters were not intended to convey a fee simple to the grantees, but only to secure to them pre-emption rights of purchase from the Indians. The charters simply intended this: We pledge the royal faith that no other Europeans shall intrude upon the lands granted, but you must settle your own terms with the Indians. And the same thing has run down through grants and treaties to the present day. It is only according to our conception of the value of lands, that the poor red men experienced such hard bargains. But it should be borne in mind that the construction of their social economy was essentially different from ours. They were not an agricultural nor a pastoral people. They did not, to any extent, till the soil, and had no conception of its value growing out of the necessities and conveniences of civilized life. "Black Will's" sale of Nahant to Mr. Dexter for a suit of clothes and a jewsharp, though a good bargain for the purchaser, may also have been a good one for the vender. Nahant was worth little as a hunting ground, and nothing for cultivation. And there was not much activity in the market for wigwam lots.

The Indians understood, as far as they could be made to understand a thing so entirely beyond their accustomed mode of viewing matters, what rights were acknowledged to be theirs. And though they would dispose of land which to a European would be of very great value under the operation of the arts and employments of civilized life, for a hatchet or a shirt, they might have received a fair equivalent. Farms and mill privileges were to them of no account.

And then again so loose were they in the matter of titles that it was often difficult to determine what individuals were proprietors. Rev. Mr Higginson, the first minister at Salem, in a letter dated in 1629, states these facts, which are well worthy of consideration: "The Indians are not able to make use of the one fourth part of the land; neither have they any settled places, as towns, to dwell in, nor any grounds as they challenge for their own possession, but change their habitation from place to place." And this confirms certain statements of Mr. Turner.

Notwithstanding the many villainous frauds practised upon them by individual settlers it is yet undeniable that the colonial governments without perhaps an exception, endeavored to enforce the strictest honesty of dealing in the purchase of Indian titles. But the cupidity that characterized many of the first settlers, found means to circumvent the wholesome laws.

It has been said that New Jersey is the only state in the old Union in which every foot of land was obtained by honorable purchase. This may be so. The land of the puritan pilgrims, the territory of the peaceful Penn, the rich domains of New York, Virginia and Carolina were all tainted by glaring examples of injustice.

To the honor of the Dutch settlers, however, it may be remarked that they appear generally to have pursued an honest course, extinguishing the Indian titles by fair purchase. And the few Swedes and other colonists from the north of Europe seem to have acted in like manner. The possession of power is apt to beget arrogance, which, in its turn, becomes the parent of much that is unrighteous; and hence it would be unsafe to assume that had these been as powerful as the English, they would have been less rapacious. To judge of the Dutch by their conduct in the East Indies we certainly should not form a very favorable opinion of them.

It may be asked in regard to the royal charters themselves, What right had the European governments to assume the power of thus granting? The reply is, that the claim to American territory was founded on discovery — that is, the subject who discovered this or that portion of the continent, and planted his national flag upon it, claimed it, by that act, as rightfully belonging to his sovereign, against all other established powers. This was sanctioned by the comity of nations. England, France, Holland and Spain, the leading powers of that period were governed by this doctrine. But as regarded the natives of the countries discovered, it was not denied, in theory at least, that the fee simple was in them. In other words, the territory belonged to the discoverers against all the world excepting the natives. Good faith was generally preserved among the nations on this point. The occasional outbreaks between the English and Dutch and in later years between the English and French settlers, we find generally arose from disputes about priority of discovery or from difficulties agitating the parent countries.

The considerations growing out of the course thus assumed by the civilized nations are of great importance and interest. The native tribes were unable forcibly to dislodge the settlers and by a kind of moral pressure seemed doomed rapidly to disappear before them. And many a pious mind has perceived, in the whole course of events, a special interposition, for the benefit of God's people, similar to instances recorded in the sacred volume.

And, taking a broad view of the question, What amount of moral wrong do we find involved? Divesting the subject of all false drapery, what is the verdict of those elevated conceptions which can at one view embrace the welfare of the whole human family? Man is commanded to subdue the soil. The Indians would not fulfil this command. They would not till the soil. They would not subdue the wilderness. It was inconsistent with the progress of our species as well as with the command of the Creator, that so immense and fair a portion of the earth should be suffered to remain a wilderness, yielding comparatively nothing for the sustenance of man. Inasmuch as the Indians would not labor upon the ground was it not fitting that those who would, should become its possessors? The whole earth was given as the vineyard in which the great family of man was to toil for sustenance, and no nation, no tribe, no individual has a right to hold any portion in an uncultivated state when what it would produce is required for the support of others.

And does it not seem that the change which a couple of centuries has wrought in this fair portion of the heritage, is in accordance with the order of nature, the progress of our species?

What was the aspect of our country at the time of its discovery by Europeans? What but that of a wilderness, dark and wild, with a few thousands of the great family of man scattered sparsely over it; and they, degraded and savage, warring upon each other and delighting in the grossest occupations of existence; possessing scarcely any knowledge of the useful arts or conception of the higher duties and enjoyments of life. Science had not shed its vivifying rays upon them, expanding their intellects and refining their tastes. Nor had a rational religion elevated their minds and purified their hearts.

What now is the aspect of the land? What but as fair as any on which the sun shines. Thirty millions of the human family are sustained in plenty and happiness within its borders. The wilderness has been subdued and the earth made to yield a mighty increase. And starving thousands of the old world have been grateful recipients of bounty bestowed from our surplus agricultural products. It was by the ordering of Divine Providence, and for the benefit of the human race that in this goodly portion of the great vineyard, the indolent and unprofitable should give place to more faithful laborers.

Another thing should be borne in mind by those who entertain so much bitterness towards the settlers regarding the extinguishment of Indian titles. The Indians themselves always admitted that the land was not originally theirs, and that their forefathers took forcible possession, driving those whom they found here through a path of blood into the sea. They boasted of this fancied bravery of their ancestors in the face of the whites, menacingly assuring them that they would be similarly dealt with as soon as the red warriors could be assembled in sufficient numbers. Thus exhibiting a title resting on a similar foundation to that of the New Zealand chief, who claimed certain lands because he had eaten the former owner. And we leave this point with the simple remark that if it can ever be justifiable to steal from a thief, it seems as if the early settlers might set up the plea.

We remarked that under the Indian dispensation this now productive region supported but a small fragment of the human family. It is difficult to state with any degree of certainty, the amount of the Indian population. Their own assertions could not be depended on, if for no other reason, because of their ignorance of numbers. In their limited traffic but little knowledge of arithmetic was required. And it is a notable fact that the large body of them could not count over fifteen or twenty. Those who could go as far as two hundred were highly accomplished in the mysteries of mathematics.

It may detract something from what has been lauded as indicative of their high poetical conceptions and striking metaphorical mode of expression, yet it is no more than just to say, that their comparing numbers to the stars of heaven, the leaves on the trees, the sands on the shore, and so forth, arose from sheer inability to count. One whose arithmetic failed him at twenty would be very likely to designate three hundred as equal to the stars of heaven, or to make some other equally poetic and just comparison, having no more conception of the numerical magnitude of three hundred than of three million.

The Powhattan confederacy, which was one of the most powerful in the territory that now constitutes the United States, embraced thirty three tribes, and occupied a large portion of the immense Virginia territory lying between the Blue Ridge and the sea. Yet the whole population seems not to have reached ten thousand. Other portions of the country appear to have been much less densely populated. And it is asserted in history that the renowned chief whose name the confederacy bore, sent messengers to England for the purpose of counting the people there; which he of course would not have done had not the state of his own country induced him to believe the thing possible. Indeed, had not the population been few and weak, the settlers would have been exterminated, notwithstanding their big guns and catechisms, that great source of reliance of which the good Mr. Higginson was led to boast.

In view of these remarks, the writer will not be deemed one given to indiscriminate laudation of the ancient occupants of this soil, a few specimens of whom we have yet lingering among us, but from whom we are cautioned to form no judgment, as they are degraded by contact with ourselves.

The romantic efforts of some to present the Indians as the most magnanimous people the world has ever known, are unjust. It is perhaps well that our minds are so constituted as to revert with glowing interest to the scenes transacted in former times upon the soil we call our own. And it is natural that those scenes and the actors in them should be invested in a drapery growing more brilliant and fanciful as time recedes. But yet, unless the historian constantly endeavors to present his subject in the attitude of nude truthfulness he betrays his trust. The Indians should not be denounced as the most miserable and depraved fragment of the human family that ever cumbered the earth. God never made a tribe of our species in which he did not implant conceptions of truth and duty, and in which there were not individuals whose conduct was guided by lofty principles.

In reverting to the history of the red men we must not conclude that they all possessed that magnanimity of character of which we have some bright examples. That would be as unjust as it would be for those in ages to come, when our own nation has become extinct, to conclude that we were all Washingtons and Franklins. Neither must we conclude that they were all treacherous and blood thirsty as we find so many fatal assurances was the case with far too many. They were human beings, with passions like our own, and with undisciplined intellects and undeveloped moral attributes were chiefly governed by the lower propensities of our common nature. But sometimes the bright rays of exalted virtue and intellectual vigor burst through every cloud, shining forth with unquenchable lustre. As warm a heart has beat beneath the Indian blanket as beneath the vesture of purple and fine linen. As sweet a lullaby has been sung over the papoose as he was rolled in his bear skin, as was ever sung over the cradled offspring of our own fathers.

But these virtues spring from the instincts of nature. And if their instincts taught them to love their friends they also taught them to hate their enemies. And more appalling, bloody, and in every way fiendish scenes were never enacted on earth than were some of those in which these children of nature displayed their fealty to the great master of evil. We speak of them as the children of nature, as if that were an argument in favor of their virtue, not realizing that to many minds we thus furnish the strongest argument against them. Human nature is corrupt, and, as none will dispute, prone to evil as are the sparks to fly upward.

From the first moment that the whites set foot upon this soil the Indian nations began rapidly to decay. There is now but a small remnant left. And ere long they will have become entirely extinct. The fire of the wigwam will have gone out and the ploughshare will have broken up the graves of their fathers.

It is sad to contemplate the utter destruction of a people. Reflections, however, press upon the mind, not unworthy of being entertained. A little more than two centuries ago this whole country was occupied by a people as different from ourselves as one nation can well be from another. But the red men have passed away. And so have the race who preceded them. And must not we, in the progress of coming centuries also give place to another people? And of what generation of our children will be the last, the forlorn wanderers, who will in sadness turn from these shores beholding the land in possession of strangers? Vainglorious people! Why should we boast?

So pass away, in mysterious procession, one nation and kindred after another. In the striking words of Ossian: "The chiefs of other times are departed. They have gone without their fame. . . . . The people are like the waves of the ocean: like the leaves of woody Morven, they pass away in the rustling blast, and other leaves lift their green heads on high."

The reader may have been struck with what Mr. Turner says, under date of 1637, regarding certain wonderful discoveries; particularly the discovery of tracks imprinted in the rocks at Nahant. And there is a tradition connected with these tracks, that so happily illustrates several prominent characteristics of the times, that we feel constrained to introduce it here, fully confident that no intelligent reader can mistake our object, whatever views may be entertained as to the credibility of this or that part of the relation. Legends and traditions are sometimes very useful as illustrations, and may supply what would otherwise be wanting. When introduced in their proper character they cannot mislead, though historians do well to be wary of them.

The lovely peninsula of Nahant was within the territorial limits of the Third Plantation. It has long been celebrated as a watering place. Anciently it was a famous place for shore fishing. Various kinds of the most delicious of the smaller specimens of the great finny tribe abounded in its waters, and those piscatory disciples who visited its bold cliffs for purposes of sport or profit, met with a rich reward. Wild fowl, too, were taken in vast quantities, for a long series of years. And in the days of the first settlers four-footed game was plenty in the dense woods that overspread the uplands.

No sooner was the peninsula traversed by the whites than it was discovered that Nature had laid it out as a tract of surpassing loveliness. And it has increased in the affections of the refined and the lovers of nature, to this day. And now, every watering season, hosts of the fairest and bravest of the land assemble there, to enjoy the affinities of friendship and love, to breathe the free and uncontaminated air, to gaze upon the magnificent and beautiful in nature — and thus to renovate the flagging spirits and restore declining health.

To follow the traditionary accounts, we should say that it was near the eastern point, on an extension of ledge that now projects somewhat into the sea, that the aforesaid tracks were to be seen. It is asserted that they were clearly defined, and resembled, in a remarkable degree, the impressions of cloven feet. There were perhaps twenty of them, the faintest being more perfect than are most of the specimens of footprints in rock preserved in geological cabinets. They were all of about the same size, and one might have imagined them to have been made by an enormous ox, to use Mr. Turner's comparison, had such an animal been wandering around there while the rocks were in an unhardened state.

These appearances excited much alarm at one period, and were frequently visited by the curious, as is said. But at what period they were lost sight of, cannot now be determined. By the action of the waves they may have been gradually worn away, or the shore may have so changed as to leave them in deep water. Taking their existence for granted, we cannot wonder that in the old colony times they should have been the occasion of much perplexity and apprehension. It is said that various theories were proposed by the learned of the times regarding their origin, mostly having reference to the attempts of the evil one to plague the settlers.

In 1641, as appears by an account given by Mr. Turner, under that date, a wonderful serpent was declared to have appeared in the vicinity. And certain Indian traditions regarding a marine monster are also alluded to. These, taken together, may account for the origin of the stories prevalent at this day about the venerable Sea-serpent, who is so accommodating as to make his appearance off Nahant, just at the time when attractions for summer visitors are most needed. And it is extremely natural that these same accounts should have led our forefathers to settle down in the belief that the veritable old Serpent who beguiled our great mother, had, for some infernal purpose, best known to himself, thought proper to appear here in his most natural guise, ready, of course, to assume any other that exigencies might require. And it is not to be wondered at that they should have been very much distressed under this conclusion. And a pious old dame lately declared to us that she should not be surprised, if after all, it turned out that the Sea-serpent was the Devil, it being so undeniable that he is always around here, in some shape. The last mournful truth stopped our mouth.

The first discovery of these extraordinary footprints, by the whites, from all that we can gather seems to have been in this wise: Abel Ballard, a half blacksmith, half fisherman and half sportsman, as well as half drunkard — if there is any half way in drunkenness — lazy, ignorant and reckless, took it into his head to visit Egg Rock, alone, one afternoon. In the boat with him he took his gun, fishing line, rum keg, and sundry other things necessary for a right jolly time. The same difficulties that now attend a landing on that famous rock then existed. The surf ran high at the point of debarkation, on the afternoon in question. Considering this, and the fact that the rock weed is so slippery that even well-balanced steps are not always sure, it was very fortunate that he was able to reach safe footing, with no further disaster than the loss of his pipe and the knocking out of one tooth by a slip, as he jumped from the boat.

Abel was not long in catching a great many fish and finding a large number of birds' eggs. In a grove which then had possession of the soil near the summit, a short distance southward from where the light house now stands, he built a fire and cooked his fish and eggs, which, with the stores he had brought, furnished a very good meal.

After the feast, Abel concluded to take a little rest before pushing off for home. Being undisturbed he dozed away for an hour or two; when, suddenly waking, he found that it was growing dark. Springing up, and rubbing his eyes for a clear view, he perceived that a very threatening cloud was moving rapidly up from the west. And he heard the thunder muttering away among the distant hills. No time was to be lost, for the storm would soon break in fury. Hastily gathering up his chattels and throwing them into the boat, he pushed off. But before rowing half a dozen rods, he stooped down to take a drop of inspiration from his keg, when lo, that dear companion was missing. Instinctively, as it were, the prow of the boat whirled back toward the rock, and with all speed he landed and hastened to the scene of his banquetting. There he soon spied the blessed keg meekly reposing on a stump beside the rocky protuberance that had furnished him with the conveniences of a table.

Seizing the keg, Abel ran back to the boat and pushed off again, just as an ominous clap of thunder shook the very foundations of the cliff. He instantly perceived that it would be imprudent to attempt to gain the main land. And so, without wasting time to count chances, he at once directed his course towards Nahant, the nearest point of which was something within a mile. Lustily bending to his oars and receiving the opportune aid of a benevolent wave, he succeeded in beaching his boat and attaining the upland just before the fury of the storm broke upon him.

About where the large Hotel now stands there was a thick wood, in which was a rough little shanty built by the proprietors of the land for the convenience of those who might be overtaken by storms or other perils while working there. Into this structure Abel ran, almost out of breath and threw himself down, fainting with fatigue and fright. Night drew on, and he was soon in a disturbed sleep. How long he remained so, he was never able to tell. But at, as he reckoned, about midnight, he was aroused by a terrific crash, occasioned as he afterwards ascertained by the thunder striking Pulpit Rock and demolishing a section of its base. Terrified beyond measure, he was just endeavoring to rise, when, by the almost continuous lightning there was revealed to him, stalking in at the door, a strange, hairy object of about the size of a stout man. Erect, and with a steady step he came and stood over the spot where Abel lay, now speechless with fear.

Eyeing the prostrate settler for a moment, the monster broke out into a broad laugh, opening the great mouth of his dog-like head and shooting out his huge tongue in the strangest manner. Presently he began to exercise himself as if playing on a fiddle. And then he began to dance in the most fantastic style. Suddenly stopping, in a commanding voice he bade Abel arise and dance too, declaring that he was fiddling for

E*

him, and that it would be good for him to take a merry round.

But Abel did not come to time. He probably had too much discretion to trust to his legs, or was too much frightened. So the graceful visitor danced around a while longer, his red tongue leering out at the corner of his mouth, at an enormous length, and a blue flame occasionally shooting from his nostrils, diversified, as he now and then sneezed, which he seemed to take a mischievous pleasure in doing, by a sort of miniature volcanic explosion.

At length he stopped, and again standing over Abel, bade him arise and dance, calling him a jolly old toper, and saying that he would have a jig with him. Presently, however, assuming a serious air, he declared that he was as dry as a fish and must have some good drink; adding that if Abel did not tell him where his keg was, he would give him a kick that would send him back to Egg Rock, and thence, by a bounce, to the Swampscot shore. He raised his foot as if to bestow the compliment, whatever might be the reply. And it was then that Abel perceived that his tormentor had a huge cloven foot; a discovery that did not add much to his comfort.

In the hope, however, of terminating the unpleasant conference, Abel's courage so far revived as to enable him to articulate, that the precious object of his inquiry was in the boat. At this, with a laugh that almost shook the door of the shanty from its leather hinges, the intruding monster frisked out, leaving a powerful brimstone smell. And Abel sank away, whether in sleep or some other condition he could not afterwards determine, but entirely oblivious of what next took place around him.

When Abel aroused and opened his eyes, a bright sun was just emerging from the ocean. His first object was to endeavor to bring his mind into working order by the restorative that he had not forgotten was left in the boat. Hastening to the cove, his mind still roiled and laboring, he with horror perceived that some one had taken his boat by main strength, carried it several rods, and deposited it on a sort of rocky shelf, entirely out of his reach. And that mischievous some one, he had not a doubt, was the Devil.

The boat was bottom up and much damaged. And every thing that he had left on board was gone. Can there be any wonder at his astonishment and fear? With hair on end and stiffened jaws he stood gazing around. Then happening to look down he beheld near his feet, imprinted in the solid rock, divers marks of cloven feet. He had no doubt now, if he had before, of the character of his midnight visitor. No one but the Devil could leave such footprints.

This discovery, instead of actually prostrating Abel, as it would have affected many others, seemed to impart to him additional powers of locomotion. And uttering one yell, that might have been heard at Deer Island, had there been any one there with ears, he started at the very top of his speed to the cartway that led through the woods to the beaches. Nor did he stop till he had run more than a mile, losing his hat and one shoe by the way. He now met a teamster going down to the shore for seaweed. But the man was disposed to give him a wide berth, he acted so wildly and appeared in such questionable guise. Abel was, however, presently recognised, and in as connected a manner as he could, undertook to relate what had happened.

The teamster listened patiently to Abel's account.

But the latter was very much surprised, when he had finished, to hear the cool remark, that though he had unquestionably seen a devil, yet it was a devil of his own make; that the evil spirit was in his own brain and no where else; and that he got there out of the rum keg. And the benevolent man was particular to inform Abel that more devils come from rum kegs than from brimstone beds; at the same time expressing a hope that as the one in question had now sailed away in the old keg he would not get a new keg to breed more. He further admonished him that a man's head was too good a place to be occupied as a dancing room for such evil spirits; and then, with the remark that all would go well, if he took heed to these warnings, without the least concern drove on. Abel thought him very cool; but before he had a reply digested and ready for utterance, the team was on the other slope of the hill.

The conviction remained immovable in Abel's mind, that the evil one had paid him a visit. And he conducted many a doubter to those remarkable footprints, and pointed to the rocky shelf whereon his boat was laid, in proof. And he succeeded in silencing the doubts of many a pious neighbor.

If these wonderful impressions were ever there, they were probably made at the remote period in the world's history when other similar impressions were. And if still in existence, it is not improbable that at some future day they may come to light again. The place is not above half a mile from the summer residence of Professor Agassiz. So we may possibly, through his talismanic power, some time or other learn all about them; unless, indeed, their distance is not sufficient to lend enchantment.

Assuming that the footprints were there, Abel may, indeed, have been the first white man who saw them; but they might have been there ages before. The waves, no doubt, battered his boat and lodged it on the rock where he found it. And, finally, the teamster was no doubt right in his location of the evil spirit. Delirium tremens often furnishes those optics keen that enable people to see what is not to be seen.

Under date of 1657, Mr. Turner makes mention, in what seems like a hurried postscript, of a harrowing tragedy just then reported to have taken place. And we presume that it was from the tragic fact, or from the report — and we cannot tell from any thing further in the journal whether or not it turned out to be a mere report — that the somewhat embellished narrative that has appeared under the title of " Stony Brook" took its outline. The incidents are of a peculiarly touching character, and, unfortunately, too faithful illustrations of many occurrences in those days. By the tradition, as it has come down the course of time, we learn that Mr. Anderson resided on what is now Boston street, and was the father of an extremely beautiful daughter, who was an only child. They had not been long in America when the alleged fatal occurrence took place. And before leaving England, the young lady had become the affianced of a youthful officer in the public service, named Wells.

Some two years after Mr. Anderson removed hither, he became involved in various speculations, mostly connected with Indian lands, which created for him not a few violent enemies. Yet it is claimed that he was a man of public spirit and warm domestic attachments. About this time, Capt. Wells arrived at Boston, and soon found his way to the pleasant home of Mr. Anderson, where he was received with the most unfeigned affection.

Miss Anderson seems to have been greatly beloved by all about her. And presently a pic-nic party, as we should call it, was formed in honor of the young soldier and his intended. The place selected for the festivities was a short distance in the woods, near the centre of what was afterwards called Hemlock Swamp, and through which flowed the little brook, subsequently so famous under the name of Stony Brook. It was a lovely afternoon, in summer, and their sports were carried forward in great glee. The baptismal name of Miss Anderson, the tradition asserts, was Julia; a name not very common in those days. And Julia, on this occasion, as might readily be supposed, was made presiding queen. She was crowned with the choicest wild flowers and conducted to a mossy throne erected on a flat rock, close by the brook.

Towards evening, as the joyful party were still pursuing their sports, old Rattlesnake, a Natick Indian, mentioned by Mr. Turner, who had become an uncompromising enemy of Mr. Anderson, suddenly appeared on the other side of the brook, and by one of his terrific yells struck petrifying terror to each young heart. Without giving time for their recovery, he hurled his tomahawk at the head of Julia and she fell dead into the brook. Capt. Wells, however, soon recovered his self-possession, and dashed toward the savage. But his courage only added another bloody trophy to the red victor's hand.

Rattlesnake marched off into the deep forest, with the curling locks of Julia and her betrothed dangling together from his wampum belt. And upon the green bank of the brook, side by side, lay the two cold and scalpless forms.

The whole settlement was, of course, soon in pursuit. But we find no reliable record of the result; nor, indeed, anything more reliable on the subject than the traditionary accounts now given.

But to return to the Subject of our sketch. The spirit of patriotism which Mr. Turner so early expressed continued to develope itself in the community, and ultimately placed us where we are in a political point of view. His prophesies, apparently founded more on a knowledge of the workings of the human mind than the tendency of outward events, have been in many instances verified to the letter. And we think ourselves fully justified in all that we have said in his praise.

That he experienced the common vicissitudes of life it is needless to state, for none are exempt. From a remark or two in his journal we are led to think that he was one of those self-relying people who are slow to believe that men are not able, in a general way, to shape their own fortunes. Yet he was honest and discriminating, while so opposed to anything like materialism or fatalism. And his charity for others was boundless. We never find him, like some of the proud worldlings of this generation, turning upon a less fortunate neighbor and upbraiding him as the producer of his own misfortunes. We all realize the value of our own exertions, and should also realize that good and ill fortunes are dispensed to the deserving and undeserving, by rules unknown to all but the great Distributer himself. We are not ignorant of the expressive lines of Goldsmith, so often quoted on this point. But there is more sweetness in his poetry than truth in his philosophy. We are all on the great Sea of Life, subject to its winds and storms. And it is as unreasonable for one to declare that the course of each is in his own keeping as to declare that the ships upon the ocean can hold their way in spite of wind and storm. Yet, as it is unbecoming in the mariner to fold his arms and indolently yield to fate, so it is unbecoming in those on the stormy voyage of life to spare exertion to improve their condition.

As before observed, Mr. Turner was quite aged when he escaped from this world of tribulation and toil. His funeral was attended by a very large concourse. Much wine and cider were disposed of on the occasion; but no stronger drink was provided, in obedience to his dying injunction. His remains were interred in what we now call the Old Burying Ground. It was not then so generally the practice, as now, to have monuments erected over the dead. Whether a stone ever marked his resting place we know not; but if there was one, it has long since disappeared.

He laid down trusting in a merciful Redeemer, and, we doubt not, will receive the recompense of a good and faithful servant. And it is fortunate that one possessing so honest, genial and unprejudiced a mind, should have left such a record as he has. He seems to have extenuated nothing, and he surely set down nothing in malice.

It is by no means difficult for the most ignorant and dull to discover faults in others; and the censorious may never be at a loss for opportunities to reprehend. But it is a recognized truth that very few are sufficiently wise to discreetly praise; and it is among those few that Mr. Turner is entitled to be ranked.

He was not censorious, nor was he inclined to indiscriminate laudation.

Some people are naturally of such crooked growth that it is utterly impossible for them to be straight with any one. In thought they can dwell only upon the evil and the dark; in speech can only magnify the blemishes of their neighbors; are never communicative excepting in the way of fault-finding; are full of suspicions and insinuations; and are prodigal of dolorous "buts." Happily, however, there are others of opposite character; those who are forward to think and speak of the good qualities of those around them; to find comfort in every vicissitude. The one class wail along the journey of life always begirt with clouds; the other rejoice along a way of sunshine. And it was in the great procession of the latter, which has been for ages filing heavenward, that Obadiah Turner passed away.

In perusing a volume on the plan of the present, it is convenient to keep in mind a variety of the common facts of history. And hence, in these earlier pages, we have felt the propriety of recalling some things that might to the intelligent reader at first appear impertinent. To some extent we have been compelled to make our pages thus far rather initiatory, though we trust they have not proved barren of interest. But an unincumbered field for the display of our Jewels will presently be attained.

We are gratified in having been able to introduce Mr. Turner and Mr. Hart. Historians have generally overlooked them. But the former, especially, would have become conspicuous generations ago, had not his invaluable journal remained sleeping in a garret, embalmed in catnip, and watched over by surly spiders. And Mr.

Hart, too, through the favorable notices of him, would have become a historical hero.

As to Mr. Turner, he seems to have been a man of peculiarly quiet habits, and averse to having his name blazoned. We do not even find, on examining the Colony Records, at what time he took the freeman's oath. And it is possible that he did not take it at all, for down to 1664 no person could take it unless he were "a member in good standing of some congregational church." And there is some doubt about his having been a decided congregationalist. Many well disposed persons, too, were prejudiced against taking the oath. And he might have been one of them. He was evidently no office seeker or political ranter, and many of the privileges secured by the oath were not such as his habits would naturally have led him to covet. Indeed, we cannot find, by the Colony Records, that even Thomas Newhall and Thomas Dexter, two others of the most respectable and enterprising settlers of the Third Plantation, and of whom biographical sketches will appear on subsequent pages, ever took the oath. Mr. Newhall was the father of the present great Newhall family of New England, and Mr. Dexter was the progenitor of the illustrious Lord Timothy, as well as other notables. It is barely possible, however, that the whole four — Mr. Hart, Mr. Turner, Mr. Newhall and Mr. Dexter — may have taken the oath at the Quarterly Court, though we do not think they would have descended to an inferior tribunal while their neighbors appeared boldly at the bar of the Great and General Court.

In 1638 the town lands were divided and a record made of the amount apportioned to the different inhabitants. But unfortunately the record has been lost;

though a copy of some three pages is extant. We do not, however, find in this remnant of that important record, the name either of Mr. Hart or Mr. Turner, and hence are unable to determine with what number of wild acres they became encumbered.

And now, in closing, it may not be inappropriate to recall to the reader a fact or two regarding the good old way of manufacturing Freemen. It was under the first Charter, or down to about the year 1689, that the custom of qualifying individuals as freemen, prevailed. We find little or nothing about it after the time when the rampant colonists seized Sir Edmond Andros, that popular uprising seeming to be under the dawning of a new political light.

Down to 1664, as just said, no person could take the freeman's oath, unless he were "a member in good standing of some congregational church." But during that year a royal order allowed such residents to be admitted as produced certificates that they were of good moral character, and sound in doctrine, signed by some clergyman in regular standing to whom they were well known. By the oath they bound themselves to be faithful subjects to the Commonwealth — to yield assistance and support thereto by person and estate — to endeavor to maintain all the liberties thereof — to submit to its wholesome laws and orders — to avoid all plots and evil practices against it — to give votes and suffrages in good faith and under a conscientious endeavor to promote the public weal — doing all "without respect of persons or favor of any man." And a variety of other things which the good citizen of this day endeavors to do, without taking an oath.

Freemen alone had the right to vote for rulers or hold offices. But these were rights not so much esteemed then as now; perhaps because the emoluments were not so great. And it must not be imagined that people were then so enlightened in these matters as now. With us it would be rank political heresy to say that a right to vote were not a most precious right. And as to office, it would be still ranker heresy to deny the right to scramble for that. Not so in those times of ignorance; and hence we find that many prominent individuals were not freemen. Those who were not freemen were termed residents. And all of these, who were twenty years and upwards of age, and who had resided in a place six months, were required to take an oath of allegiance to the government.

The whole body of freemen were required to meet at Boston, annually, and in a General Court of Elections, to choose a Governor, Lieut. Governor and other magistrates. And this practice was continued till about the year 1670, when the greatness of numbers rendered it inconvenient. It was then required that the freemen should assemble in their several towns for the purpose of voting. And so commenced that time-honored Yankee institution, the annual Town Meeting for the choice of State Officers.

The custom of qualifying freemen, as before observed, fell into disuse about the year 1689. But for some years previous to that the distinction between Freemen and Residents seems to have been by degrees growing less and less marked.

THOMAS NEWHALL.

> "He was of noble parentage,
> and he was father, too,
> Of sons brave, virtuous and sage,
> and daughters faire and true."

WE find Mr. Newhall here in the Third Plantation as early as 1630. Perhaps the remark on page 114, that he was the father of the great Newhall family of New England, was a little too liberal, for we find that Anthony Newhall, and one or two others of the stock, came over at an early day. Indeed the stereotype assertion of historians, when speaking of New England families, that "three brothers came over," may be made of the Newhalls with an average probability of truth.

The name, in this country, has always been variously spelled — as, Newhall, Newall, Newell, and even, in the last mode, with the extraordinary prefix of an h to the last syllable. And it is not easy now to determine which spelling was first adopted here. Newhall, at all events, is a very ancient style. And that must be the right one, unless the reputed origin of the name be fabulous. As elsewhere remarked, we feel little interest in tracing ancestry. But occasionally a leisure hour may be agreeably spent in the service, especially when so honorable a line as that in question is concerned. Many members of that family who have not become acquainted with the curious learning respecting their origin may be gratified with a brief sketch. And those readers who are n*o*t so happy as to be members, may have similar reason to be pleased with a hasty glance into the fountain whence sprang the blood that flows in most American veins. Let us then, for a moment, dig together some distance back among the clods of time; for it is often with families as with carrots, the best part being under ground.

Some fourteen hundred years ago, or during the first half of the fifth century, a grim, barbaric host, calling themselves Saxons and hailing from the small islands at the mouth of the Elbe, and the Baltic shores, made their appearance in England. They had been invited over by the Britons, who were then weak and much exposed to the inroads of the Scots, Picts and other fierce adventurers. Previously, for some centuries, perhaps all the time from the days of Julius Cesar, the Britons had been protected by the Romans. But the latter had recently withdrawn, as Rome needed all her forces at home to defend against the Goths and Vandals.

The Saxons were a warlike, shrewd and persevering race — much like uncivilized Yankees — and soon beat off all the enemies of the Britons. But it turned out that the Britons were no great gainers by the valor of the Saxons, for no sooner were the invaders driven off than the Saxons completely subjugated the Britons themselves and erected a government of their own. And they kept up a continual scene of petty war and rapine, holding the poor Britons, as long as there were any left, in the most abject condition.

It has been said that the laws of a nation are the surest index of their character and condition. And it must be so; for the laws of a community proceed from its very bosom and business. The humanity, the moral and intellectual state and degree of civilization of a people may be unmistakably ascertained by this medium — also their warlike, agricultural or commercial characteristics. And hence a slight glance at the Saxon jurisprudence may be useful.

The Saxons recognised the trial by judicium Dei, as they called it; or ordeal. First, there was the fire ordeal, designed for the more eminent of criminals. The person charged was adjudged to walk bare footed and blindfolded, over nine red hot ploughshares laid lengthwise a little distance apart. If he passed over without treading on them, or treading on them was unhurt, he was considered innocent. Emma, the mother of Edward the Confessor, is stated to have gone through this ordeal unharmed, thus purging herself of the charge of unchaste commerce with the bishop of Winchester. Second, there was the hot water ordeal, by which the guilt or innocence of a party was determined by thrusting the arm into boiling water. If the arm came out unharmed, the person was adjudged innocent; otherwise, guilty. Third, the cold water ordeal, in which the accused was secured by a cord under the arms and plunged overboard. If he sank, and remained at the bottom for a certain specified time, he was deemed innocent and drawn up. Floating was considered evidence of guilt. Such were trials by ordeal; and they seem to have originated in the extraordinary genius of the Saxons. And while we can hardly accept them as evidence of a peculiarly intelligent conception of Christian truth, they yet show a reliance on the special interposition of Providence for the relief of the innocent and punishment of the guilty, more talked about than apparently believed in by the good people of this day.

The Saxons were really but a shade above savages in character, and in their diplomacy depended much more upon their clubs and battle-axes than upon the justice of their cause.

Christianity was probably introduced into Britain during the Roman occupation; perhaps as early as the days of the apostles. But it appears to have existed only in spots. If the Saxons, in the early part of their occupation made any pretension to Christianity, it was of a curious kind and mixed up with many dark and unsavory superstitions. At all events, it seems certain that nothing that could properly be called the Christian religion prevailed through the land before the seventh century. Whatever their religion was, in it they were extremely gross and addicted to cruel and bloody rites, believing in auguries and charms and frequently sacrificing human beings. They had, indeed, improved but little on the Druidism of the former age. The whole Saxon policy was based on selfishness and violence. Intelligence and just dealing were hardly known. Pecuniary satisfaction was received for all manner of crimes, and every kind of corruption prevailed. In short, the early Saxons were ignorant, unprincipled, blood thirsty barbarians.

We have thus endeavored to recall to the mind of the reader one or two points in the character of the people whose blood some of our fourth of July orators and lyceum lecturers instruct us to be very proud of having in our veins. But yet there were in those stern old Saxon souls germs of true greatness. And as they increased in civilization and embraced a more rational religion, they began to discover most excellent traits. And we are justified, to a considerable extent, in feeling proud of our inheritance from them. But do we not rather overestimate our obligation? Strong will, independence of thought, and freedom of action, are unquestionably Saxon traits. And are they not just as unquestionably Yankee traits? They are what distinguish Americans from all people not of the same lineage.

The first settlers of New England were impatient of control and extremely jealous of the centralization of power. Like the old Saxons, each one claimed for himself ability to sustain a part in the administration of public affairs, and was fond of having his claim allowed. And this has grown with our growth and strengthened with our strength, till we have become the most ravenous office seekers on earth. This would perhaps admit of a show of justification were the great purpose to have affairs administered aright. But when the scramble is merely for emoluments or honors, it is about time to ask if the ship is not heading for breakers. Nevertheless, the great point that all should have an equal chance, is manly.

The Great and General Court of our early colonial days was, as before remarked, composed of the whole body of freemen. And when the numbers had so increased that the assembly became too numerous to be held within doors, they did not, like the Icelanders, hold annual assemblies of the whole people in the open air, which would have been but a carrying out of the principle they so highly regarded, but established the Annual Town Meeting, at which all the freemen could meet in their own towns and elect from among themselves such as they were willing to trust their interests with in the General Court. The individuals so elected were at first called Deputies, afterwards, Representatives. As the towns increased in population city organizations were resorted to for obviating the inconveniences of large assemblages. But the people came slowly to this. Boston, the first city in the Bay State, did not receive her charter till 1822, and then had a population of some 45,000. Within the last twenty years, however, several places have adopted the more aristocratic form of government. Lynn, the bright blossom of the Third Plantation, made the year 1850 memorable in the annals of the world by then taking her rank as a city. But all such changes so far increase the distance from elementary freedom. And if they add to the facilities for governing they also afford the better opportunities for ambitious politicians to successfully pursue their ends.

Our forefathers, to a considerable extent, eschewed the formalities that seem necessary in conducting our more complicated public business. Nor were they scared at any cry about legislating for men's consciences or the hazard of departing from precedent. It was their way to determine every matter by its own merits, unhampered by old forms and precepts. And the Saxon blood that was in them led to this independence, as well as to watchfulness against approaches towards a centralization of power.

Now the policy of the Normans, who in 1066 subjugated the Saxons, was directly the reverse of the policy of the latter. They were for centralizing political power; taking it, as far as possible, from the people, and lodging it with the sovereign and aristocracy. In short, the Normans established the feudal system.

And as regards the two lines of policy — Saxon and Norman — there is no doubt that by the Saxon the strength and energy of a people are much more surely brought into action, though there may be danger that rampant ambition will work ruin. The natural power of a people resides in the lower classes. And any polity that has a tendency to repress it, is cramping and wrong. The Norman polity was calculated to blunt the national energies, though it gave greater stability to affairs. Mere peace and security, however, to the American mind seem but a poor return for the abridgment of leading natural rights. The influence of the English Church was deemed by our fathers favorable to centralization and an aristocracy — the Squire's pew and his Lordship's tablet had met their eyes in the sanctuary — and hence sprang much of their hatred towards it. The Papal Church was inclined to the very extreme in that direction; and hence there never was much love for it in minds partaking of the Saxon element.

But we have said enough of those bluff old Saxons. they were introduced here for the laudable purpose of showing from what brilliant ancestry the Newhalls descended; for, on the maternal side, the first Newhall was a pure Saxon.

The great male progenitor of the Newhalls was a Norman. It was in the eleventh century that the Normans invaded England and under William the Conqueror made themselves masters of the land. They were of the Scandinavian race, and came chiefly from Norway and Denmark; were fierce and warlike, but much in advance of the Saxons, in several respects. They secured the supremacy at the battle of Hastings, October, 1066. And it was a conquest overwhelming and complete; almost as destructive to the Saxons as was the Saxon conquest to the poor Britons.

The Normans had a better religion and more polished manners than the Saxons, and evidently considered themselves as belonging to a better race. But they had a more imperfect conception of individual right and responsibility. It may be mentioned as an illustration of certain differences of character between the two people that the night before the battle of Hastings was spent by the Normans in prayer and religious exercises and by the Saxons in drunkenness, rioting and buffoonery. Yet the Normans were predatory in their habits, perfidious and inhuman. Their administration was sustained by force and sanguinary violence. And a most cruel disregard was manifested for the claims and rights of those whom they had subjugated.

The Christianity of the Normans was evidently not of a very elevated type though better than that of the Saxons. Their lawsuits were determined in about as rational a way as that of ordeal. They introduced the trial by battle, or single combat; that is, plaintiff and defendant had a regular fight, and judgment was pronounced in favor of the victor. Our phrase "throwing down the glove" comes from the custom. The appellee threw down his glove and declared himself ready to defend by his body. The appellant took up the glove and replied that with his body he would make good his appeal. The battle was fought with batons. In a murder case, for instance, if the one charged could maintain the fight from sunrise till early starlight he was acquitted; otherwise he was adjudged guilty and immediately hanged. And it is remarkable that this singular feature became so woven into English jurisprudence that the right of appeal to battle was not abolished till within the present century; though the taste, or more probably the courage, of the people did not often lead them to resort to it during the last century or two. And we cannot avoid remarking that were it revived and established as an imperative proceeding, in civil actions, in our American courts, the dockets would probably soon cease to groan under such interminable lists of cases as they now do.

In August, 1817, one Abraham Thornton was tried at Warwick, England, for the murder of Mary Ashford, a gay country girl; and though there were circumstances appearing much against him, yet he was acquitted, the judge, Holroyd, considering that an alibi had been fully proved. Soon after the acquittal, however, a brother of the murdered girl was induced to proceed against Thornton, for a second trial, by the ancient Writ of Appeal, which process rather demanded punishment for the private and particular injury than for the offence against the public. Thornton was again arrested and taken to London for trial in the King's Bench Court.

Now it happened to occur to Thornton's shrewd legal advisers, that the same old law that enabled Ashford to take out his writ of appeal also enabled the one against whom it was brought to meet it by Wager of Battle. So when the case came on, Thornton astonished not only the court and bar, but the whole nation, by the plea: "Not Guilty. And I am ready to defend the same by my body." Then he threw his glove upon the floor. The next proceeding was for each party to present in regular form all the facts upon either side of the main question; the appellant endeavoring to show that the appellee was guilty, and the appellee endeavoring to show his innocence. Then the eminent counsel, Chitty for the appellant and Tindal for the appellee, elaborately argued the cause.

And, finally, the court determined that it had not been made sufficiently clear that Thornton was guilty to deny him the right of battle. This placed things in rather an ominous position, for it happened that Thornton was an athletic man and Ashford quite a stripling. The court, however, without formally announcing a determination to allow the battle, made some suggestions. And before a decision was promulgated Ashford prayed for leave to discontinue his appeal. His prayer was granted and Thornton of course discharged. This, as remarked, was in 1817; and it appears to be the last case on record in which this singular right was demanded. The attorney general, soon after, brought in a bill to repeal the strange old relic of Norman jurisprudence. Thornton had respectable connections, but does not appear to have been of the best habits. Soon after this occurrence he came to America, under an assumed name. And it has been said that a stranger who died at Lynn in 1820, was this same individual.

By the Norman customs the pugilistic propensities of our nature became regulated by scientific rules. The prize ring is a Norman institution. And we find the "noble art of self-defence" fostered among all people of the Norman lineage. Christianity has not extinguished the savage propensity of some to pommel and be pommeled; nor the delight of others, more careful of their own heads, to witness such ennobling exhibitions. The great contest in England, in April, 1860, between Heenan, the American champion, and Sayers, the British, created a thrill throughout both countries about equal to that produced by the battle of Bunker Hill, and afforded a rather remarkable illustration of the refined taste of all classes.

It is well determined that the Feudal System was

established about the year 1075; though some have imagined that traces of it could be found among the Saxons. But it seems quite clear that the Saxons had no settled tenures of a feudal character. Lordship and vassalage have justly been denominated a Norman principle. William the Conqueror divided the kingdom into what may be called baronies. And these were granted to men of superior military prowess and fidelity; the condition being that they should hold themselves in readiness to furnish a stated number of knights or soldiers and a certain amount of money at the call of the sovereign. The people became the miserable and slavish subjects of the barons, whose lordly castles began to tower up in grim grandeur all over the land. The freedom of the masses became extinct.

A very few of the old English castles date back as far as the earlier Saxon times. But they were not probably erected for such purposes as were those of the feudal times. And many of the venerable erections that the English now call Saxon are Norman. During the brief interval from 1016 to 1041, when the Danes under Canute the Great, Harold Harefoot and Hardicanute, held the supremacy, probably not one castle was erected. But the Normans, on introducing the feudal system, completed a large number. They were generally built on an extensive scale and in the most substantial manner. Sometimes they were erected near rivers and sometimes on eminences. When upon a site easy of access, they were surrounded by moats with bridges that might be drawn up; and the ponderous walls were proof against any warlike engine of the day. From the turrets of these lordly castles, extensive views were had, and an enemy stood small chance of approaching undiscovered.

In these castles the old barons dwelt in lordly state, surrounded by their tenantry and vassals, who tilled the soil and devoted their lives to their lords. Sometimes the barons made war upon each other, marching forth with their little armies and devastating the territory of their hostile compeers. Little attention was paid to learning or the elegant arts and refinements of life. The chase, the tournament, feasting and reveling occupied most of the time spared from the service of the sovereign. A chivalric spirit was fostered, and a rude but hearty hospitality reigned. Devotion to the fascinations of female society and a spirit of undefined knight errantry inspired the young; wine and wassail edified the old. We look back upon that period as enveloped in a radiant mist. It was a transition period. And from its rugged inspiration the more ennobling traits of English character began to develop, though with no great rapidity.

The baronial establishments so increased that at the close of Stephen's reign, in 1154, more than a thousand castles existed. And a large portion of them continued to lift their frowning battlements for a long series of years, furnishing strongholds for contending parties during the turbulent times of the Plantagenets, the Red and White Roses and the early Tudors. Around them clusters much of the most stirring romance of English history.

The barons, when united, possessed an irresistible power in the kingdom. They even extorted from King John, in 1215, the Magna Charta, which remains indisputable evidence of their power, for kings had rather part with their teeth than their prerogatives. To this day the great charter is known as the bulwark of English liberty. But the sturdy barons were human beings, and as such often grossly inconsistent, denying to their inferiors some of the dearest natural rights, while making the most exacting demands for themselves.

At times, the recognised power of the barons over the peasantry seems to have been almost unlimited. And in many instances that power was exercised in a cruel and mercenary manner. The extraordinary right of the lord to be the first occupant of the peasant's bridal bed was sometimes compromised at a most desperate sacrifice on the subject's part. In a word, the rule of the barons was harsh and spirit-crushing in the extreme.

The way seems now prepared to come more directly to the romantic origin of the Newhall family. We have said that the great father of the line was a Norman of pure blood, and the great mother a Saxon of blood equally pure.

There was in Wiltshire, in the reign of Richard Cœur de Lion, a wealthy baron, of unmixed Norman lineage. His castle was on a bold and commanding site among the highlands that rise not far from the western border of Salisbury Plain. His domain was extensive and rich, and his tenantry among the most happy in the realm. His magnificent castle was one of the first and strongest, and had withstood many a fierce assault. Its ponderous walls and deep moat showed that at the time of its erection it was expected that the mad waves of war would beat against it. Its stern old towers and mossy turrets overlooked a glorious landscape. And within, it was fashioned to meet the exigences of sudden invasion as well as the demands of a most extensive hospitality. The capacious banqueting halls were sufficient for the many gentry who assembled at tournament or other festival; and their retinues found ample room and unstinted cheer. There, the fairest maidens of the land displayed their charms, and fascinated by their feats of grace and daring, in field and forest. And there the devoted knight, unknowing fear when meeting hostile knight, knelt humbly for the favor of his lady-love. The huntsman's horn rang out at break of day, and the answering hounds bayed their readiness for duty. The hawker cried, and the sanguinary bird wheeled from its airy height, eager to do its murderous work. In peaceful times, the days passed in almost unbroken festivity; and when the solemn notes of the curfew bell came sounding over the hills, the tired revellers were quite ready for repose.

Among the tenantry of this Wiltshire baron was an enterprising and trustworthy householder who had always stood high in the estimation of his lord, and been the recipient of many favors. His most loved occupation was husbandry, though he was not unskillful with the sword nor wanting in valor, as was fairly shown on more than one occasion when he had supported his superior on the field. He was entrusted with such duties as not unfrequently required his presence at the castle; and there his intelligence and good manners secured for him a reception more like that of an equal than a dependent. Now this tenant was of pure Saxon blood. He could as directly trace his pedigree to the Saxon fount as could the baron trace his to the Norman. He took great pride in his descent, and professed much satisfaction in transmitting to his children untainted blood, for his conjugal bed was shared by one of as pure Saxon origin as he. And many a bantering did he and his good humored liege engage in as to the merits of their respective races; such contests usually terminating in the sportive remark by the baron that in pity for the rest of the world he hoped that at some time a way might be opened for the production of a race of demi-gods by a union of such purity and power; and darkly hinting that even then means seemed preparing, by which a consummation so devoutly to be desired might some day be attained.

The home of this favored tenant was graced by a daughter of rare endowments. To her beautiful Saxon features was added a charming delicacy of manner. And her sparkling wit and graceful assurance were irresistibly fascinating. From earliest childhood she had been a sort of pet at the castle, whither she often went with her father. And the inmates, in a companionable way, instructed her in arts and accomplishments more befitting the lordly condition than that in which she was born. She loved with the jovial lordlings to sport through the ancient halls, dimmed by the grim armorial hangings; to listen to the wandering legendary's tales, the harpist's lays, the jester's merry turns. But more than all she loved to steal away to a quaint little room far up in the old tower, where alone she might scan the glorious landscape, with its glistening streams, green woods and flowery meadows, and contemplate the bright picture of her own dear cottage home nestling in the hill side copse, with the lowing herds and bleating flocks dotting the broad fields. In that undisturbed retreat, too, she loved to sit and ruminate upon such subjects as might well be expected to agitate a young and susceptible heart in that age of gallantry and romance. And as the darker shades of twilight gathered, she might be excused for the fancy — if fancy it were or an excuse were needed —

that she beheld some brave knight galloping athwart the plain to meet his lady-love, at the far off castle just descernible upon a frowning crag among the dim hills; or some hapless fugitive, fleeing for shelter within the sacred precincts marked by the gray convent tower.

And could fair Haroldine — for such appears to have been the baptismal name of her of whom we speak — have been permitted, in one of her contemplative moods to have thrown a glance into the then far future, even to this our day, what would she have beheld? In the picture unrolled would she have found most cause to rejoice over an array of virtuous sons and daughters, zealous to do good, and honoring the line of which she was the great mother — we mean the Newhall — or to weep over an army of blockheads and heartless worldlings, zealous to do evil, and clouding it with dishonor? Would the picture have been one calculated to impart fresh inspiration to her young heart, and lead her to tread those halls and lawns with a prouder step, or one calculated to so roughly touch her tender nerves as to induce a headlong plunge from that frowning parapet? Answer that, to your own consciences, ye of the lineage.

We have given the baptismal name of this fair daughter of the Saxon race, but are unable to determine the name by which the particular family was distinguished. Surnames were then just coming into popular use in England; and a great many of those most common with us had their curious origin at that period.

When she had arrived at a suitable age, Haroldine had many admirers among the higher class of the baronial tenantry. And though a little coquetish, she was not of a temperament to withstand the tender advances of young Arthur, the manly and promising son of a neighboring tenant; especially as those advances were supported by the approval of her parents and their well-wishers at the castle.

Arthur and Haroldine became affianced.

He was of her own position in life, virtuous, and in every way worthy of her hand. Brave and loyal, he was looked upon by the lord as one whose strong arm might some day be relied upon to do valiant service in support of the barony should perils beset it. He loved the excitements and dangers of the field, and had already by his courage and prowess won a noble suit of armor, in which, with glittering helmet, his erect form rivalled the bravest knight. Yet, though he might dream of wars to come, and renown upon the battle field, or even a crusader's glorious benediction, he must still meet the realities of life in the field of the husbandman and the duties of a dependent.

The sweet, dreamy period of betrothal passed rapidly and the nuptial day of Arthur and Haroldine was appointed. And it was arranged that the ceremony should take place at the castle.

It was a calm autumnal day. The sun had hardly begun to decline, when the spacious grounds of the castle were alive with the joyous tenantry, all in their best attire, come at their lord's bidding, to make merry and greet with smiles and good wishes those on whose account the festivities had been appointed.

And then, as the first shades of twilight began to gather, beneath the patriarchal branches of an ancient hawthorn, stood Arthur, his manly form erect and his countenance bearing the impress of serious realization of the responsibilities he was about to assume, blended with happy anticipation of the pleasures in store for him. By his side was Haroldine, radiant in beauty, gazing up to him as to the loved warder of all her earthly happiness. The good hearted baron and the ladies were there. And there too was the jolly old priest in his cleanest robe.

The setting sun seemed to linger a moment for some kind breeze to sway an interposing bough that it might bestow a last kiss on the virgin lips of Haroldine. Presently the wind lent its friendly aid, and with the kiss offered the incense of flowers.

The sun set; and Haroldine was a bride.

The occasion of the nuptials was made by the liberal souled baron such a one as even a petty noble might envy. The spacious apartments were thrown open to the joyous tenantry; and the brilliant lights shed their lustre on boards loaded with a feast of fattest things. And when all had eaten and drank, the old harpers played, the minstrels sang, and the legendaries chanted their tales. Then the stalwart youth donned the old suits of armor and engaged in friendly tilt with halberd and foil; while in the group of shy and blushing maidens, the aged crone dispensed her fortunes by her palmistry and mirror of love.

The hour of midnight came. And presently all was silent at the castle. The tenantry had withdrawn to their quiet homes, each bearing some simple memorial of the occasion from their lord, and the blessing of the priest. None remained, save Arthur and his bride. They, in compliance with the ancient custom, were to remain till morning.

Soon, the midnight silence of that lately laughter echoing hall was broken by an earnest debate between Arthur and his lord. The baron insisted on exercising

the right that was his by the strange old custom
respecting the first occupation of the peasant's bridal
bed, to which we have alluded. And even now, in
the most sumptuous lodging apartment that the castle
afforded were the maids disrobing the beaming bride.
It was long in vain that the bridegroom urged upon
his lord the claims of nature, of honor and love; and
as long in vain that he offered all his money and goods.
But the liege's heart was not of stone. He relented,
and giving his faithful subject a warm grasp of the
hand, playfully challenged him to refer the question
to the bride herself. And in the same spirit the challenge
was accepted; neither, most certainly, doubting
as to the nature of the answer she would return.

A trusty page was despatched to the bridal chamber.
And he soon returned with the strange and unexpected
reply, that the custom having been observed by her
own revered ancestors, from respect to their memory
she could interpose no objection to its course. Who
would have anticipated such an answer? Truly, the
female heart is an inexplicable mystery. Had Shakspeare
lived before, and given his celebrated definition
of frailty, poor Arthur might have adopted it in bitterness
of soul. Yet, one may readily conceive of reasons
that might have strongly urged Haroldine to such
a decision, even without taking in view the character
of the age; an age when derelictions in the conjugal
relation, and even maiden purity, were not viewed in a
light like that of the present day; an age in which
many a fair Rosamond bloomed unblushing on the
baronial manors.

The lord did not banter his chilled tenant on the
unanticipated success that had met his challenge. Neither
did the tenant give vent to his feelings. The

bright hopes that a few hours before had made him the happiest of men had suddenly become so clouded that he was now the most miserable. Yet he uttered no curses, no lamentations. But there was a terrible emphasis in his silence.

Without speaking a word Arthur walked forth into the cool air. With his own strong arm he lowered the lightest draw-bridge and passed the moat. And the first streak of morning light found him away upon Salisbury Plain, hastily journeying toward the far-off town whose tall cathedral spire could be discerned even from the castle tower.

But what could have been the feelings that swelled the breast of Haroldine when the maidens had left her alone in that gorgeous chamber? Reflection, stern and uncompromising, must have claimed at least a momentary sway. With what blushes must her radiant Saxon face have burned. And how wildly must her disquieted heart have beat. Formidable must have been the struggle in which the loved image of Arthur was forced to disappear before supposed duty or frail inclination.

A few months passed, and we find Haroldine mistress of a delightful little cottage on the bank of a small stream that flowed from one of the noble hunting parks of the barony. She had a matronly adviser and gay companions. But though supplied with every outward appliance for enjoyment, her grave demeanor plainly declared that she was not at peace within. She had received no tidings of Arthur since the night of his bootless bridal.

A pretty garden lay between the door of the cottage of Haroldine and the pleasant road. Noble trees, choice vines and shrubs added their stately beauty and grace to the landscape, far and near. At the embowered gate-way was not unfrequently seen the caparisoned steed of the baron himself, for he found the cottage an agreeable resting place in his hunting and other equestrian excursions. And the bay of the hound and scream of the hawk often startled the adjacent woods.

From the night that the old priest pronounced him the husband of Haroldine, Arthur had never been seen within the barony. It was supposed that he had gone to the foreign wars. And many thought that he would soon make his name famous and return to England loaded with honors and wealth.

Presently, great improvements were to be made on the baronial grounds, for the sovereign was to visit the lord and spend a few jolly days. A new hall, or lodge, as such structures seem indiscriminately to have been called, must be first erected for the huntsmen's bouts. And soon, in a fine old grove, just in sight of the cottage of Haroldine, did the fantastic walls of the new erection begin to appear. The work went bravely on, and in a little time the hall was ready for dedication.

A grand fete was held on the inspiring occasion of dedicating this famous new hall. The gentry from far and near assembled. The day was spent in the free sports of the field, and the evening in boisterous hilarity. And midnight found the revellers within those new walls, enjoying in full tide the unpolished hospitality of the chief of the barony.

At that solemn hour of mysteries there came in haste a squire with a message for the baron's ear. And what was that hastened message? It was even that there had been a birth in the cottage by the brook. The fair Haroldine had ushered into the world a lusty little soldier of fortune. Why did the lord's fine Norman eye so suddenly blaze with delight? Why did he instantly call his boisterous company to silence? And why did he with so many pleasurable emotions inform them of the happy event and bid them fill their cups to the brim with choicest wine to drink to the mother and her son? In rude eloquence he expressed many generous sentiments, and said that the little one should begin the world with a surname; a surname that in after years might become renowned by the nobility of those who would proceed from him; and it should be a surname, too, that would commemorate the event that had called together, in such a friendly way, so many of the Wiltshire gentry.

Then they all stood in silence, with their bumpers raised, the baron pondering. Presently he cried out, in a voice that almost shook the walls:

"His name shall be NEW-HALL!" The wine was gulped and the name enrolled.

And now, gentle reader — for you must be gentle to have gone unmurmuringly with us on this long historical airing — we will return to the neighborhood of our subject. We have stated the old tradition regarding the origin of the Newhall line. And without holding ourselves responsible for its truth — though we have heard many truths much more wonderful — beg leave to remind such of the family as have yet done nothing to its credit, that it is not now too late to begin the good work.

In the first Newhall we behold a union of two unsanctified races; yet the immediate father and mother — the Norman lord of the grandest castle in Wiltshire, and his beautiful Saxon subject Haroldine — were perhaps well enough, excepting as regards the particular occurrence of which that first Newhall was a consequence. But the Saxon and Norman races were both, as we have seen, of commanding ability, energy and enterprise; though we have been careful about praising their morals or manners. And the history of all after time has proved that they were more reliable as a stock than any other that could be named.

It is not our purpose to trace the pedigree; for, as elsewhere remarked, we could not go far back from the present time before meeting individuals whom we would rather avoid. It is enough for us to give the origin. Others can follow the lineage. Black sheep they will find; but not in greater proportion than in other folds. In some individuals the Saxon blood seems to predominate; in others, the Norman. After so many years of adulteration, perhaps no reliable mark can be fixed on. The beard, however, has been considered an important matter among mankind from Samson down. The Saxons wore their beards long. The Normans shaved close. So, possibly, the taste of an individual, as regards the appendage in question, may indicate the character of his blood.

Perhaps some foe of this august family may derisively smile at the moral blemish that attended the first born. But this might be perilous; for possibly it could be shown that he came from no purer source. The whole world might be drawn into the contest and the Newhalls come out as bright as any; for it is not recorded that even Adam and Eve had a marriage certificate.

The first white child born in the Third Plantation was a son of Thomas Newhall, our subject. And it was baptised by Mr. Batchellor, the first minister. On the same solemn occasion, one or two other children appeared at the sacred font. It happened that little Tommy was handed up first. But the minister shoved him aside, and gave precedence to another. Then the snapping of those enraged little Saxon eyes which had so lately deigned to open on this miserable world, the commotion within the swaddling blanket just about where two little feet might have been supposed to be, and above all, the vigorous exercise of those infantile lungs, showed that there was a will if not a way to offer a suitable return for the indignity. The recital of this interesting little occurrence to a moody member of the family, gave occasion for the somewhat petulent reply that in just such a way the Newhalls have always been shoved aside to this hour. But we do not see cause for any such feeling. Types of all the orders of New England greatness have appeared in the family. Numbers have crossed their legs in legislative chairs. Others have sat in the courts of law; if not on the bench certainly in the criminal dock. Some have beat pulpit cushions with their apostolic knuckles. Others have made books. Pedagogues, editors, doctors, lawyers, shoemakers, merchants, farmers, fishermen and gentlemen, have appeared in the family procession. In the army of the Revolution there were brave representatives from Colonel Ezra of the Massachusetts line down to the red nosed drummer Ephraim. The Jersey prison ship held a Newhall. And one of the first that followed Paul Jones on board the Serapis at the most terrible hour of the whole war, was also a Newhall, though he appears to have shipped under a different name. One was a voyager in the arctic regions, and another a traveler in the Arabian deserts. The bones of some lie at the bottom of the ocean, and of others in the golden clods of California.

We do not mean to say that any particularly brilliant stars of the race have arisen from the Newhall branch—local luminaries always excepted. But we do maintain that it has presented an enviable average; few have attained very high places and few have gone very low. Not one is brought to mind as having been in Congress or in the State Prison; but which is the high or low of these two places may admit of a question. The eagerness with which some seem to strive to win a passport to the latter, which, to say the least, is the most safe and peaceful, would indicate that they esteemed that rather the more elevated and desirable. Two of the family, however, attained very considerable heights. One, braved the ascent of the Himmalay mountains about the time Bishop Heber was in that region, and in defiance of the good prelate's admonitions; but he was punished for his temerity by being turned into pillar of ice. In other words, he froze to death. The ascent of the other was at Boston. But he remained up a short time only, when the centripetal force upon him was so great as to violently jerk him through a trap door; and had he not been providentially secured to a beam above, by a rope about his neck, his legs would inevitably have been broken. As it was, only his neck was broken. By a strange coincidence this event happened on the same day that his neighbor Hart, alluded to on a preceding page, met a similar fate.

Those who expect to find a family without an unworthy member, will as surely be disappointed as those who expect to find a tree on which none but fair fruit ever grew. A good average is all that we should expect in any thing. And of such, as already observed, this family can certainly boast.

We desire to say all these things with becoming gravity; for we are convinced that writers often seriously damage themselves and their cause by indulging in what they call wit, satire or irony — and so do talkers, as to that matter. But satire pleases readers, especially when it is aimed at their neighbors. And through this infirmity an author is very liable to be fooled. If a writer could always keep in mind that the reader cares nothing about him, his honor or interest, he would proceed with a better understanding. It is fair to conclude that for every satirical ebullition at least six enemies are made. Dean Swift, we believe, varies somewhat from this number, in his estimate; but perhaps he calculated a little too directly from his own remarkable experience. However, it is this conviction that danger lurks in raillery, that induces us to be so circumspect in our language. And the reader will please give us the benefit of our care.

Assuming again to speak for the great Newhall family in America, we are once more reminded of the common saying that it is a person's own fault that he is not somebody in the world. How often it is said that a man can make himself whatever he desires to be. But the idea that one can shape his own destiny, as before declared, is all a fudge. And it is wicked; for it arrogates to man a prescience that belongs only to his Maker, and altogether sets aside providential intervention. One day Mr. Newhall was in the woods searching for the northeast bound of a wood lot. During the search he came to a spot where three paths met, only one of which could lead to the object of his search, and which that one was he had no possible means of determining. After deliberately weighing the probabilities, and being warned by the declining sun that his time was short, he took one of the paths and perseveringly pursued it. But if he had followed it till this time he would not have reached the bound, excepting that he might have stumbled on it in one of his circuits of the earth. It was not the right path. It led into a deep valley of hemlocks, where a rainy night, sundry wild beasts, and, as he thought, a legion of devils amused themselves over his distresses till morning. Now just so it is in the search after the good of life. So do not persist in declaring that families or individuals have power to shape their own destinies.

Another discouraging circumstance might be named in this connection. At least three feminine members gave extraordinary promise. But as their lofty and lustrous qualities began to develop, they must needs transplant themselves into new families and turn their backs upon the very name of Newhall. One became a Pendergrubb and another a Bottleshock. And we see from the present reputation of those names, what excellence the Newhall blood imparted to its new connections.

Dean Swift said that a man who caused two ears of corn or two blades of grass to grow where only one grew before, was more worthy of praise than the whole brood of politicians; or something like that. And we say that if this be true, Mr. Newhall, our subject, was entitled to much praise; for he caused many ears of corn and many blades of grass to grow where few grew before. The broad acres that he cleared and planted were his incontrovertible vouchers for this.

He was one of the first as well as best farmers in

the place; had a comfortable house and good stock of pigs and poultry; also two cows and some sheep. He likewise had a yoke of cattle and two horses at one time. His dwelling house was one of the best that had been erected since the Plantation began. Its frame was of oak, rough hewn, to be sure, but firm and durable. The thick, unplaned boards of the exterior, overlapped each other in a workman-like manner, rendering shingles or clapboards unnecessary. True, the weather soon warped them to a degree that made it necessary to use considerable seaweed and clay in filling the interstices to defend against the blasts of winter; and this made it look a little like a beggar who had run a race and strained open the seams of his garments; but then there were few eyes around that were accustomed to look upon more comely architecture.

The habitation faced due south; a peculiarity of location quite common in those days. It enabled the occupant to secure the greatest benefit of the sun in winter, and to keep the time of day by marks on the window sill. The luxury of time pieces was then almost unknown; and the sun and shepherd's clock had important duties to perform beyond those expected of them in the present age, when their usefulness in horometry has been superseded by the ingenuity of our Connecticut brethren. Hour-glasses, however, were considerably used, being, indeed, a sort of necessity in cloudy weather; but they required much attention. The peculiar location of the houses made them occasionally look awry as regarded the street. But the streets themselves, at that time, were very accommodating, often changing their course for the sake of having a handsome house smile square upon them.

There was a front yard to Mr. Newhall's house, enclosed by a fence of untrimmed cedar rails. And in that garden bloomed, in glorious state, divers hollyhocks, marigolds, and sunflowers, with the graceful pumpkin vine winding among them. And the useful artichoke, too, sent up its prim spires. Ambitious gourds, also, here and there wound fantastically up the friendly shrubs, ostentatiously displaying their vulgar fruit, as if exulting over the barren maples that shaded the highway. Skirting along the fence, were the wild rose and sweet-briar, the blue blossoming nightshade and red lily of the wood, all shyly approaching their cultivated kindred, even as the dusky maid of the forest approached her pale sister.

This beautiful adjunct was well cared for. And it was delightful to see the smart little Huldah Arlington, the adopted daughter of Mr. Newhall, and the flower of his household, on a bright rosy morning working among the balmy assemblage with watering dipper and wooden spade, her glossy hair bound up by rich wampum strings, the gift of an Indian princess, and her bonny face radiant with health and intelligence. She was indeed a rare maid; accomplished in all the simple household duties of the day; as able to spin, bake, brew or milk as any dame in the settlement.

The house was two stories in front, and sloped regularly down to one, in the rear. And the whole back part was devoted to kitchen purposes, including conveniences for the spinning-wheel and weaving-frame, for candle dipping, soap making, and cloth dyeing. It was a glorious old kitchen for all domestic purposes, and a right jolly place for the noble winter game of blindman's-buff. It was one of the very first houses built in that style, which, being so convenient, afterwards became quite common. True, it was rather easy for the mischievous Indians, who were always playing pranks, to scale the roof. And it is said that the very first morning after Mr. Newhall took up his quarters there, he was astonished, as he went to kindle a fire on the hearth to have a dead rabbit come pounce upon his head; and more astonished still, on running out, to discover a score of forest dignitaries seated along the ridge-pole, gravely snuffing in the morning air and expressing their approbation of the prospect by unearthly grunts.

The large kitchen fire place, sufficient to accommodate the four foot logs with ample room to spit and snap upon the ponderous andirons, and still leave space for wooden blocks in the corners; the capacious oven and yawning receptacle for the rapidly accumulating ashes; the ponderous trammels with enormous iron pots depending; the great dressers adorned with trenchers and wooden bowls, with a pewter platter or two glistening behind; the high-back settle, destined, perhaps, to receive into its cosey embrace the fair Huldah and her happy lover, before the radiant fire, safe from the jealous blast essaying to work its way through some undiscovered crevice; the leather covered grandsire-chair, whose hospitable arms would be capacious enough to embrace the same lovers, even were she encircled by the nine-foot crinoline expanse of this our day; the long table, sustained under its load of wholesome cheer, by its innumerable legs; and the old family portraits all in painted plaster; — these, and many other luxurious appliances of the day were in the noble homestead of Farmer Newhall.

And could we have looked in upon that worthy family as they were assembled on some winter night, we should surely have concluded that luxuries, such as are most zealously striven for in these days, are not prerequisites to happiness. There was the manly form of the household's head, his countenance browned by toil, but beaming with benevolence; his hands rough as the ancient oak, but always pliant to grasp the implement of useful labor and relaxing at the call of charity. What if he did wear a coarse gray roundabout, greasy leather vest, and deer skin small-clothes? What if enormous shoes of rough hide, ornamented with huge iron buckles did encase feet of such dimensions as a youthful elephant might envy? And what if, as he drew off his old striped leggins, he did reveal gray stockings that had long been accustomed to the friendly offices of the darning needle? — He was a man for all these.

And there was the careful matron and the sweet Huldah nestling by her side, the same ruddy beams from the hearth lighting up the countenance of the one, calm and contented in her walk beyond the agitating scenes of youth, and that of the other, flushed in joyful hope on entering upon those eventful scenes. There, also, sat the hired man and the sturdy boys, happy in their freedom from out-door duties, and eagerly pursuing their simple games.

And seeing these, who would not have felt that there was a hearth, around which existed true happiness, though it were composed of unshapely stones laid in ungraceful forms? And who would have thought that the rough, unplastered walls, or the little windows of diminutive panes, so knotty, wavy and coarse, as even in full sunshine to distort every object abroad, were comfortless or unseemly? And who, finally, would have failed to realise that there are pictures of domestic life, always beautiful, however rude may be their setting?

Mr. Newhall, the subject of this sketch, was the first person hereabouts, so far as we have learned, who undertook to raise bees. His apiary was picturesquely situated in the capacious back yard, beneath the shelter of a large tree, which also threw its cooling shade upon the corn barn and a part of the swine's quarters. A rustic seat, erected against the gnarled trunk, furnished a convenient place for such visitors and idlers as had enough curiosity and not too much fear, to sit and watch the proceedings of the busy and buzzing colony. And at the same time their ears might be regaled by the music of the cloven footed songsters that now and then erected their graceful heads above the pen and gave specimens of their vocal accomplishments, illustrating their own appreciation of their skill by those wonderful whisks and twitches of the caudal appendage, that no creature on earth but a pig need ever hope to compass. The bees were successful in gathering honey, and their master was successful in selling it after robbing their hives. The heaviest part of the burden fell on the workers; as is usually the case in this unequal world. Mr. Newhall prospered in this enterprise for three or four years. The honey became quite celebrated for its purity and flavor; perhaps because so much of it was drawn from the flowers that Huldah cultivated. And at that time the vulgar notion prevailed that bees only could make honey; it being left to more modern genius to discover that it can be produced by mixing sugar and lard. Bees, perhaps, have cause to rejoice in the discovery, so far as the enjoyment of the products of their own labor is concerned. But they have equal cause to lament that men will be guilty of unblushingly putting forth such abominable counterfeits in their name.

Mr. Newhall's experience with bees came to an end in five or six years. As the worthy farmer was one day busy in his garden, bare headed and with his shirt sleeves rolled up, all of a sudden there came a terrible buzzing about his ears. And presently, without asking leave, an immense swarm settled right down upon his head. As might be supposed, his terror was indescribable. And losing that presence of mind which is under all circumstances a man's best safeguard, he began exercising himself in a manner more becoming a maniac than a rational being. The bees, not fully comprehending his state of mind, became highly incensed and began to show their anger in the way most natural to bees. They entirely forgot their allegiance, and resentment, or fun, for it is barely possible that they might have had the latter in view, became the order of the hour. At all events, the good man came out of the contest blind, smarting, and declaring vengeance. As the readiest way of avoiding another such experience, he went forth, that very evening, armed with a platter of burning brimstone, with which he forever stifled their mischievous spirit. Afterwards, his enterprise began to develop in other channels of usefulness.

One favorite object with Mr. Newhall was the building of roads; certainly a most valuable object among new settlements. His scene of action lay more particularly in the woods. The great Dungeon Way, as it was anciently called, was a result of his enterprise. And Bonaparte was not more proud of the Simplon than he of that. It traversed the swamps and wound over the hills, and really was a work of great labor;

and though rough and obstructed by rocks, quagmires and stumps, answered a good purpose. He also worked many a day with his cattle in removing obstructions from the road to Salem, which, for a long time, was choked by boulders and charred stumps. Some of the roads, too, in the principal parts of the settlement, received his attention; particularly what are now Boston, Federal, Market and Nahant streets of Lynn. He was a man extremely well fitted for the occasions of a new settlement, possessing good judgment, without the slightest fear of manual labor.

But notwithstanding the efforts of Mr. Newhall, the roads were not always found in good condition. Other settlers did not take so much interest as he, in the the matter; and he often in vain entreated for suitable pecuniary appropriations. By the records of the Quarterly Court, June, 1639, we find that "Linn was fined 10s for their bad wayes." It is hardly probable that this refers to moral ways. And applying it to the highways, it looks a little as if he had given the town a gentle stirring by slily making complaint to the Court.

Mr. Newhall was a man of capacious mind. But his utterance was not sufficient for his ideas; a difficulty experienced by many. A full head and full flow of words are seldom found in one person. The reason is that the sluice exhausts the fount. But he often had ideas that no human language was competent to express; unless, perhaps, some of those graceful Indian words which are long enough to fill half a line, might have answered the purpose. And in his lingual struggles he is represented to have really appeared as if his thoughts were endeavoring to work their way through such learned words as quttianatamunach, kukketassutamoonk, nutahquontamounnonog, and sagkompagunaiinnean, all of which may be found in Eliot's first translation of the Lord's Prayer. We do not know that there is any particular lesson to be drawn from this peculiarity of his, though it may not be inappropriate to remark that many people who have really meritorious ideas have such an infelicitous way of expressing them that they fail to secure due credit. And, on the other hand, some, by felicity of expression, do very much to conceal their mental poverty. This may be observed quite as often in books as in speech. Voltaire said that words were means by which to conceal thoughts. And with the artful they are extremely effectual means. A little careful practice will enable one to use words with wonderful skill in controverting sentiments that his conduct clearly supports. There are many, however, with heads in which pure wisdom is distilled, so very careless in managing the faucet, that most of the virtue is lost.

There is certainly more damage done in the world by speaking than by silence. It is very often, for instance, that a politician destroys his influence and bars his success, by making speeches, even such as his partisans applaud. There is a silence, bold and stern, that overawes and scares; and a silence, quiet and insinuating, that leads captive. Mr. Newhall had a crooked neighbor who well knew the value of this negative commodity. He had many selfish ends to answer, but was never known to press his claims by rhetorical persuasives. And he has been known to carry a point at town meeting, when every interest but his own was on the other side, by simply keeping silence; accompanying the silence, to be sure, by opportune shakings of his clenched fist, that the timid voters might be certified as to what they were to expect if they had the hardihood to act against his interest. And if we recollect aright the United States Senate was considerably disturbed, a few years since, by the attempt of a member to control some movement by a similarly unparliamentary effort. In that case, however, there was no fistial display; the honorable member, to use a popular phrase, only looked daggers. Some men attempt to influence others by appeals and assaults directed to their physical nature alone; others direct their efforts only to the moral nature. But the most successful are those who take judicious cognisance of both.

One excellent habit of Mr. Newhall we desire most strongly to recommend. And that was the habit of making a note of every thing that it was important to recollect, instead of relying on memory, which is not trustworthy even in the best of people. And it is a singular fact that those who are most positive in their assertions based on memory alone, are generally the most unreliable. Indeed, positiveness, in most people, is only a way of fortifying uncertainty or lying. It is a great blemish in a historian to always write in the positive style. Perhaps the most serious defect of Macaulay is to be found in this particular. Our Subject, being a man of probity and rigid carefulness, always carried a crayon wherewith to note down all engagements, important occurrences, or duties. And the wear of the button-hole from which it depended showed that it was much in use. It would be interesting to avail ourselves of some of the records he made, in bold strokes, such as:

"Hunnie com to Widdo Alinn, 1 pownd & haff."

"Ponder more on ye godlie discourse of Mr Whiting touching sanctification; & kerry him a load of woode."

"Kickt ye boy Ioe into ye brooke ffor lyjng, sayjng y^t Bridges should haue iijs ffor corne ett by cowe, ye agr^em^t being ijs. Did not mean to kick soe harde. Sorry ffor ye same."

"Git Mr Dexter putt in bilboes ffor prophane talke, sayjng dam ye cowe. But see ye minister firste."

"Go to ye tavern, to-night, & iff Iohn Olliver is there drounke get him home. Give him pep^rm^t. Take no flipp while there."

"Pray ffor raine."

"Ask Mr Whiting his mind on Indjan damnation, & ask him if sinn is sinn whether or no — be itt from ignorance or hardnesse. Praise his discourse att Goodman Hawkes his funerall."

"Digg stumpes, blast rockes, fill hollows and cutt bushes in Middle Roade." [Market street.]

"Tell William Turner y^t he cann not haue Huldah. Saw him in ye tavern drinking flipp."

"Pay ye D^r for curing feever. Give pork & corne. Haff peck, or pownd each visit."

"Gather harbes ffor wife to dry."

"Advise Mr Dexter to eate no more clamms in Augt and to drink no more blackberrie punch."

"Deal with boy for evill speache. Pray for him."

"Visit Widdow Johnson and kerry meale and one of Huldah's pies. Also dow-nutts. Feed ye hungry. Give drinke to ye thirstie. Not fire water. Also kerry towe cloth enow ffor short gownd. Some of wife's best. Fight the Devill."

"A jagg of ye mapil woode to nayboure Burton, by sunn downe, 2d daie."

"Strong drinke is a cuss. Also tobacka."

But we must forbear making further extracts, and say a word or two on another of our Subject's characteristics.

Mr. Newhall was quite a philosopher, and reflected elaborately on the great purposes of human life, and the events and providences connected with it. Like all persons who exercise themselves in that way, he sometimes arrived at conclusions decidedly at variance with the commonly received opinions of mankind. One theory that he held to with prodigious tenacity, may, perhaps, be called the theory of compensations. He conceived that in the great economy, every evil was balanced by a good; that for every tear there was a smile; for every birth a death; for every bitter a sweet; for every disease a remedy; and so on. Now if we look to a grand average of every thing in creation, perhaps this view is not so untenable. But if we descend to particulars, probably not many would offer their own experience in support of it. Nevertheless, it has been declared a most comforting truth by a profound moral philosopher of the present day. Be all these things, however, as they may, Mr. Newhall derived much consolation from it, and diligently employed many an hour in the effort to search out the compensatory good for the evils and discomforts that beset his path. But we are persuaded that if as he left the world he reviewed the matter, he must have concluded that the place which he was leaving and that to which he was going have their interests connected in such a way that things cannot be entirely squared here.

We feel compelled, in view of what has been said of the direct Newhall line, in this country, to at least allude to collateral lines that diverged in the old world. Very eminent and illustrious personages have proceeded from some of these. Among others might be named Archbishop Tillotson, Sir William Herschel and Mrs. Hemans; Gen. Greene, Hannah Adams, John C. Calhoun and Mrs. Madison. And we cannot avoid adding that a sort of prescience possesses us, strongly pressing to the conclusion that but few more years are to roll away before a star of the first magnitude will ascend from the direct line. And we trust that the soil of the good old Third Plantation, on which so many Newhalls, descendants of our Subject, still continue to reside, will be the favored place of ascent.

Almost any one who takes a retrospective glance, when about to quit the world, probably perceives that his life has been one of experiments rather than results; and that he has been inconsistent in all his ways. It has been said that anxiety to appear consistent is evidence of a little mind; a great soul having nothing to do with such a commodity. But if the inconsistent were always great, where should we look for the small? It may, indeed, be true that to cramp one's self for the mere purpose of appearing consistent, is like taking concern for a shadow; but it is also true that every one realizes the unsafety of relying on a weathercock. While, therefore, truth and right principle should never be forced to yield to mere consistency, it becomes us to be most careful not to stray into paths that truth and right principle may require us to abandon.

And this leads us to remark that if there was any thing for which Mr. Newhall strove, through life, with most meritorious consistency and unwavering constancy, it was to be in the right way in all his walks. He was extremely careful, in the most trivial as well as important matters, to have his face set aright before he went a-head. By such a course, though he gained the reputation, among the impetuous, of moving slowly, he yet moved surely. And he secured a very enviable reputation; one which gave him a commanding influence.

And how great is the benefit of such an example to any community. Most men, being too indolent to reflect, submissively follow the lead of others. They do not proceed on principles of their own, and take too little care about the right or wrong of the course of their exemplars. Could such be induced always to follow the lead of one like Mr. Newhall, they might be safe. Still, those who are good from imitation rather than principle, may not be entitled to the highest ultimate reward.

This propensity to blindly follow a leader we find developed among men as prominently as among sheep. It is so in matters of the highest interest as well as the more common. Do we not find it in melancholy prominence even in religion? Who, in short, is disposed for a moment to dispute that the great bulk of mankind constantly act from habit or imitation rather than principle?

These few concluding reflections began with the intimation that the lives of most men were rather lives of experiments than results. But, turning to our worthy Subject, we are gratified by the sight of one who differed widely from most men in this respect. His life was rather one of results than experiments. And have we not named such good results of his earthly labors as will render his name more enduring than would a shaft of lying marble, as tall as Pompey's Pillar?

OLIVER PURCHIS.

"He faine would plant faire Libertie
her flag vpon this soyl;
And manie, manie hours did he
in her good service toyl."

AMONG the notables who appeared in the Third Plantation at an early day was Oliver Purchis We find by the Colony Records that he was admitted a freeman in 1636. He was born in 1613, and appeared here while quite a young man. But it is not necessary for us to say much of his early life. Perhaps it is as well to go no farther back than the year 1660, at which time he was first chosen Deputy, or Representative, to the General Court. He was then in the vigor of manhood, being forty-seven years of age.

The first few days of Mr. Purchis's experience in the hall of legislation, brought under his notice several abuses, as he deemed them; and he forthwith set about regulating public opinion, preparatory to reforming them. He began by circulating small printed leaves — for his missives were not entitled to the dignified name of pamphlets — among those who could not enjoy the blessed privilege of being within the sound of his voice; much as members of Congress now do with their speeches, though under the disadvantage of not being able to saddle the expense of the circulation on the country, through the franking privilege.

The first reformatory attempt of Mr. Purchis was to abolish corporeal punishment in Harvard College. It may not be generally known, at this day, that delinquent students there were sometimes most unmercifully flagellated. He insisted that if the custom were not abolished, all the manliness would be finally whipped out of the colony. For little children, he said, it might do; but for those old enough to realise the importance of learning, every blow was more damaging to the spirit than the back. He urged his points with strong arguments and grotesque diction, qualities that will draw attention to any writing. But his success was not equal to his zeal. Many years rolled away before the walls of old Harvard ceased to echo back the screams of students under the raw-hide dispensations. Yet he had the satisfaction of receiving a vote of thanks from those then exposed to the evil; though that very vote, he afterwards learned, with sorrow, was the occasion of more pitiless whippings than had taken place for a twelvemonth before. Lucky it was that the day of presentations had not arrived; for had the poor students been guilty of such an indiscreet manifestation of their gratitude as to have presented him with a shiny pewter tankard, a handsome hour-glass or a glistening brass candlestick, the enraged professors would surely have broken their backs.

In 1686, Mr. Purchis was chosen Town Clerk. And from that time we find him quite conspicuous in public life. And his character and position at that period, so far as we are able to delineate them from the materials at hand, may be briefly stated in this wise: Though a warm politician, he was respected by his neighbors; a phenomenon that can only be accounted for by supposing him possessed of some overawing traits of greatness. In his domestic relations he was provident, pleasant and generous, though in public life exacting, enthusiastic and stubborn; characteristics, by the way, not uncommonly meeting in the same individual, anomalous as it may seem. His bright hazel eyes, as occasion demanded, were suffused with tears of pity for the suffering and forlorn, or flashing with indignation on the oppressive and uncharitable. His sinewy arm was bared to protect the weak and to thrust the unworthy from the seat of power. And to crown all, he was deeply pious and very judicious in his zealous efforts to promote the cause of religion.

In 1688, Mr. Purchis received a grievous mutilation of the left ear. And that organ was never restored to its original comeliness, though its usefulness was not greatly impaired. In its mutilated condition it went with him when he removed to Concord, in 1691. And when he went down to his peaceful grave in 1701, it was still with him, a memento of his patriotic strife. The reader may desire to know how the injury occurred. And as it was in some sense connected with important political events, it may be useful to alight on the year 1682.

It was at that time, as the reader is well aware, that serious complaints were made in England against the colonial governments. Some were jealous of the prosperity of the settlers; some had been unsuccessful aspirants for colonial honors; and so, among these and all enemies of the Charters enough was trumped up to obtain a hearing.

In June, 1683, Edward Randolph, then public accuser, exhibited against the Governor and Company of Massachusetts, articles of high misdemeanor; whereupon an inquiry was instituted.

At the opening of the General Court called to sit in Boston, November 7, 1683, the Governor gave notice that since the last sitting of the Court, Edward Randolph had arrived, " & had presented him wth his maj'jes declaration & proclamation, wth the quo warranto y^t was isued out ag^t the Gouno^r & Company, &c."

The King's proclamation graciously stated, among other things, that though a " writ of quo warranto against the charter and priuiledges claymed by the Gouno^r and Company of Massachusetts Bay in New England, by reason of some crjmes and misdemeano^{r}s by them comitted," had been issued, yet private interests were not to be damaged; and if before further prosecution upon the quo warranto they would render "full submission & entire resignation" to the royal pleasure, the Charter might be continued, with alterations for such and such purposes. And various other pleasant things did the Merry Monarch say to the misdemeaning colonists.

These proceedings induced the colonists to look about them with very sharp eyes. Increase Mather, that great father in the New England Israel, declared that it was a plot to make shipwreck of their liberties; and the country, by complying, would act neither the part of good Christians nor true Englishmen.

Things did not take a more favorable turn that year. And at Trinity Term, 1684, the High Court of Chancery gave judgment against the Massachusetts Government and Company, "that their letters patent and the enrolment thereof be cancelled." So died the Charter which had weathered so many storms and become so dear to the hearts of the people.

At this juncture, February, 1685, Charles himself was summoned under a quo warranto from the High

Court of Chancery above, by the grim messenger Death. And the next April, James II. was proclaimed at Boston. The Charter having been annulled, it became apparent that something must speedily be done for the poor colonists. So in the same year, Joseph Dudley was appointed President of the Bay Colony, with authority to administer the government much after the old fashion, though without a revival of the Charter. This temporary government existed for a few months. And then came a stirring period in colonial political history.

Massachusetts was not alone in her hard fate. Other colonies had been served much in the same way. And thus stood the governments when in 1686 the notorious Sir Edmond Andros was commissioned for the arbitrary government of New York and New England. The infliction of such a government naturally created a great ferment.

The neat little piece of legerdemain that was practiced when Andros went to Hartford to receive the Connecticut Charter was very amusing to the world. The Assembly was in session. The discussion had been protracted, for Governor Treat had been talking against time, in the forlorn hope, perhaps, that a favoring Providence would in some way interpose at the last moment. The precious document had already been brought forth; and there it lay upon the old oak table looking up from its winding-sheet of green baize with becoming resignation.

Night had shut in, the candles were lighted, and it appeared as if preparations were made for holding a wake. The final moment for the yielding up of the charter ghost seemed to have arrived. Then, presto! out went all the lights! With the greatest possible speed they were relighted. But gas — we mean the illuminating material made from coal, not such as proceeds from the human head — and friction matches not being then in use, a little more time was required than now would be for the same performance. And when the hall was again radiant with the beams of tallow-dips, behold, no Charter was to be found. It had escaped in some mysterious manner. Sir Edmond twitched up the green baize; it was not under the table. He gazed up to the ceiling; it was not flying about there. Governor Treat gaped and rubbed his knee buckles with the palms of his hands. The Secretary puckered his mouth as if he had just bitten a crab apple, and looked bewildered.

But all these did not bring back the Charter nor discover its hiding place. And the chagrined Andros was obliged to close his eyes that night unblessed by a sight of it. Nor did he ever see it again. He however took formal possession of the government, and annexed it to Massachusetts. But, strange as it may appear, the little joker afterwards, and just when it was most wanted to save the interests of the Connecticut people, turned out, safe and sound, from the hollow of an old oak. Its long sleep had been refreshing, and it came forth with renewed energy. And that tree became much venerated in after years, in consequence of the protection it had thus afforded to the fugitive Charter.

The Charter Oak weathered all the storms and revolutions even down to 1856, when it yielded to the irreverent blast. After its prostration it afforded material enough for more canes than would be needed in giving every rogue in christendom a caning that the most sanguinary pedagogue now in Connecticut would quiver to behold; or, had not the halcyon days of snuff taking gone by, to have made snuff-boxes enough to hold material sufficient for sneezing off the head of every man, woman and child in the land. Indeed it possessed, in no small degree, the extraordinary property of the famed pilgrim ship May Flower. And blessed was the Providence that so endowed that favored ship, for without her wonderful endowment, she never could have brought over, on her renowned voyage, an amount of trumpery that would have loaded down half the British navy.

It was after the accession of William and Mary, and the expulsion of Andros, that the Connecticut Charter came out so bright from the old oak. Leading English lawyers gave opinions that the colony had not surrendered her Charter; and as there was no judgment annulling it on record, it was not vacated. So the old government was continued. No judgment on record? It was even so. But how there happens to be a hiatus in the English State Records just about where a judgment would have been recorded, none can tell, though all can imagine. Connecticut generally seemed more successful in her political moves than her sister colonies. She appeared to be a sort of pet child. Perhaps she had some friend at court more powerful than they; or perhaps the extraordinary power of her soil to supply a certain tropical production, much used in spicing flip, had begun to develop itself, raising hopes that something still more valuable might spring from her wonderful bosom.

To go back a little. Andros, when he arrived at Boston, in 1686, had with him a squad of soldiers, to enable him to enforce his measures. The number, however, was too small to create much fear. The professions of the new ruler were at first kind, and in his intercourse he was affable and conciliatory. These things, however, had but little weight with the colonists, as they could not keep out of view the extent of his powers and the disabilities and inconveniences they labored under from the loss of their charters. Perhaps their feelings prompted them to meet Andros in an antagonistic attitude and to treat his advances in a manner calculated to aggravate his sensibilities; for he certainly was not altogether a savage as some appear to imagine.

Andros soon declared that the vacating of the Colonial Charters annulled real estate titles; and that an Indian deed was no better than the scratch of a bear's paw. If he had limited his meaning to mere looks, not many would have dissented from him. But when he insinuated that a bear's title was as good as an Indian's he was shamefully wrong. The people were required to take out new titles or grants. And for these, enormous fees were demanded. This proceeding created much excitement.

Andros also imposed serious restraints upon the press. Newspapers, it is true, were hardly known in the world at that time. There were none in America. The first one here, the Boston News Letter, did not come into existence till April 24, 1704. But little pamphlets and circulars were vehicles of thought; and the restraints were viewed as a great grievance, for people much love to behold their wise thoughts in print. And that love is not always to be deprecated. If the reader suspects that even the book now in his hand was conceived in some such spirit, we shall not attempt to combat his innocent suspicion.

Sir Edmond also interfered to some extent with the

religious observances; among other things, prohibiting public Thanksgiving without a royal order. This was certainly touching our fathers in a tender point. And besides the loss of the gastronomic gratifications attending the loved New England institution, the absurdity of denying men the privilege of giving thanks to God at any time they might desire, was well calculated to excite minds disciplined as were those in this religious domain; particularly as there can be but remote danger that people will ever be too forward in offering thanks to their divine Benefactor.

This brings to mind a proposition made at one of the religious anniversary meetings at Boston, in 1859. It was, to commence efforts for the discontinuance of our good old annual Thanksgiving. But it grated hard; for people venerate institutions that were dear to their fathers; especially when they bring luscious banquets to their own tables. And the old "Election," which was abolished in 1830, after having given joy to young and old hearts for about two hundred years, had hardly, as it were, ceased to be wept over. The reason given for the desire to discontinue Thanksgiving was that it had come to be loosely observed. But to abolish it for that would seem to be a weakness. ¡Why not abolish Sunday, for the same reason?\ Rather, why not endeavor to restore the old way?

This leads us to remind the reader that the Puritans here, early undertook to abolish the observance of Christmas. In 1651 an act was passed, ordering that "whoever shall be found observing any such day as Christmas or the like, either by forbearing labor, feasting, or any other way upon any such account as aforesaid, every such person so offending shall pay for every such offence five shillings as a fine to the county." The pretence was to get rid of the evils attending the observance; but it has been thought that the real object was to show spite towards the English church, which regarded that day as the most note worthy in the whole calendar. The Puritans made many such laws and were fond of attaching to them an array of whereases, which often raised a fog; though through it the real purpose might sometimes be readily discerned. (One should always beware of whereases, however. / There is mischief in the mist; excepting, perhaps, when they lead off in a mittimus. In that case it is sufficiently plain what they point to. At all events there is one close at hand to explain.

Under the better spirit of the present age Christmas has come to be quite generally observed by most denominations. And the Massachusetts Legislature in 1856 passed a law establishing it as a holiday, whereon the General Court and the courts of law should not sit, and the public offices should be closed.

Various oppressive burdens besides those named, were imposed, and irrational requisitions made, by the Andros government, to which it is not necessary for our purpose, to allude. And numerous were the imprisonments made of those who refused to comply with the tyrannical demands. Perhaps, however, nothing that the new Governor did, created such determined opposition as the ground he took in regard to real estate titles. This touched the colonists in their homes and their pockets. On principles they might not have been so inflamed.

And this brings us back to Mr. Purchis — or Purchase, or Purchiss, as it is variously spelled on the Colony Records — with his mutilated ear.

Edward Randolph, before named, who was now Secretary to Andros, having a little spare time, set about looking up a pleasant spot whereon, perhaps, to locate. And presently his beautiful light gray eyes were fixed admiringly on Nahant. This is sufficient evidence that he was a man of taste; but unfortunately men of taste are not always men of principle. He spent a day in pleasant rambles on the peninsula, with sundry dignitaries of the town. He feasted his eyes upon the charming views and his palate on the piscatory banquet liberally spread upon the rocks, under the careful episcopy of Mr. Purchis, in the vicinity of Cold Spring. He quaffed the invigorating breeze, and, with a little stimulating addition, the equally invigorating waters of the spring.

But it turned out that from quaffing one or the other, Mr. Randolph, during the afternoon, became a little jolly, as they used to say. Perhaps it was the delightful air that so exhilerated him. Any way, he became quite antic, and talked and acted in a manner more comical than becoming in one who had held the high office of Public Accuser, in England. Presently he insisted that Mr. Purchis should dance with him, on a flat rock, to which he pointed, in very dangerous proximity to the sea. Now Mr. Purchis would as soon have thought of hanging himself as dancing, at any time. And the probability of losing his life would have been no greater under the process of hanging, than under terpsichorean exercises in a place so dangerous. He promptly made known to the Secretary his entire unwillingness to engage in any such performance. This caused the wind to instantly veer with the merry official. He now insisted upon having a fight with Mr. Purchis; and divested himself of his outer garment in preparation. But fighting was quite as little to the taste of our Subject as dancing; and he peremptorily declined the challenge. This so inflamed the impatient champion that he declared his determination to whip somebody, before he resumed his coat.

Without uttering another word, Randolph made a pass at Mr. Purchis, which, had it fulfilled its design, might have rendered it necessary for the town to choose a new Clerk. But as it was, the wary man just stepped aside, and away went Randolph over the cliff into the sea. The whole company instantly skipped down to the rocks that jutted into the surge, and did their utmost to save him. A repentant wave, which had borne him a short distance into the offing immediately on his descent, and there amused itself with his stuggles, presently thought best to bear him back for a gentle chafing against the rocks. And while he was undergoing that discipline, they were able to seize him by his floating hair and thus disappoint the sea of its prey.

And we cannot avoid the reflection that had not Mr. Purchis and his companions been so fortunate as to rescue Randolph, the whole course of political events in New England and New York would probably have been changed; for it is evident that he was to Andros a sort of evil right hand.

Randolph came from his experience in the deep but little bruised, and on the whole rather refreshed. He was very cordial in his expressions of gratitude for the deliverance. And they were surprised at his sobriety and good manners during the rest of their stay.

But how astonished were the entertainers of Mr. Randolph, soon after, to learn that he had petitioned Andros to grant the whole of Nahant to him. This was repaying their kind attentions with a vengeance. The matter immediately assumed a very serious aspect, as it became apparent that Andros viewed the petition with favor. The town was notified, and informed that they could have a hearing. This was in 1688. A town meeting was forthwith held and a committee chosen to act in the strait. One of the committee was Mr. Purchis; and a better man could not have been selected. At this time, as before intimated, he was Town Clerk.

The whole population became excited. There was much more scolding, and, we fear, swearing, than there was during the great Shoemakers' Strike in 1860. Mr. Shepard, the minister, entered zealously into the affair, as well in the pulpit as out. He even appears to have assumed a sort of leadership; but for such a position it occurs to us he was not well fitted. Calm perseverance would be far better in such an emergency than rampant zeal.

During the excitement Mr. Randolph rode out to Lynn, bringing various letters in his pocket and a smile on his countenance. After parleying and passing compliments for an hour or two, it was determined to hold a meeting, at the house of Mr. Purchis, that very afternoon, to talk over matters. And by the time appointed, some half a dozen of the principal men had assembled.

Randolph had now delivered all his letters and dispensed with his smile. And furthermore, he appeared impatient and assuming at the meeting. Perhaps he mistook that as the best aspect under which to open the talk. For an hour or more he was the talker and they were the thinkers; that is, if silence is evidence of thought; it certainly being the only evidence we have, in many grave cases. We know that what Mr. Calhoun denominated a masterly inactivity, often accomplishes a great deal. And so does a masterly silence. But yet people are sometimes inactive from natural indolence, and silent from mental penury. So a judgment resting on such ground may not always be sure.

Randolph soon had the mortification to discover that his eloquence, instead of falling like a shower of millstones on their heads, was more like a shower of feathers falling on millstones. They would assent to nothing proposed by him, and were as immovable as the rocks on which they had eaten their chowder at Nahant. And very naturally his anger began to kindle. Presently he so far forgot himself as to hurl epithets of a quality by no means the most select at the heads of those around him. Mr. Purchis was astounded by a terrific one directed at him. And its flight taking place in his own house, his own castle, he felt called upon to assume a clearly defined position; for having once heard Mr. Shepard read Magna Charta, in Latin, he felt his individuality, his rights and his responsibilities.

The others, still preserving their masterly silence, Mr. Purchis, after fidgeting a little, got upon his feet, and when fairly poised, with his throat cleared and his nose wiped, he opened a battery on poor Randolph, who stood upon the other side of the ten-legged table, that, to use a very vulgar expression, made the feathers fly. His arguments and denunciations fell upon that partially bald head like so many fifty-sixes. The Secretary was in his turn astounded. He did not know what to make of it. He threw up his chin, puckered his mouth, grasped his left arm as if a shot had struck it, and in various ways manifested great perturbation. But the storm did not abate.

Presently Mr. Purchis surprised himself as well as all the others by a furious launch at the great Sir Edmond. This afforded a propitious opportunity for Randolph greatly to magnify himself in the eyes of his absent superior. To defend an absent friend is always an act worthy of gratitude. And the infrequency of so deserving an act renders it the more conspicuous. Randolph instantly perceived his chance, and, availing himself of a lull in the rhetorical tornado raised by the other, replied in a way that one rascal might be expected to adopt in defence of a brother rascal.

For some minutes Randolph spoke in a manner that would not only have crushed to the earth those present, but the whole town, yea, and the whole colony with them, had there been power in the human voice to do it. Beautiful Nahant was probably looming up inspiringly before his mental vision. There is no stronger incentive to eloquence, after all, than the expectation of a commensurate reward. We are sure that it is so at the bar, and beg leave modestly to ask if appearances do not indicate that it is likewise so in the pulpit.

Simple words not being competent to effect his purpose at once, Randolph resorted to gestures. And these he adopted in threatening variety. But as yet, the table, being between them, was the greatest sufferer, meeting the common fate of go-betweens. It danced and creaked under the inflictions; but its antics and complaints were unheeded. All this was perhaps very well as a finality, but as a prelude, the same can hardly be said of it.

Another moment, and with startling suddenness the demure witnesses of the scene were brought to their feet by a horrid shriek from the champion of their cause, hastily followed by Randolph's yelling out, that the ears of his bold antagonist should pay the forfeit of the slanders of his tongue.

The fact was, the insanely excited Randolph had, with the rapidity of lightning, whipped a little knife from his pocket, and actually almost severed his antagonist's left ear from his head. The blood ran in a stream, and the poor man danced round as if he were bare-footed on hot iron. His friends instantly gathered around him, and in the confusion Randolph hastily retired, not even bidding them good-bye. Without one moment of fond lingering to contemplate the beauties of the improved landscape, or to reflect upon the result of the friendly conference, he mounted his horse and rode rapidly away, taking a last look at Nahant, as it lay in the misty distance, over his left shoulder.

Randolph never became the owner of Nahant.

And the reign of Andros soon terminated.

It was early in 1689 that the colonists received intelligence of the invasion of England by William, Prince of Orange, for the purpose of dethroning James, who, aside from every other consideration had shown himself entirely unfit for his position. On receiving the news, the people were elated beyond measure, and many from the country rushed to Boston. There they immediately united with the uprising citizens, seized Andros, Randolph, and of their most obnoxious coadjutors forty or more and imprisoned them.

The people from the country are stated to have been headed by Mr. Shepard the Lynn minister. And we are inclined to think that on that occasion he did not manifest a particularly meek and lowly spirit, for a writer of that period says, " the country " came in at about eleven o'clock, " headed by one Shepard, teacher of Lynn, who were like so many wild bears; and the leader, mad with passion, more savage than any of his followers." And the writer adds that " All the cry was for the Governor and Mr. Randolph." Mr. Purchis and two or three of the dignitaries who had met the Secretary at his house, and who had eaten and drank with him at Nahant on the exciting occasion before alluded to, were there, supporting Mr. Shepard, and it was quite natural that the cry should be for Mr. Randolph as well as the Governor. And had Mr. Randolph been handed over to the disposal of Mr. Purchis, nothing but the great humanity of the latter would have saved him from a worse mutilation than a half severed ear.

After the Andros government had been thus disposed of, the former magistrates were reinstated to act as a council of safety till authentic information could be received from England. Sir Edmond and some of his right hand men were kept securely, excepting for a brief interval of escape to Rhode Island, until they were ordered home for trial.

But every thing remained in a turbulent and doubtful state till the tidings arrived that William and Mary were firmly seated on the throne. Great rejoicing followed.

One of the first things that Mr. Purchis did was to illuminate his house. And he came near being a serious loser by his patriotic display; for one of the unwatched tallow candles in the garret window undertook to play some pranks with a bunch of pennyroyal that hung near, which flared up, and indignantly blazed away upon some innocent catnip. And then the catnip must needs run a fiery race upon a basket of mullen leaves. And finally, the spread of the contagion was not arrested till half the roof was burned.

The people of the Bay Colony were now zealous in their endeavors for the revival of the old Charter or the grant of a new one. The question of the Charters was not, however, immediately acted on. But authority was given to the council to administer the government, till further directions, according to the old Charter.

That memorable year of smiles and tears, of mystery and sightless zeal, 1692, brought a new Charter for Massachusetts, and it included Plymouth, Maine, and other territory. The Governors under this Charter were appointed by the Crown. And Sir William Phipp was the first Governor.

And now a new era, as it were, commenced in New England. A fresh spirit seemed to be awakened, and new and enlarged views began to prevail. The people conceived that they had other great problems to work out than those of a strictly religious character; that temporal interests of leading importance in the wide world demanded their attention; that commerce should be extended, the arts encouraged. Those branches of education more directly bearing on the business of the world began to receive greater care. And the press was looked upon as an engine more worthy of being secured for the support of justice in the ever occurring conflicts for popular rights.

We have spoken of Mr. Purchis as being a Representative to the General Court as early as 1660. In 1668 he was chosen County Commissioner. He was several years Town Clerk. And at the Court of Elections held at Boston, in May, 1685, he was elected to the dignified office of Assistant; but the record adds that he "declined his oath." Now all these things show that he was a man for whom the community had great respect, and in whose judgment and fidelity they relied. And his conduct in the knotty matter of the Randolph petition showed that he was by no means deficient in courage.

And now Mr. Purchis must be allowed to prance before the reader for a moment in quite a different character. And we must go back some twenty years, for in this sketch we have chosen rather to preserve unity in subject matter than chronological order.

In 1665 an order was made for the promulgation of a certain declaration under this title: "A declaration by the General Court of his majestjes colony of the Massachusets Bay in New England." With the declaration itself the reader would not be interested. But with another order, that followed, we are certain that the case would be different. It was this: "And it is hereby ordered & desired that the declaration shall be published by Mr Oliuer Purchis on horse backe, by sound of trumpet, & that Thomas Bligh, the trumpeter, & Marshall Richard Wajte accompany him, & y^t in the close he say, wth an audible vojce, 'God saue the king.'" Now it was no hardship for Mr. Purchis to declare the matter of the order; nor was it probably any hardship to have his trumpet blown, either literally or metaphorically. But as to the closing supplicatory ejaculation, that was not quite so easily disposed of. There is, however, always some back door of escape from the performance of an unpleasant duty. He was no partisan of Charles, having many a time made himself hoarse by huzzaing for Cromwell and the Commonwealth. And, providentially, on the very day when he was to perform his duty, a powerful cough came to his rescue; and what was a little remarkable in its operation, a spell was sure to seize him, just as he was about to pronounce the last word. So, during the explosion, something would gurgle out, that might have been interpreted king, curse, or commonwealth — whichever the hearer might most strongly desire to have saved.

Mr. Purchis received many compliments for his dignified manner and stentorian enunciation, as well as much sympathy on account of his tormenting cough. One benevolent dame followed him for a quarter of a mile, with her tow cloth apron thrown over her head, to recommend a curative syrup that she had lately concocted, and to offer him a present of some if he would call on his return. And not the least remarkable thing about the cough was that it disappeared as suddenly as it came. Immediately on his return from his official airing, his lungs were at rest; and that even without a resort to the syrup.

We have just alluded to Mr. Purchis's attachment to the Commonwealth. And in connection with that point in his character it seems appropriate to relate an occurrence that took place as early as 1660, and which was greatly approved of by his patriotic townsmen. By very shrewd management he saved from arrest an eminent fugitive who sought shelter beneath his roof.

On a cold evening in the winter of that year, just as Mr. Purchis had drawn up his great flag-bottomed chair in preparation for partaking of his evening meal, which was already smoking on the table, he was a little disturbed by a loud rap at the door. He hastened to obey the summons, and found upon the step a venerable looking stranger. His hair fell in silvery curls over the stiff collar of his coat, and his three cornered hat was brought low upon his head, as well, apparently, for the purpose of concealing his countenance as protecting his ears from the chill wind. He stood erect, and his whole presence was commanding. His dress was of the finer kind of cloth, and though plain, exhibited no sign of poverty in the wearer, save that an outer garment, of which he was destitute, would have been desirable on so cold a night. He carried a formidable staff, though it did not seem necessary for his support.

As the stranger manifested considerable impatience to be within doors, and cast hasty and anxious glances up and down the street, Mr. Purchis began to have his suspicions aroused, and so placed himself in the doorway as if taking a position to defend the castle. Perceiving this, the man smiled, and looking the other directly in the eye, said a few words, in a low tone. But those words were talismanic. The door instantly flew wide open, and the brawny arm of the lord of the mansion was thrown around the stranger, who was drawn with irresistible force into the spacious hall. Then the door was shut and securely barred. And then and there, in that cold, dark hall, might have been heard the echoing emphasis with which the expansive hands of the patriotic townsman were brought together, and his stentorian voice exclaiming:

"God-a-man! Thou art welcome! Thou shalt lodge under my roof! Thou shalt eat of my bread, and be warmed by my fire! The Devil hath set snares and traps for thee, but we will deliver thee out of them! Go to, thou damned ones!"

Then it was agreed, in whispers, that the stranger should be known as John Rivers, a traveler, while he remained. This settled, Mr. Purchis grasped the other's hand with a fervor that admitted of no doubt of his sincerity, and led him into the great kitchen. Without a formal introduction he whispered a few words to the older persons, and for the ears of the little pitchers had something to say in more audible tones about friend Rivers, the traveler, who perhaps might tell them of his wonderful adventures.

They all sat down to the well supplied board, and the stranger, seeming to forget his fatigues and dangers, conversed with a freedom and pleasantry that charmed them all. Even the young folk quite forgot their sweet cakes in his sweeter words.

After supper, Mr. Purchis and the new comer withdrew to the little back room that was warmed by the kitchen fire, and there, by the dim light of an aromatic bayberry candle, remained for an hour or more in earnest conversation. Occasionally the excited settler's hands would be brought together with terrific force, and he would let down a withering denunciation upon the heads of the "hunting devils."

But the conversation ended, and Mr. Purchis came out of the room leaving the other there with the candle and a book. Without saying a word he put on his great fox skin overcoat and grotesque fur cap, and strode down to the principal store in the village, where he very diligently employed himself for an hour or two in picking up all the news there was afloat, all the while exercising the utmost discretion in concealing all knowledge of the precious life protected by his roof. Digesting what he had learned, on the way home, by the time he reached his house, he had become a little agitated, but concealed his state of mind as much as possible. He had another private interview with the stranger, and at its close conducted him to the little corner chamber in which he was to lodge, and which was directly over his own bed-room. After bidding him a good night he carefully closed the door, and as he was doing so, in an emphatic whisper, charged him if he heard a certain noise in the room beneath, which had been agreed on as a signal of danger, to start with the utmost speed, and to be sure that he took the right road.

At a seasonable hour the whole household retired, and presently all was still. But Mr. Purchis was watchful and apprehensive.

About midnight, as the moon was near setting, two or three individuals, closely muffled, made their appearance, and concealing themselves in the shadow of the house, close to the window of the very room in which Mr. Purchis was lying, not, however, sleeping, held a short conference, speaking in low tones. But there happened to be a broken pane near the head of the bed, and it was not difficult for the one reposing there, with his quickened senses, to distinguish some parts of the conversation. Presently they turned the corner of the house and loudly rapped at the door.

Hardly had the rap been given, when Mr. Purchis slipped from his bed and silently raised the window. Then he seized the little table, and with all his might dashed it against the wainscoting. This done, he jumped out of the window, and at the top of his speed rushed up the street. The villains at the door caught sight of him, as he designed they should, and gave chase. It was a spirited race.

Mr. Purchis had not a shred of clothes on, with the

exception of his short under garment, his night-cap and shoes. His long legs, disencumbered as they were, stood him in good stead, and he easily distanced his pursuers. Nevertheless, he occasionally slackened his pace, lest they should give over in despair. The gallant race was continued for nearly two miles, he, conscious of his superior powers of foot, keeping just within a tantalising distance ahead.

By this time, however, he began to fail a little in wind, and a range of friendly pines whispering their willingness to afford him shelter, he dodged into cover.

The moon went down, and he had no difficulty in making a detour and reaching his home in good time, all of a fine glow from his healthful exercise. But what was most satisfactory, his venerable lodger had in the mean time escaped, and was at that moment, no doubt, warm in bed at his new retreat. And where that was, our hero knew well enough, for he was not absent so long in the evening for nothing; nor was his last conference with the stranger without a purpose.

That stranger was Goff the Regicide.

Whally and Goff, as is well known, reached Boston about the middle of the year 1660, and remained dodging around there, and in the vicinity, mostly at Cambridge, for eight or nine months, or until they got off to New Haven. During that time they had many hairbreadth escapes, for there were numerous rascals, who, under pretense of loyalty, but really to obtain such rewards as they might, were ready like hounds to hunt the poor Judges, and if possible deliver them into hands that would delight in shedding their blood. It appears that on the day when Goff so suddenly appeared at Lynn, he had narrowly escaped capture, and had made his way on foot from Cambridge. And his uneasiness on reaching the house of Mr. Purchis is accounted for by his apprehension that he was pursued.

And now a few more words regarding the legislative career of Mr. Purchis. At a General Court held in Boston, in May, 1685, he, with seven other wise men, was appointed " to revise the laws and especially such as have binn made since the last comittee had the pervsall and revisall of the body of them, and to make a returne at the next Court of Election." So it seems he was called to lay "his huge paw on the statute book," to use the expressive phrase of the immortal Someone, that fell so movingly on the sensitive ears of the politicians in the exciting presidential campaign of 1840.

Massachusetts has always had a propensity to keep revising her statutes; and, we might add, a propensity always to keep them in a state to need revising. Over legislation has been her weakness. She has been almost smothered under her laws. And had it not been for the safety valve afforded by the power of one Legislature to undo what its predecessors had done, it seems as if she must have breathed her last long ago.

In 1860 another revision was published. And it is hoped that it may fare better than its predecessors, retaining its identity a little longer. The hope, indeed, resolves itself into expectation, in view of the fact that the members of the Legislature are now paid the round sum of three hundred dollars for the whole session, be it long or short, instead of so much a day, with the privilege of extending the session to any length. The new arrangement, which went into operation in 1858 has already had a wonderful effect in shortening the period of their labors. We have been particular in mentioning this, on account of the useful lesson involved.

One other thing: By referring back it will be found that Mr. Purchis and his coadjutors were required to make return to the next Court. This was having the thing done up in time. Those employed on the 1860 revision occupied some five years. It may be said that their labors were great. But that may possibly be met by the reply that the same could not be said of their industry.

But revising commissioners, before our day, have been caught lagging. The records of a General Court held as early as 1640, contain this: "Whereas, a breviate of lawes was formerly sent fourth to bee considered by the elders of the churches & other freemen of this comon welth, it is now desired that they will endevor to ripen their thoughts & counsells about the same by the Generall Court in the next 8th mo." That, however, does not appear to have been, strictly speaking, a revision. But it is worth mentioning, on account of what is disclosed regarding the deference paid to the elders of the churches in forming the laws. From the little heed taken of that class now-a-days, in such matters, one would imagine that the element they represent was not considered of much account in law making.

The first revision of the statutes, under the constitution, was made in 1822; the next in 1836. And every year since, the Legislature has inflicted such an avalanche of new laws, and made so many alterations in the old ones, that the lawyers have been obliged to be more industrious than was ever before characteristic of the profession, to keep up in their reading.

And we are not at all surprised that some have been driven to suicide. Dr. Johnson declared that he could always discover when an author had amended his writing, it being impossible to avoid leaving imperfect joints. But in our amended laws, it would require great sagacity to discern which is patch and which original.

And the Bay State legislatures have certainly, during the last few years, made unmerciful havoc with old principles. Perhaps in no particular has there been more upheaving than in what relates to the connubial connection. The tendency of our legislation, and the same may be said of legislation in other states, has been to make separate, if, indeed, not antagonistic, the interests of husband and wife, in regard to property. It can by no means now be said that husband and wife are one in law. And it must necessarily follow, that if all other interests are made separate, the connection itself will by the very force of circumstances, be made easy of severance. If this thing goes on for many years, gaining as it has of late, the marriage relation will come to be regarded both popularly and legally as a mere civil contract capable of being dissolved at any time by consent of the parties themselves — instead of a *status*, the continuance of which should not be determined against the interests of society at large. We very much question whether the tendency of these things is not to disturb the peace of families without rendering an equivalent. Indeed, can any thing compensate for the destruction of domestic peace? The union of husband and wife should be as perfect as possible. And the declaration of the elegant writer and sound moralist of a century and a half ago, that in his opinion separate purses between husband and wife are as unnatural as separate beds, might be profitably heeded.

Legislatures have great power, and we often see that they not only exercise what they have, tyrannically, but assume what they do not possess. Jefferson said, in a letter to Madison, as early as 1789, that the executive power of our government was not alone to be feared; that the tyranny of the legislature was then most to be feared and would continue so for many years. And the truth involved in this is conspicuous in our day.

The assertion that every man who is fond of fun is a good man, may not be true. But it is true that every good man is fond of fun. Fun, however, should not so monopolise our being as to crowd out all other virtues, as sometimes comes near being the case. Indeed it often appears with an individual as if he were so crammed with this or that particular excellence that no room was left for any other; much as it might be with a boy when half through his Thanksgiving dinner.

Mr. Purchis had a well balanced fondness for fun, and as he loved it in moderation, so he loved it in purity. Now there is enough of the commodity in the world, and any one who is disposed to search a little can find it in plenty. But Mr. Purchis did not need to spend much of his valuable time in the search, for he knew just where to look for it. He was favored above that numerous class who are doomed to spend one half of their lives in unsuccessfully searching for the blessing named, or some other, and occupy the other half in lamenting that they cannot find it.

The General Court was the great fountain of fun from which Mr. Purchis drew abundant supplies. And the inspiration thus received did not subside during his life. Many a winter evening did he spend, when gray headed, in entertaining his neighbors with recitals of the funny occurrences there while he graced one of the seats. It is astonishing how long, in most memories, such things will retain a place, after more weighty matters have faded away.

He became quite noted for his narrations, and being always sure to attach some excellent moral to them, was regarded as a sort of village Gamaliel. The schoolmaster frequently urged him into school, to instruct the little ones from his stores of wisdom. And he never arose to deliver his talk, as he modestly termed it, without the little eyes sparkling and the little ears erecting.

But it would not perhaps be desirable to extend this sketch, though other interesting events in the life of Mr. Purchis press forward for notice. It however gives us great pleasure to dwell on such a character, a character wherein the merits so far transcend the failings. It is to such as he that we are indebted for the noble foundations of our greatness and prosperity. And let no one who values the blessings that crown these days, sneer at those sturdy fathers whose hardships browned their visages and gnarled their hands, and whose knowledge of the polite arts and the learning of the books was, in most instances, necessarily circumscribed.

In closing, we feel bound to remark that Mr. Purchis had eccentricities. And it is not to be disguised that these gave occasion for some to speak evil of him. Now in a moral point of view, it is perhaps better for one not to be spoken of at all, than to be spoken against; in other words to remain unknown rather than to be known through evil report. And it is certainly most congenial to the honest and sensitive to be spared from censure though it might be maliciously and falsely bestowed. Indeed there is no one, however brave he may think himself, who is not disturbed by animadversions, whether just or unjust. But if we take the matter in a more worldly point of view, one had better be talked against than not talked about. It is, moreover, quite clear that for some purposes it is even better to be traduced than praised; for by being set down among rogues one may get the sympathy of that brotherhood, and they being largely in the majority, he might receive the more aid and comfort. Why, what would a politician, for instance, do without a crew of slanderers at his heels? though perhaps in this illustration it might be more exact to say, instead of slanderers, dispensers of unsavory truths. But we have no disposition to insinuate that Mr. Purchis had any reprehensible ambition, or desire to manufacture a reputation in any illegitimate way. His course was straightforward and manly.

As before observed, Mr. Purchis removed to Concord in 1691, and died in 1701, at the age of "foure score yeares & viij." The evening twilight of his existence was serene and happy. Though he was away from most of those who had longest known him and could consequently the better appreciate his virtues, yet the christian resignation of his parting hour afforded an example that all who wept around him could comprehend and were constrained to admire.

THOMAS DEXTER.

"Lo! quick beneath his lustie arme,
 the antient forest falls;
And o'er its bounde the noble farme
 distends its circling walls."

We find Mr. Dexter in the Third Plantation as early as 1630. And being one of those destined to make a sensation wherever they may be, we are enabled to catch glimpses of him through a long series of years. The early municipal records having been destroyed, however, it is not easy to give a full account of his life. To the colony records we are indebted for most of the certain knowledge that survives respecting him.

It must be acknowledged in the outset that Mr. Dexter, at least in his earlier life, possessed an irascible temper, and that his moral principles were not always sufficient to restrain his pugnacious propensities; a condition by no means uncommon in this irritating and irritable world. One of the earliest incidents in his life here, was a quarrel with Gov. Endicott. And it seems to have originated in a dispute about the proper season for trimming that immortal pear tree brought over by the latter, and which the newspapers of this day every year inform us yet flourishes on what is still called the Endicott Farm, in Danvers. In regard to the difficulty, however, we are glad to say that the aggression seems to have come from the testy magistrate, for Mr. Dexter appeared as complainant. It may be mentioned, in passing, that Endicott was not Governor at the time the affair happened. At a Court of Assistants, held in Boston, May 3, 1631, a jury was empanneled to inquire concerning the "accon of battry, complayned of by Thomas Dexter against Capt. Endicott." And the verdict was: "The jury findes for the plaintiffe and cesses for damages xl$s$." We do not therefore perceive that in this matter much should be set down to the discredit of Mr. Dexter.

An unbecoming exhibition of temper in Mr. Dexter took place in 1632. The record of the Court of Assistants, thus discovers its nature: "It is ordered that Thomas Dexter shalbe bound to his good behav^r till the nexte Genall Court, & ffined vl. for his misdemean^r & insolent carriage & speeches to S: Bradstreete, att his owne howse; also att the Genall Court is bound to confesse his fault." It does not exactly appear what he did about confessing his fault. But we are justified in a favorable conclusion for the Court seems to have been graciously inclined at the term held Nov. 7. At that time there were "iiij$l$. of Tho: Dexter's fine of vl. forgiven him."

And we find still another case, which, judging from the severity of the penalty, was deemed of a peculiarly aggravated character. At a Court holden March 4, 1632, it was disposed of in this wise: "It is ordered that Thomas Dexter shalbe sett in the bilbowes, disfranchized & ffined xl$l$. for speakeing repchfull & seditious words against the goum^t here established, & findeing fault to dyv^{rs} wth the acts of the Court sayeing this captious goum^t will bring all to naught, adding that the best of them was but an atturney, &c." This was really a severe punishment; the disfranchising feature especially. Nor was the fine of 40*l.* a small matter, particularly in those days. And the ignominious exposition in the bilboes was of no light character. What part of the rigor is attributable to his slurring allusion to "an atturney," we cannot say. But the utterance seems to indicate that some law-mongers were not very highly estimated. And the distaste for lawyers so early manifested in the Plantation seems to have existed for many years. The venerable Benjamin Merrill, who died in Salem, in 1847, and who was for a long period one of the brightest ornaments of the bar appears to have been the first regular lawyer who settled in Lynn. He came in 1808. And a few years before his death he informed the writer, that soon after opening his office, which was in the lower room of a modest dwelling house, a deputation of the citizens waited on him with the request that he would remove from town; giving as a reason that they had usually lived peaceably and were apprehensive that the incoming of a lawyer betokened the outgoing of quiet and good-neighborhood. Now Mr. Merrill was a gentleman distinguished for excellence of feeling and suavity of manner. So he politely informed them that he certainly should not remain against their wishes; and presently removed to Salem, where he lived for many years, prosperous and greatly respected.

But to return to Mr. Dexter: The severe punishment awarded him clearly proves that the people of his day had not the blessed privilege of railing at government with the impunity that people of this day have. But here, again, good fortune attended him. A record of the General Court, Sept. 6, 1638, referring to certain doings in 1632, says: "4 M^{r}ch Thom: Dexter being fined 40*l.* there was 30*l.* of it remited to him." The fourth of March is a lucky day, as well as an honorable one in American annals.

But it is not agreeable to dwell on occurrences like those named; occurrences that impel us to the aforesaid acknowledgment that our Subject was unfortunately possessed of an irritable temper. However, his antagonists seem to have been among the more eminent personages. If a man must fight, it is more to his credit to grapple with a worthy adversary. "Capt. Endicott" and "S: Bradstreete" were Governors under the first Charter, the former in 1644 and the latter in 1679. And his assaults upon the government show that he shot among lofty game. Yet he may have engaged with more lowly adversaries, differences with them being adjusted without the intervention of the august courts; for, after all, irritable people are not usually very particular in choosing their antagonists.

There is no doubt that Mr. Dexter was a man of enterprise and public spirit. We find him zealous in the furtherance of every operation promising to be of public benefit, particularly when connected with his own personal advantage. Enterprise, indeed, was a characteristic of the family from the time when their great progenitor began the manufacture of Dutch cheese, in North Wales, down to the time when the renowned Lord Timothy sent warming-pans and skates to the West India market.

And the men of enterprise, after all, are those who are most frequently in difficulties with those about them. Many oppose them from selfish motives and many from jealousy. Quiet and indolent people have little opposition to encounter. They do not jostle their neighbors because they do not stir among them. If a person never steps he will not tread on the toes of others. And by never stirring, he accomplishes little or nothing. True, the old saw teaches that the deepest water runs stillest. But passing by the important question recently agitated, whether still water runs at all, it might be suggested that something depends upon the quality of the bottom.

Some people are so given to planning and the changing of plans that they arrive at the time to die before they have fixed on a way to live. It seemed necessary, however, for Mr. Dexter to change or supersede some of his plans, for two or three were of such magnitude that had he been required to live a sufficient time for their accomplishment, he would not at this hour have been beyond middle life.

One or two of his enterprises certainly arose to the sublime, if, indeed, they did not shoot a little into the adjoining territory. And on the whole, we are persuaded that under conceivable circumstances he might have become as conspicuous as Walter Raleigh, Cromwell, or Van Tromp. But in the pent up Third Plantation he was simply Farmer Dexter. Are not characters formed by circumstances? Had Franklin been bound as apprentice to a shoemaker in some country village, is it probable that he would ever have been known as any thing more than a jolly cordwainer? Why should there not be jovial Franklins in village shops as well as mute Miltons in country churchyards?

Mr. Dexter did much service in clearing away the woods, fencing pasture land, and reducing the richer acres to an arable condition. That excellent kind of fencing, the cobble-stone wall, still so common in the Bay State, was put in requisition at a very early period. Indeed, in clearing the lands, these walls could be laid very cheaply; and were so easily repaired and so durable, that for miles hardly any other kind of fencing was in use. Many of the walls laid by the first settlers still adorn the landscape, mossy with age but enduring in strength. And many a valuable land title has been established by these unsubornable witnesses.

Not long ago an important cause was decided in the Supreme Court, wherein an ancient stone wall on land that once belonged to Mr. Dexter, and the line of which is still visible, was made, through the mirage of the law, to loom up in a manner most perspicuous and satisfactory. And it is not improbable that the worthy Subject of this biography himself assisted in laying that very wall. Perhaps, also, an occasional set-to with a boosy workman, served to relieve the monotony of the labor. Alrac, when so fiercely battling the Romans, declared that he was always at peace with stone walls. Without stopping to inquire whether they were fortress walls, with which, no doubt, he found it expedient to be at peace, we proceed to remark that Mr. Dexter was not only at peace but in love with stone walls of the kind just now under notice. He was a lusty and accomplished hand at their erection, and so substantial was his handiwork, that on one occasion, in 1658, the frost, which had for several years been trying in vain to level a small piece, was forced to call to its aid a spirited young earthquake before the end could be accomplished.

In common with all men of public spirit, Mr. Dexter was not always successful in inducing others to think as he did. Had it not been for this difficulty, some of the wonderful improvements that have been reserved for this age would have gladdened the eyes of our great-grandfathers. And some others that now never will be made would have cheered the same eyes.

Lynn Beach, that lovely extent of glittering sand and curious pebbles and shells, which the old geographer declared it worth a voyage across the ocean to see, would have had a sea-guard that all the sapping and mining power that old Neptune had at his command could not have overthrown. Mr. Dexter foresaw the encroachments that the ungovernable billows would make, as soon as the trees were removed; and sagaciously considering that in the abundance of material then at hand, an impregnable barrier could be erected at comparatively little cost, set about compassing the object. But the colonial authorities viewed the matter with indifference. And magnates of the lesser spheres thought the undertaking altogether too great to be engaged in. Some ridiculed the project. But ridicule is one of those weapons that none but the most skillful should attempt to use.

A member of the General Court, who had given an airing to his powers of irony in a speech concerning the proposed erection, during an afternoon session, got a blow in the face, on his way home, a little after dark, that sent him staggering against a rail fence. It was never ascertained who gave the blow, though a great noise was made on account of such a daring assault being made on a public functionary. It is not even clear on whom suspicion most strongly rested.

Mr. Dexter arrived home rather late that night. But there was nothing particularly suspicious in that. Neither was there any thing particularly suspicious in the fact that in the morning one or two small patches of skin appeared to have escaped from the knuckles of his right hand; for work upon stone walls is apt to occasion injuries of the hands. But there was a little something calculated to awaken suspicion in his tart reply to the goodwife who at the breakfast table sympathetically inquired how he had so injured himself—"Ask me not, ask me not, dame. The pain will not be yours to bear."

Perhaps, however, Mr. Dexter would have been more successful in securing his end had he not connected with the project named another so unquestionably chimerical as almost to create a doubt as to his sanity. Indeed he loaded his omnibus so heavily that it could not be dragged. This latter enterprise was to clear off all the trees and other vegetation on Egg Rock, shovel the surface earth into the sea, and then boat over sufficient yellow loam to form a miniature plantation. But what he expected to raise there that could not be better produced on the main land, we are entirely at a loss to determine. We however conclude, from something found in Obadiah Turner's journal, that he fancied he could there raise a kind of cane that would be useful in chair making and which required, in growing, a constant and abundant saline evaporation. Any way, by perseverance during an entire season he managed to get a considerable quantity of new earth there. The lonely keeper of the light house, has now the benefit of his wonderful labor. And when that functionary contemplates his stunted cabbages and wilted squash-vines, listless upon their beds of red sorrel, he should drop a tear to the memory of Goodman Dexter.

The project of Mr. Dexter for the erection of the sea-wall, was put forth and received as an enterprise for the public benefit. But yet, it is not difficult to perceive its connection with a private interest. He had purchased Nahant from an Indian chief and naturally had an eye to the improvement of his newly acquired possession. And this we must set down as indisputable evidence that he was a shrewd, wide-awake man; for do we not award such a character to those among us who manage in exactly the same way?

Another scheme of Mr. Dexter, was to straighten Saugus river. Any one ignorant of the course of that stream, by taking a look from the highlands in the vicinity, will at once conclude that there is need enough of its being straightened. First, it appears to have made up its mind to run this way. Then, after going some rods, it seems to have found it expedient to go back and take a fresh start. Again, it diverges to the right, as if determined to run up the hills and off towards Boston. Soon repenting of this, it flows rapidly back and keeps on towards the left as if bent on undermining the cedar hills on the bounds of Lynn. In short, for a mile or two, it seems aiming to illustrate the picturesque or endeavoring to elucidate some occult geometrical problem.

The account given by the Indians of the formation of this river, is worthy of being considered. They gravely informed the settlers that when the Great Spirit had got the earth nearly prepared for its garniture, he happened to be walking around one fine morning, somewhere up at the north, and espied an enormous serpent, basking in the sun, among some spare boulders. Seizing one of the boulders, of many tuns weight, he hurled it at the monster. Unluckily the aim was imperfect, and the serpent started, with great speed, for the ocean. His assailant, however, rapidly followed, dealing a blow whenever within reach. And it was only by exercising all his powers, both of speed and cunning, sometimes dodging back, between the legs of his pursuer, and sometimes gliding to the right or left, that he was finally able to reach the sea. The earth not then having quite hardened, the serpent's body sank somewhat; and thus was ploughed the tortuous channel of Saugus river.

The Indians added that there were accounts of the serpent's having been occasionally seen near the shore, after the country became inhabited, and of some being afraid to go out in their skiffs for fish. What reflective mind will fail to connect the wonderful serpent here spoken of with that pet of summer visitors to the coast of New England, the Sea-serpent? And what pious mind will fail to connect them both with that old serpent, the Devil, who is ubiquitous?

There is some obscurity about Mr. Dexter's object in straightening Saugus river, though he seems to have had something connected with mill privileges in mind. His purpose, however, might simply have been to make straight the crooked ways of nature. But be that as it may, he was no more successful in obtaining public aid here than in his beach enterprise. And there is little wonder, for he overdid the thing, running into the same weakness that defeats many worthy objects in these days. Perseverance is much more effectual than zeal, with one who desires to obtain public favor. Some of the witnesses whom he produced made most extraordinary statements while under oath before the Court. Among other things it was sworn that five people who lived in the vicinity had been made cross-eyed by looking on the river.

In his private enterprises, Mr. Dexter's genius sometimes outrode his resources. In other words, he could not always find the means necessary to carry out his plans, and so found himself, now and then, in the wilderness of pecuniary embarrassment; a condition unfortunately by no means uncommon with the most enterprising in all times.

Perhaps the most notable of Mr. Dexter's speculations was the purchase of Nahant from the Indian chief who did honor to the euphonious English name of "Black Will." That charming headland, now so extensively known and as extensively admired as a watering place, where on every hand rise the costly villas and nestle the unique cottages of the sons of fortune; and where, during the warm season, congregate the beauty and fashion of the land — that gem of the blue ocean, with its magnificent cliffs, its silvery beaches and green uplands, was, in 1630, sold by Black Will to Mr. Dexter for a suit of clothes and a jewsharp. The parties occupied nearly a whole day in settling the details. And it was not till Mr. Dexter had gone four miles into the woods and played six tunes on the harp, before the assembled tribe, to convince them that the tongue was not leather, that he was able to procure what he conceived to be a sufficient title-deed.

There was nothing remarkable in the mere act of purchase. It was the after rumbling that elevated the matter to the position of an important event. The town treated the bargain as a nullity, declaring, Andros like, that Will's deed was no better than the scratch of a bear's paw. And vexatious litigation soon began to drag its slow length along. The cause was finally determined against Mr. Dexter; but not till years after Will had worn out the clothes. The jewsharp, however, survived, but in a damaged state. By constant use it soon lost its tongue and was then sold to a neighboring chief for land enough to make a modern farm, the purchaser coveting it as a personal ornament for a favorite squaw. So Will was safe from making restitution, when the title failed. And as to the quarrel between his grantee and the town, he cared not a crow feather which beat in that. He no doubt thought himself shrewd. And why should he not be praised for his shrewdness as well as good christian people when they conduct in like manner?

Nahant was by no means the only land purchase that Mr. Dexter made of the Indians. He also bought a large tract lying about a mile north of the iron works. For this he gave an iron kettle, a pewter spoon, four pumpkin seeds, and one of those never failing jewsharps. Our ancestors early found that music had charms for the savage; and had they possessed a dozen hand organs, they could at once have made themselves owners of half the continent. The worst thing about this purchase was, that the Indian and Mr. Dexter, while perambulating the bounds, got into a quarrel. Their combat took place at the edge of a swamp, near a growth of dogwood, and fortunately or unfortunately they seized the weapons nearest at hand, and both became so poisoned in using them that they were laid up for three weeks. The gross amount of punishment was about equally divided between them. And it would be highly beneficial to have all such quarrels terminate as equitably.

Mr. Dexter's purchase of Nahant, as before intimated, like some of his other speculations, did not turn out to be very profitable. The town having disputed his title, the matter was kept fermenting in the cauldron of the law for a good while, till it finally settled bright and clear against him. A survey of the whole peninsula was then ordered, and it was laid out in lots, which were distributed among the inhabitants. But the litigation concerning Nahant lands did not end with Mr. Dexter. A taste was reserved even for this generation. The surveyors were too liberal in certain instances, here and there throwing in little tracts to compensate for deformities and deficiencies of nature. As the land increased in value and the proprietors began to look up their rights, it was found, on measuring, that in this or that range of lots there was more land than was required to give each his portion. And as it is generally as difficult to manage a surplus as a deficiency, disputes arose as to the ownership of the overplus, at once perplexing and irritating. There was much scolding; and as to fighting, that has not ceased to this day, at least such as could be carried on by the more genteel weapons of the law. Some, not apprehending the true cause of the difficulty, declared that the earth had grown since the original surveys, and that the increase should be disposed of as a gratuity bestowed by nature. The more the land increased in value, the more obstinate and acrimonious became the controversies. And though at this day most of the territory is in undisputed possession, yet in regard to the few outstanding claims, it may be said that they are contended for with a zeal which, did it characterise men's efforts to secure possessions in Paradise would surely not prove unavailing.

Myriads of cod fish sported in Massachusetts Bay at the time of the early settlements. The noble promontory now known as Cape Cod took its name from this circumstance. They were easily taken, and soon came to furnish a profitable article of export. A hardy and industrious race of bay fishermen, of whom the Third Plantation furnished her full share, were early known. And from them ultimately grew the foreign marine of

New England, the indomitable naval material, the right arm of our nation's defense. In the early stages of the fishing business — to say nothing of the late — many a shrewd landsman furnished the means for outfitting, and in return had the lion's share of profits.

And this leads to the statement that we have a lurking apprehension, from certain facts that have turned up during our historical researches, that Mr. Dexter, in company with his enterprising fellow townsman, Thomas Laighton — he from whom the Laighton Bank takes its euphonious name — went into the cod fishing business, exported the fish to Barbadoes, and, we say it with blushes, sold them for rum. This was a kind of trade that flourished amazingly, among the morally pretentious colonists at a certain period.

The partnership of Dexter and Laighton did not exist for a great while, the former becoming dissatisfied with the result of some speculations. They kept a small store in a little frame building that stood where Exchange Building now stands, on Market street. And the business of the store was left almost entirely to Mr. Laighton's management.

Now Mr. Laighton was a confidence man — not in the modern acceptation of the term, for both he and Mr. Dexter were scrupulously honest — but a man confident of his own abilities. He was famous for laying down maxims for the guidance of human conduct; and generally, when he showed his sincerity by acting on them, found his interest more or less compromised. He laid it down as an invariable rule, for instance, that a rogue can never look an honest man straight in the eye. Now rogues are not usually bashful and can often look honest men out of countenance. It is the naturally diffident, such as are commonly found among the most innocent, who are apt to cast their eyes downward. As Mr. Laighton held tenaciously to this maxim it was not remarkable that he should as well put it in the converse form, assuming that all who could look others in the eye, were honest. The absurdity is patent in this form if not in the other. It would be a better maxim to adopt, that all who boast of their ability to discern character in any such way, are of the unsophisticated school with whom the worldly wise profess to be less inclined to deal than with rogues.

We remarked that the store was almost entirely under the management of Mr. Laighton. And he did not, as do the more ambitious traders of the present day, deem it important, excepting in the most busy season, to be very constantly at his post. He was to be found there on rainy days, evenings, an hour or two at noon, and at various odd intervals. Sometimes his neighbors would desire articles at such hours as the store was closed. They must then look him up at his house, in some workshop or on some field of public duty; or, perhaps, they would find him seated in the shade of a tree, conferring with Mr. Dexter on their mutual interests. And being found, he might hand them the store key, and bid them go and help themselves, making a charge of what they took, upon the day book, which was usually kept lying open on the counter, blurred and blotted by maple molasses and sanded with dust and meal. But he was never known to thus trust one who could not look him straight in the eye.

We think these things quite sufficient to justify our assertion that Mr. Laighton was a confidence man. But there must have been a blessed state of society at

I*

that time. If one of the traders whose elegant stores are now upon the very spot he occupied should fall into his way of conducting business, the whole capital of Laighton Bank, the good settler's own memorist, would not keep him afloat for six months.

We have alluded to this foible of Mr. Laighton, more because of its singularity in such a character, than from any particular instruction that is to be drawn from it. He was really a man of excellent parts; had keen perceptive powers, much natural intelligence, and a good judgment, well disciplined by a varied experience. And his moral integrity was unquestioned. For a number of years he filled the office of Representative to the General Court with credit to himself and usefulness to his constituency. The foible named only goes to confirm the truism that there can be no human character without its weak point. Taken for all in all, if one third of the people in the world were as good as Mr. Laighton, the human family could boast of a much better average than we find.

The store was an unpretending edifice, without paint or clapboards, and the front was adorned with odd little signs of different lengths and widths, announcing that "Corne Meale," "Candells," "Salte ffish," "Tooles," and "Towe Cloth," were for sale within; and also that "Pype Staves," "Hoope Poles," and "Cydar," would be taken in exchange for "goodes."

A noble beach tree stood in front of the shop door, spreading its patriarchal branches to a great extent, and bestowing the blessing of refreshing shade. Near its trunk were sundry rough troughs for the convenience of baiting hungry horses. And an oaken bucket, benevolently provided for transporting water from a spring that bubbled up from beneath a rock on the other side of the road, hung alluringly on a peg in the tree. It was an inviting spot to way-worn man and beast. And often of a summer noon an eminently picturesque scene was there presented. A rude bench stood on either side of the shop door, for the convenience of those village fathers who at evening assembled to discuss the news and debate on public affairs. And there, while considering their glorious privileges, they would occasionally become so elated, as spontaneously to break forth in songs of pious joy, such as would echo over the little pond that quietly smiled in its rushy zone a few rods west of the store, and roll murmuringly along the distant hills. And then the whole surface of the water would become studded with the green heads of charmed bullfrogs, who, emulous of harmonious sounds, would, after putting forth their best endeavors, and failing to satisfy themselves, sail away to hide their diminished heads. It is said that Plato had such a perverted ear, or practical mind, that he desired to banish the heavenly maid from the commonwealth. Luckily it was not so with our fathers, for had it been they would have failed to possess one of the most effectual of all means for subduing the savages.

At the risk of being charged with digressing — a thing of such rare occurrence in this volume — we are constrained to say a word about a very singular article that it has been said Mr. Laighton at one time wore for the protection of his head, and of the distressing event that induced its adoption.

The article in question was a racoon skin, all in full fur, worn as a wig, with the tail hanging down behind, like an ill-shapen cue.

And the disaster which rendered it necessary for

him to adopt some such head dress may be briefly related in this way:

One warm day Mr. Laighton was cutting white pine wood in the Dungeon Pasture. He had trimmed some of the larger limbs from a huge tree and cleared away the rougher bark, preparatory to felling it, when, being much fatigued, he concluded to partake of his noon repast and then indulge in a little rest. Having accomplished the first, in pursuance of the latter, he threw off his hat, and seating himself near the devoted tree, soon fell fast asleep, his venerable head, often weary from carrying its great burden of knowledge, falling back against the trunk. His sleep was sound, for he had an undisturbed conscience, and somewhat protracted, insomuch that when he awoke, the declining sun and cooled air betokened the near approach of night. A little startled, he was springing to his feet, when his head was almost wrenched from his shoulders, and he perceived that by some unaccountable means his meridian member had become a real estate fixture. He put all his philosophy at work to solve the mystery. It did not seem consistent that his head should have suddenly died, leaving his body alive; so he would not entertain such an idea. Nor was it more rational to suppose that his head was determined to have a little more of that sweet sleep, in spite of the disturbances of its wakeful adjuncts.

In making a second effort, however, his eyes became literally opened, and so widely, that it seemed questionable whether he would ever be able to close them again. The mystery was solved.

From the wounds he had inflicted on the tree, the pitch had copiously flowed; and as the air cooled it had hardened, holding the matted body of his hair as firmly as the scalp held the roots. His condition was any thing but agreeable, no effort that he was able to make, giving the slightest promise of release. He had no knife, and the slow process of relieving himself by his hands, even were it possible to endure the pain and keep his arms in the agonising position necessary, for a sufficient length of time, seemed entirely out of the question. He might have starved to death or been eaten up by wild beasts before he could have effected any thing in that way.

By all that appeared he would be obliged to remain a prisoner at least for the night, and perhaps be forced in his crippled condition to defend himself against savage beasts and satanic emissaries, the woods at that time abounding in such gentry. In the extremity of terror, arising from reflection on his dangers, he roared out in such a strain as to induce the most terrific responses from far and near.

Presently, with mingled feelings of joy and apprehension, Mr. Laighton perceived, stealthily emerging from the thicket, a stalwart Indian. The red man grinned at his contortions, and approached with some boldness, for he could perceive from the writhings of the body and the fixedness of the head, that from the latter at least there was not much to be feared. Mr. Laighton at once hailed his red brother, and gave him to understand that he desired a little christian aid. But this appeal not exactly striking home to the dusky heart, as was indicated by a surly grunt, he without more ado threw himself upon the Indian's generosity and honor as a man, a fellow being; taking, in short, the course that very many do when they are in a strait and cannot help themselves. And the sincerity of Mr. Laighton's appeal was evidenced by a copious flow of tears. It used to be said that tears were a great dread to the Indians; and that nothing on earth could cause them to shed any, but the tooth ache. Be that as it may, Mr. Laighton succeeded in gaining the friendly offices of the one who had so opportunely appeared.

"Me vum," growled the savage, "Master Lakum in ye stocks, jest as poor Indjan was. Now me give him a dam preach."

This last was in allusion to the circumstance that when that same Indian was once undergoing the useful discipline of the stocks, Mr. Laighton had his christian sympathies so stirred that he stood for an hour in the broiling sun lecturing him on the danger of his sinful ways.

The red rascal now planted himself before his victim, and went on with a "preach," more plain than pleasant. It contained all the tattle and slander that he had picked up during his many visits to the settlement. The charge on which the dusky orator dwelt with the most passionate ardor was that of his having sold a leather tongued jewsharp to an Indian. But another charge, which seemed to be considered hardly second in importance to this, was that of his having, in conjunction with Mr. Dexter, sent Indian prisoners, taken in the wars, to the West Indies, with their salt fish, and sold them for the same sort of return cargo that they sold the fish. That such nefarious things were done by some of the christian colonists we are afraid is undeniable. But there is no reason that we can find to suppose that any thing of the kind was ever done hereabouts. This Indian had probably somewhere heard of the horrible traffick and used the information to embellish his discourse. And do not we behold, in these enlightened times, quite as questionable a way of embellishing often resorted to?

The dusky orator's discourse was delivered with great unction. And having finished, he drew his knife, saying, "Now me let Master Lakum out ye stocks."

With a ceremony in imitation of the proceedings on the release of a culprit from the stocks, and brandishing his weapon in a mysterious way, the Indian approached the tree. Scarcely had he looked down on that defenseless head, when all the sanguinary impulses of his cruel nature became aroused. And he could not resist the temptation to become possessor of one more white man's scalp. With the rapidity of lightning his knife flew to its favorite work; the warm blood gushed along the artistic curve; and then, in completion of the labor, he set up a frightful yell, at the same time pricking his victim in the back. Mr. Laighton, not doubting that the savage intended to kill him outright, gave a desperate spring. And away he went, freed from durance and freed also from his scalp, with the speed of a camel, off towards Tomlins's Swamp. And there remained the grinning Indian unloosing the venerable scalp from the old pine tree.

The red villain was never seen in the Plantation afterward.

Mr. Laighton's dreadful wound healed in due time. He found it convenient to adopt the comical substitute before named, the racoon skin, for the natural covering of his head; and though singular in its appearance it excited mirth in no one, for all knew of the calamitous event that called it into use.

We remarked, a few pages back, that there is cause for suspicion that Messrs. Dexter and Laighton were engaged, to some extent, in that discreditable Barbadoes traffick. The Barbadoes rum was the true "fire water" of the Indians. And it was imported in such quantities as to become a terrible scourge to New England, not only as regarded the colonists themselves but also the miserable Indians. Had Hugh Peters seen things as they certainly were here at one period, his conscience never would have permitted him to make the boastful statement that he did to Parliament, to wit, that he had lived seven years in New England, and had not heard a profane oath nor seen a drunken man in all that time. These seven years were probably from 1635 to 1642. And it gives us pleasure to add that most of his time was spent in the vicinity of the Third Plantation.

But there seems to have come from Barbadoes something besides fire water, that greatly troubled the colonists. The first Quakers that appeared in New England came from that productive island; the first, at least, who openly professed themselves of that order. It was in 1656 that Ann Austin and Mary Fisher arrived and commenced promulgating those doctrines that ultimately created such a ferment.

A biographer never fully performs his duty without treating to some extent of the personal appearance of his Subject. The reader is always pleased with this, for if the character is a worthy one, it facilitates his power to trace resemblances in himself; and if an unworthy one it aids him in the pleasant occupation of tracing resemblances in his neighbors.

In Mr. Dexter's physical construction there was nothing very remarkable. His forehead was full, with a vertical wrinkle or two, rather expressive of conflicts within. His gently bulging nose, slightly rubicund, and shining as if kept well varnished, stood out in rather more than ordinary prominence from the facial plain of sandy red. His eyes were gray and deeply set in their sockets, surrounded by ruddy circles, indicative of inflammation, occasioned, it might be, by exposure to the weather; or, perhaps, by overstraining from looking at Saugus river. His hair was thick and bushy, and while he was yet in middle life, took pity on the lonesome condition of his eyes and changed so as to bear them company in color. He interposed no obstruction to its growth, in defiance of the law forbidding that any man's hair should extend below his ears, and kindly avoided disturbing its equanimity, on ordinary occasions, by any comb finer than his spread fingers. His noble beard, too, was treated with great consideration. He would as soon have thought of clipping his ears as that. In form, he certainly approached the faultless. His chest was broad and full, and his arms and nether extremities would have done honor to a gladiator. On the whole, we feel fully justified in pronouncing Mr. Dexter a man of more than ordinarily commanding presence.

We have remarked that we hold it important for a biographer to describe the physical peculiarities of his Subject just as they are, and given cogent reasons therefor. And it is desirable further to say that in these days of scientific light a more perfect idea of character may be thus formed than by any details of actions. The old fashioned idea that a man's doings are to certify what his character is, has exploded. His phrenological or physiognomical developments are to determine the question. And we have found it necessary in keeping pace with the progress of science to somewhat mar the fair face even of our big Bible by annotations. For instance, after Dr. Trapplescorn, the phrenologist, was here, against the passage declaring that by their *works* we may know men, we had to put, "Mem. By their *heads* we must know them." Then came Dr. Addlesop, the physiognomist, and we had to put again, "Mem. 2d. By their *faces* we must know them." After Professor Hodgcapp, the geologist, was here, against the passage in Exodus, xx. 11, "For in six days," &c. we had to write, "For in six periods each of six hundred thousand years, more or less," &c. True, it made mischief in another way; for what becomes of the seventh day, the good old Sabbath which men for so many ages have delighted to honor? But then what is the Sabbath when it opposes the theoretical deductions of masters in science?

Like most men of philosophical turn, in the matter of dress Mr. Dexter thought less of appearance than of comfort or convenience. As it was said of one that he did not live to eat but ate to live, so of our Subject it may be said, he did not live to dress but dressed to live. His coat of gray woolen was indulged with an airing on Sundays and other notable occasions. And his brown velvet small-clothes, with their graceful continuances, all fashioned in the father land, received the same favors, illustrating the benefit of being adjunctive to greatness. But the every day habiliments of Mr. Dexter were not such as to distinguish him as a Brummel. A homespun frock, from beneath which protruded a pair of boots of uncurried leather, enormous in size and grotesque in shape, and a scarf of striped cloth about the neck were the chief things observable, save the round topped hat, with immense brim, flabby and flapping. As he walked, that brim would beat on his shoulders like an elephant's ears; and if he ran, it would play such pranks as to greatly offend the eyes. To obviate this difficulty, he sometimes resorted to the expedient of passing a piece of cod-line over the crown and tying it under the chin; thus making all taut, as the sailors say. And whenever this was done the rebellious eyes would readily return to duty, congratulating the ears on their prospect of protection from the cold.

We have said something of Mr. Dexter's ancestry; and a word or two may be added. He belonged to a very ancient family, which can be traced to the times of the Plantagenets. In the reign of Edward III. they stirred up great political strife in Anglesey, and one restless spirit would have found his head and four quarters suddenly parting company had he not claimed benefit of clergy. The success of the claim proves that though he may have been a villain he yet had some learning; probably about the amount that makes it a dangerous thing. At any rate he had some, for no one was entitled to that inestimable benefit, who could not at least write. That singular subterfuge, the ægis under which every species of roguery flourished, and which from its origin in the Middle Ages, continued for centuries, sprang from the mysterious reverence for learning which even now is often found to exist in the uncultivated mind. Any criminal, even up to a murderer, could escape punishment from the temporal power, by claiming his benefit of clergy, though he may have been already convicted in a law court. On setting up the claim, he was handed over to the ecclesiastical power, which, perhaps inflicting the terrific punishment of excommunication, let him run. If he was sufficiently learned to write his name, he was entitled to the benefit, though he might not be able to intelligibly read his Bible, or was beyond caring for its teaching if he could. And progressive Massachusetts seemed to have waked to a similar reverence for learning when in 1857 she amended her constitution so as to deny the right of voting to those who could not read and write.

Perhaps the benefit of clergy would have shed its sanctified light on our day had not that magnanimous sovereign, Henry VIII., shaken off the old popish harness because his Holiness would not sanction his villanies in the matrimonial line. The unswerving determination of Clement VII. to firmly oppose such great wrongs as those committed by Henry, made the world stare, and should have been more justly represented and more honored than it has been by some historians. When he knowingly lost the allegiance of a kingdom, by a course of unflinching justice, as instanced in the cases of Catharine of Aragon and Anne Boleyn, something better should be said than that he had no political sagacity and was not fit to govern. It should have been said that he chose rather to lose England, with all her power, than sanction the disgraceful immorality and meanness of her sovereign. But mankind have not yet arrived at that blessed condition where it is possible for some individuals to conceive that others can have such a strong sense of right that temporal advantage cannot overcome it. Such Ephraims do not understand how any one can do right merely because it is pleasing to God and their own consciences.

But we are admonished to draw this sketch to a close. Little has been said of Mr. Dexter's domestic relations, and little need be said. He did not rear a large family; neither was he childless. A few very worthy descendants might be named, showing that what was lacking in quantity was amply made up in quality. In most families the rule works the other way.

When the head begins to whiten it is time for the asperities to begin to soften. But is not the reverse most frequently the case? Mr. Dexter, in his old age, had the reputation of being somewhat testy. And he certainly did occasionally flourish his staff in a manner better calculated to repel than attract, and express his views in a tone that evinced little anxiety to keep his affairs private. Now an ill-tempered old man is a very pitiable object; almost as much so as an ill-tempered old woman. But things are often called by wrong names. We are persuaded that our Subject was to a considerable extent misunderstood; though we frankly admitted in the outset that, unfortunately, he was quick of temper; a failing by no means always evidence of a bad heart. He grew old; and having been in his progress through life so constantly subjected to the rougher usage of fortune, to the superficial observer he might have seemed as if the kindlier sympathies of humanity had been beaten out of him. Yet, we insist upon it, he had a heart capable of being deeply touched by real wo. He would, indeed, like the great moralist who flourished a hundred and more years after him, laugh or scold at one who complained of the minor annoyances of life; of heat or cold; of ill or even scant fare; of the ordinary aches and pains; more especially, he gave no quarter to such as suffered from wounded pride or defeated ambition. But no one was more ready than he to visit the widow and fatherless when truly afflicted, or to minister to all such as were in real distress of mind, body or estate. And are there not many such around us, who yet pass with the undiscerning as mean and unfeeling?

It is a great comfort to a man to have a high appreciation of his own value in the world. And besides being a comfort to himself, how agreeable it renders him to those with whom he associates. Very much is lost by undue modesty. And we are glad in being able to point to Mr. Dexter as one who was not particularly prone to the too common weakness of undervaluing himself. About all the great achievements in the world are effected by two classes: First, those who deem themselves mere instruments of Providence, placed here to accomplish certain work to which they are specially ordained, without any power of themselves to change their course; and being unceasingly guided towards the great object. These generally work with zeal, in view of meriting the high prize of the approbation of their great Director. Napoleon Bonaparte was one eminent example of this class. And Martin Luther was another. The second class embraces those who appear to think that they of themselves are equal to any thing ever heard of in the world, and grapple with the greatest enterprises, as most worthy of their efforts, fully persuaded of their own power to will and to do. It is not necessary to give examples of this class; they are common enough all about. But it may be well to add that Mr. Dexter appears to have been by nature located with these latter. Mixed characters accomplish least.

That Mr. Dexter was a little off the track occasionally, in other respects than those named, it should in honesty be admitted. But we are happy to believe that he sowed his wilder oats in early life. In the records of the Court held at Boston, October 1, 1633, we find this: "It is ordered that S*r*ient Perkins shall carry 40 turfes to the ffort as a punishmt for drunkenes by him comitted." And, "Also, it is ordered that Thomas Dexter shalbe ffined xx*s*. for the like offence." It will be observed that this false step took place at a very early period. And though some twelve years afterward he appears to have been fined as "a common sleeper in meetings," we have abundant reason to conclude that he forswore his cups. Had he been an intemperate man, he certainly could not have accomplished what he did, for we have the conclusive authority of scripture for saying that such err in vision and stumble in judgment. And who will say that Mr. Dexter erred and stumbled in those ways, save in the few instances we have been faithful to name. No, no, he must have reformed, if, indeed the instance recorded, were not a solitary instance of inebriation during his whole life — a mere inadvertence, such as happens not unfrequently in these days, according to the statements constantly heard in our courts.

As has probably been inferred, Mr. Dexter was rather inclined to change in his pursuits. The adage, "A rolling stone gathers no moss," was as well known in his day as it is in this. But he was sensible enough to realize that the stone might have some pleasure in rolling, and that there were many things to be prized more highly than the moss of mammon.

The normal state of man is laziness. Thus we see that in those countries where little or no exertion is necessary to procure a livelihood, men pass their time basking in the sunshine, like crocodiles. Industry is one of the most excellent of all acquisitions, for it opens to the individual numerous sources of enjoyment and adds materially to the progress of the species. Mr. Dexter was a most industrious man. There was no stagnant blood in his veins. And being shrewd enough to observe that those who work with their hands alone, generally remain in penury, he constantly availed himself of the efficient services of the brain. Both brain and hands were kept in vigorous motion. And we have seen something of what he accomplished. But it is a shame on any man to be industrious merely to accumulate wealth, to be hoarded up or expended in dainty food and costly raiment, to say nothing of more sensual indulgence. If no higher purpose can call one's energies into action they might as well remain dormant. We have seen how unselfish Mr. Dexter was, and how much he endeavored for the benefit of generations that were to come after him.

Notwithstanding the foibles — faults if we must so call them — that we have alluded to, Mr. Dexter appears to have been esteemed a good neighbor and useful citizen. He did his full share in supporting the ministry, and was ready with his means to aid in evangelizing the heathen around him. And he strove hard to overcome the evil propensities of his nature. Many a time, when he felt himself most weak before the crafts and assaults of the Devil, did he in humble trust seek the christian counsel and prayers of the good minister, Mr. Whiting. Had it not been for that impulsive temper, he might have passed life more pleasantly. But he fought bravely against the evil spirit to the end, and went to his final rest in the panoply of christian faith and hope.

PHILIP KERTLAND.

> "Some move with neither noise nor speed,
>   along life's crooked path,
> Who yet may drop some wayside seed,
>   that springs to mightie growth."

Another jewel of the Third Plantation was Philip Kertland. He came during the first decade of the settlement, and is represented to have been the first shoemaker in Lynn. From this circumstance, if for no other reason we feel in duty bound to do something in honor of his memory. Little appears on the regular records, concerning him, and for most that we are able to state we are indebted to casual notes and traditions. His is said to be a German name, the translation of which is Lack-land. But he did not long lack land after coming here, for ten acres were granted him in 1638.

All New England, yea, the whole country should make obeisance to the Third Plantation, and do reverence to Philip Kertland; the first, because she early encouraged ingenuity and enterprise; and the latter, because he spent his best energies in perfecting a most useful art. And both their names should be exalted for the blessings conferred by the establishment of that great branch of American industry from which has been derived so much wealth to one class and comfort to all others. Lynn not only encouraged the manufacture of shoes at an early period, but also that of various kinds of leather. Here was first established the manufacture of those beautiful moroccos that used to adorn the feet of the belles of olden time, and are devoted to so many elegant purposes, at the present day, besides the protection of beautiful feet.

Of Mr. Kertland's early life we need say but little; though one or two remarkable things require some notice. It may be observed that when about five years old, he one day strayed into his father's pasture, to indulge for a while in the boyish pastime of twitching a bull's tail. Perhaps, however, he was, like a young philosopher, endeavoring to elucidate the problem as to how far such an animal might be thrown by the caudal appendage, for he had often heard his father, who was quite a moralist, allude to such graceful experiments. But whatever his object was, the bull does not appear to have favored its furtherance. He gave a kick that sent little Philip rolling like an ill-shaped ball, into a ditch. By this accident the nose was so damaged that it ever after sat awry. His personal appearance was thereby somewhat impaired; but beyond that and a slight difficulty in compassing a genteel sneeze, he perhaps experienced no evil. For most purposes it was as good a nose as need be. A handsome man is an ornament to any community. And in those rare cases where beauty of character is added we behold an object envied by men and adored by women; for we do not accept the slanderous declaration of the ostentatious moralist, regarding the latter, that with them, character never rules in competition with person.

It certainly must be confessed that Mr. Kertland

was not a handsome man, and we shall not rest his claims upon his beauty. But speaking of personal appearance leads to the remark that it seems very foolish for people to cry out so against what they unfortunately denominate pride of person. But then envy will rankle in the human breast, and the tongue of slander will wag. There is not an individual living, in full possession of his senses, who does not feel the influence of personal charms. It is thought commendable to admire a beautiful landscape, or even a picture of it, or a piece of marble chiseled out in graceful form. Why, then, is it wrong to do homage to beauty in the most dignified object of creation? Personal beauty will often purchase what no money can; and is it not, in its nature, of quite as much value as money?

Martin Luther spoke of beauty as a noble gift, and added, " God commonly gives riches to gross asses, to whom he can afford nothing else." Perhaps it was well for Christianity that he was thus susceptible, for the smiles of a pretty nun inflamed his zeal for the Reformation. The shrewd Cobbett remarked that the surest thing to make a man feel good natured all day is for him to look upon a handsome face in a night-cap, beside him, in the morning. There is much truth in these things. The arguments of bright eyes and rosy cheeks have overcome many a man when nothing else on earth could. The wisest are not above their influence. Look at Solomon. Handsome men, as well as handsome women are the most successful in life. And now, reader, what would you take in exchange for those personal charms of yours?

Mr. Laighton, of whom we said something in our sketch of Thomas Dexter, appears to have been on very friendly terms with Mr. Kertland. The two spent many profitable hours in discussing great philosophical principles as well as important theological points, sometimes in one of their shops, and sometimes in the shade of a tree. Mr. Kertland became a thorough convert to Mr. Laighton's maxim that no rogue can look an honest man straight in the eye, and that all who can look others straight in the eye are honest. And the following little incident will illustrate the benefit he derived on one occasion at least, from his adherence to the maxim:

A sort of fair was to be held at Boston, and Mr. Kertland went up for the purpose of purchasing a new milch cow. He shrewdly suspected that there might be rogues about on such an occasion, and made bold to proclaim his suspicions to all the assembly, adding, however, that he defied them all to cheat him, as the maxim, which he discreetly repeated, would enable him to keep safe from any rogue in the crowd. Having thus defined his position, he began to look round, all the while keeping his eyes wide open, for the return gaze of the honest ones who might be straying there. Presently he discovered a tidy looking brindle with a lusty calf by her side. And he was delighted to find that the man in whose keeping they were, could look him straight in the eye. Without much haggling a bargain was concluded. Having a little other business to transact, he requested the vendor to keep his purchase in charge till he returned. This was kindly agreed to.

Having concluded his other business, Mr. Kertland returned, and there stood the cow, but the calf was gone. Not suspecting any trick of trade, he desired the man to trot out the calf and he would be gone, for his way was long and the clouds betokened rain.

With well feigned surprise the honest drover replied that he did not sell the calf, for the very good reason that it was not his; neither did the little beauty belong to the cow. It had been borrowed from a neighboring stall, and now was back with its mamma whose anxious lowings during its absence had greatly disturbed their tender hearts. And the conscientious man further reminded his customer that not one word was said by him about the calf while they were negotiating. With great frankness, however, he admitted that his customer did remark that a cow with a calf just ready for the butcher was exactly what he wanted, and that he felt of little red-and-white and commended his fatness. But he did not feel himself bound to respond to the compliments paid to the calf. And with some warmth the man concluded by reiterating that the cow only was sold, and the calf had already gone back to its restless parent, and he did not see why he should be held responsible for the purchaser's being deceived by appearances. Were not appearances often deceitful? They were so; Mr. Whiting had fixed that fact by a luminous discourse which he had preached on the very Lord's-day before.

Mr. Kertland felt the force of the drover's curt reasoning, and his anger was wonderfully softened. But he was greatly puzzled, after all. The man looked him straight in the eye while speaking, and expressed regret that he should have been deceived. Yet it was clear that he had not only been deceived, but grossly cheated. The drover would not hear to any proposition to rescind the bargain, for, as he said, the day was far spent and another customer might not appear.

Mr. Kertland's perplexity again developed itself in

extreme anger. And he promptly announced his determination to whip every one present. A crowd began to gather. Presently, at the suggestion of a peace-making though perhaps thirsty individual, a reference was agreed on. There was no difficulty in selecting three arbitrators, for Mr. Kertland had but one test of their honesty, and the first that presented themselves could look in the attractive direction demanded by the test. The drover himself offered no objection, to those fixed on, for they were all brother drovers. The red faced trio chosen seated themselves on the edge of a horse trough, the owner of the calf acting as chairman, and had the points in dispute formally presented to them.

In fifteen or twenty minutes, after leaning thoughtfully over a pig-pen and conferring in an under tone, the arbitrators announced their determination of the weighty matter. Their conclusion was that Mr. Kertland had bought the cow and could not annul the bargain; that he had not bought the calf, and consequently the calf was not his; that though there had been a grievous mistake, it was yet attributable to his own laches, and he could not take advantage of his own mistake to the damage of his innocent opponent. After announcing this luminous verdict, they had the magnanimity to add, that, considering all the facts named and the additional one that the drover had succeeded in disposing of a most miserable beast at an enormous price, he, the drover, should treat all hands. The friendly individual who had suggested the arbitration clapped his hands in approbation, and the whole crowd seemed to be well satisfied, particularly with the concluding requisition. They at once adjourned to the neighboring house of entertainment.

Mr. Kertland stood for a few moments with his hands

behind his back, in mute perplexity. But light soon appeared to break upon him. He joined the company, and a jolly time they had of it. He did not reach home till midnight. And when at that late hour he came down the street driving his cow and singing at the top of his voice, it was evident that he felt well pleased with the adventures of the day.

For some time he tried to coax a little milk from the aged quadruped that had thus fallen on his hands. The first day, she dispensed about a pint; the second, half as much; the third, half as much as that; the fourth, half an egg-shell full; and that was the last drop she ever vouchsafed.

Singular as it may seem, this experience did not in the least shake his faith in the Laightonian maxim. Indeed his faith was strengthened, though his heart sank, when he discovered that the cow herself, through whom the mischief had come, could not look him straight in the eye. Whenever he endeavored to catch a direct glance her head would swing some other way.

Mr. Kertland, though he did not live in absolute penury, was by no means a rich man. He was too benevolent to be rich; besides being, like all men of genius, rather improvident. We must never look for good financiers among men of genius or great mind. The amusement said to have been caused at one time on the exchange, by an unsophisticated holder endeavoring to raise money on a note of Daniel Webster, endorsed by Rufus Choate affords an illustration of the value of mind in the haunts of mammon. The latch-string of Mr. Kertland's door was always out for the grasp of the needy and the stranger. And he was never backward in lending a hand to a neighbor, even though his own affairs might be suffering for attention.

Some considered him rather too ready to volunteer his services in other people's affairs; but we are persuaded that this conduct arose from the overflowing benevolence of his heart. And however objectionable this propensity to interfere in the concerns of others may be held to be, is it not attributable to the consciousness possessed by most of us that we are better judges of the affairs of others than they themselves? And that being the case with Mr. Kertland, for instance, we see how naturally he must have conceived such intermeddling to be a part of his duty.

The great Shoe Trade of New England, now one of the most profitable and extensive industrial pursuits ever known in the country, had a humble beginning. Mr. Kertland's shop was a rude adjunct to his lowly habitation which cowered in a little hollow on the north side of the winding road that was the original of what is now the beautiful Boston street of Lynn. The interior was some twelve feet square, and innocent alike of plaster or wainscot. It had two diminutive sashes, and the light had to struggle vigorously to get through the little knotty panes that from appearance might have fulfilled one destiny as the bottoms of German wine bottles. The chimney ran up on the outside, at the northeast corner, and was so extremely rough and angular that the poor smoke found it a hard road to travel. And the little triangular fire place, within, was flanked by cutting-board and backless seat. A wooden block sat in front for the convenience of customers and visiters; and many and many a time did it bear the weighty forms of Zachariah Hart, Obadiah Turner, Thomas Newhall, Oliver Purchis, Thomas Dexter, Thomas Laighton, and the godly Whiting.

For a part of the time Mr. Kertland had little or

nothing to do, at his trade. He would then attend to small farming, fishing, or other useful labor. At other times he was so much driven by work that he would be obliged to call to his aid a couple of ingenious boys who knew something of the rudimental mysteries of shoemaking. There also lived in the neighborhood of Saugus river a cross-eyed man, who had some knowledge of the art; and he too, under extraordinary pressure, was induced occasionally to make a breach in his habitual laziness and take hold for a few hours.

Mr. Kertland took commendable pride in his calling and really did much to advance the art. He has been known to pay a ruinous price for a newly fashioned shoe from abroad, that he might dissect it and study the hidden mysteries of its beauty. And he once made a journey to Virginia to visit a celebrated shoemaker who was for a short time tarrying there. By such means he gained a high reputation, and customers from other places began to appear. At one time his trade was so extensive that he had to visit Boston and Salem at least once a month with a large bag of shoes on his shoulder.

What we have said shows the small beginning of a business which has steadily grown through two centuries and more till it has reached such gigantic proportions that by an honest and careful estimate not less than thirty millions of pairs of boots and shoes were manufactured on the very territory that constituted the old Third Plantation, during the five years ending with 1860 — or about the same number that would be required to furnish every man woman and child now in the United States with one pair. And is not this something that will bear a little boasting?

About the worst thing that we have learned of Mr.

Kertland is that he was not always courteous to customers; a bad failing in any tradesman. Like many others, he was apt, when a reflection was cast on his merchandise, by a purchaser, to side at once with the merchandise, resenting the indignity in terms more expressive than choice. One day while fitting a pair of shoes to the feet of a lady, she strongly insisted that his shoes were too small; and he as strongly insisted that her feet were too large. The wordy quarrel waxed warm, to the edification of the grinning boys. Presently the application of his oratory was shifted from her feet to her head. He ridiculed her enormous head-dress, eagle-feathers, and eel-skin rosetts; angrily intimating, among other indecorous allusions, that according to his way of thinking, Indian moccasins would better comport with such a display, than shoes. Now it happened that this lady was the wife of one in authority. And could it be expected that his slanderous tongue should so wag unpunished? By no means. The very next lecture day found him in durance, near the meeting house, for two hours, with the unruly member in a cleft stick. And are there no imprudent young shop-keepers at this day who might be benefited by such a wholesome experience?

We find one most extraordinary thing recorded regarding Mr. Kertland, which we cannot forbear alluding to, even at the hazard of being thought inclined to talk of wonders. We understand it, however, to relate to his early life. It is asserted that it was physically impossible for him, under ordinary circumstances, to appear uncleanly in person, his flesh possessing a powerful repulsion to all filthiness. This was noticed long before he appeared remarkable for any thing else. It is related that during one of his school vacations, when much of his valuable time was devoted to the healthful employment of constructing mud mills and transporting the material in his hat, he did not wash his face for thirteen days. Yet he appeared fresh and clean as the rose "which Mary to Anna conveyed." Sometimes for the gratification of curious neighbors, his parents would adorn his cheeks and arms with charcoal sketches, and very soon, without being touched, they would all disappear. By such facts we confess to having been greatly puzzled. But they may perhaps be accounted for by supposing that there was such an extremely healthful action in his system that impurities were driven off with a speed unknown in common cases. No doubt there is a natural tendency in the human body to repel all foreign substances. Disease must weaken the repelling power; and the power being in proportion to the degree of health, it follows that where the health is perfect the propulsion will be immediate, and where there is no health dirt will stick eternally if artificial means are not resorted to for its removal. This doctrine is no doubt correct, in a general sense. The eminent Boyle speaks of the constant passing of corpuscles out through the skin. And now if all these things be so, what an extraordinary degree of health must have blessed the early days of Mr. Kertland.

But our imperfect sketch must be drawn to a close. It is true that we have not had many extraordinary things to relate of Mr. Kertland. Yet, as he passed a useful and on the whole exemplary life he has a better title to the enduring smiles of Fame than many whose names flaunt high upon her scroll. Scarcely an individual goes down to the grave, whose biography, if penned by an honest and skillful hand, would not be found deeply interesting and instructive, however humble the life may have been or barren of stirring incident. We are all interested in seeing how others acquit themselves in the common affairs of life, for with the same realities we ourselves are struggling.

It has not been an object in these sketches, always to choose the most conspicuous characters to dwell upon, for it is very far from being true that the most conspicuous are always the most meritorious. And, besides, there are enough others to laud and magnify the already renowned. Circumstances often conspire, in a most unaccountable manner, to make one man famous, while his neighbor, infinitely better endowed, passes his life in obscurity. We feel justified in lauding such of the early settlers as we have been able to speak of. They were a hardy and self-sacrificing race; pious, industrious and prudent; a people inspired by holier motives than the greed of gain. What, indeed, would have been the condition of New England, at the present day, had the early planters possessed no more ennobling traits than do most of this mammon seeking and mammon worshipping generation? And we close with the pertinent question —

What would the good old Third Plantation have come to without such jewels as ZACHARIAH HART, OBADIAH TURNER, THOMAS NEWHALL, OLIVER PURCHIS, THOMAS DEXTER and PHILIP KERTLAND?

PART II.

NOTABLE THINGS
OF
OLDEN TIME.

"In the gray morn and purple eve,
  Spirit of Thought!
O lead me to those dim old rustic shrines
My fathers loved. Recall their lusty forms,
And let me ponder on their worthy acts;
Teach me to emulate their dignity,
And prosecute life's nobler aims!"

INTRODUCTORY REMARKS.

IN a volume of such design as the one now in the hand of the reader, it would be a marked omission not to treat, to some extent, of Things as well as Persons. Yet, in all historical illustrations, the images of the two departments so mingle together that it is to a great degree impossible to present them in any very distinguishing light. The scenes and actors must constantly appear together. And perhaps the most that can be done is to endeavor, when treating professedly of Persons, to place them in the strongest light, and when treating of Things, to pursue a similar course.

In the present case, certainly, the reader will recognise the propriety of the divisions we speak of, whatever may be his opinion of the manner in which we acquit ourselves.

In our biographical sketch of Obadiah Turner, we gave copious extracts from his interesting journal. Mention is made by him of numerous localities and institutions that in after years became famous; and not a few occurrences are treated of, the results of which were subsequently reckoned of leading importance. And it is not difficult to trace some of our cherished customs and institutions to the small beginnings of that period. No history can be more profitable than that which, while it inculcates pure morality, impresses useful lessons in the philosophy of life. Our brief details, we trust, will secure the reader's attention; and the few reflections intermingled may not prove altogether destitute of value.

We love to go back to the quaint days of our fathers; to the days of blue leggins and leather small-clothes; of huge bonnets that hid the face of innocence and beauty from every rude gaze; of gowns of tow cloth which the wearer's own hand had woven, and which were worn with no expansion of skirt beyond what was necessary for grace and ease of step. We love to think of their intrepidity in meeting perils and their uncomplaining submission to sore privation. No other people ever on earth were like them; so brave in the battle of life; so devoted and trusting in spirit. And is it not pleasant and profitable to mark the growth of those good things which they originated and by their virtuous heroism guarded and nurtured, and which have come down to bless our own generation?

THE
OLD BURYING GROUND.

"Though storms and winds rule high in air,
And men's rough passions rave,
Calm rest the weary sleepers here,
Safe in the dreamless grave!"

For a period quite beyond the memory of all living, the quaint name that we have placed above, has distinguished a consecrated spot in the western part of Lynn — a spot which by its beautiful location, its numerous trees and its neat monuments, never fails to attract the attention of travelers. In our extracts from the journal of Mr. Turner, it will be observed that under date of 1653, he speaks of "yᵉ buryal place." And it seems quite certain that he can refer to no other than this. The history of this interesting spot so runs back into the obscurities of past time that the period when it was first devoted to its sacred purposes does not certainly appear. For generation after generation it has remained a revered spot. And could the tongues that lie here in the cold silence of death be reanimated, what a history they might disclose.

In the modern cemetery one sees costly monuments assigning to the dead virtues above the power of mortal attainment; — fond conceits of mourning love. And the rich tablet, to the humble mind, too often seems but ostentatious evidence of human pride. To the gray old stones that rise beside the resting places of New England's early dead we turn. Upon their mossy fronts, in few and simple words are touching lessons to the heart, and worthy histories.

To the contemplative mind there is a serious and enduring satisfaction in retiring from the scenes of busy life to spend a tranquil hour in the community of those who are no longer disturbed by the murmuring of the waves of care nor by the raging of the storms of passion on the shore of time. To such a mind the ancient churchyard is most hallowed ground. Here, retired from the turmoil and vexations of a heartless world, and from the gaze of earth's unfeeling devotees, he reads upon the green sward and lettered stone a history of bygone years. He looks upon the grave of honorable manhood and blesses him who was a blessing to his kind; upon the grave of childhood, and with grateful aspirations that the tender plant has been removed to bloom in brighter spheres than earth affords, mingles an emotion of sorrow for the mourning hearts from whom its light and love have been withdrawn.

Men would not be harmed by retiring more often to such a place, to muse upon their course and destiny. Were they accustomed so to do, many of the rough passages of life would be made more smooth, for they would be led to perceive the hollowness of all earth's promises, hopes and attainments, and learn to lean with more confiding faith on those promises which concern a nobler life.

Some men have such enlarged and comprehensive minds, that they look forward, even beyond the bounds of time, to estimate the effects of their present conduct. But most men are so circumscribed in their contemplations that a few years entirely close up the view. Yet a hundred years will roll away just as certainly as five. And 1865 is no more sure to come than 1965. Time is not the substance of things.

Let the groveler in the path to wealth come hither at the solemn hour when "fades the glimmering landscape on the sight," and consider the purpose and end of his care and toil. How deluded, to turn from the true and only road to happiness, the training of the unearthly powers of mind, to chase the ignis fatuus that dances along the quagmires by the wayside. The ability to obtain happiness from the mere possession of wealth is not an attribute of the human soul. Why then bend its powers to such ignoble purposes? Why spend a life in gathering that which cannot make more happy here, which can afford no barrier to the shaft of death, nor purchase entrance to more joyous realms? That sanctified petition, "Give me neither poverty nor riches," contains a world of wisdom, and of instruction for the seeker after happiness. Without heed to its spirit all our efforts are vain. And in an enlarged view, what community can be more happy than that in which all have enough and none too much. If such a community exists they are in a position to enjoy the greatest amount of temporal felicity attainable by mankind. Men who ceaselessly toil for wealth spend their energies for means instead of an end; that is, instead of enjoying life as it passes, making use of their gains as means for enjoyment, they harrass themselves by unceasing endeavor to continue the accumulation of means, and finally end a miserable life without ever applying them to an end. By such a course riches have no more power to impart happiness than wind blown into the nostrils of a statue has power to impart life.

Let the aspirant for fame and worldly honor come hither, and contemplate the end of all his daily toils and nightly vigils. What though wondering millions speak his praise and on his fevered brow the laurel wreath be twined. Remember that the trump of fame sounds not beyond the borne of time, and that the wings of mortal praise can never waft one to a happier sphere.

And hither let us all come; high and low; rich and poor; learned and ignorant. Let us come and consider our ways, remembering that our earthly pilgrimage is soon to close; and remembering too that as we lie down, so must we rise again. And may we so order our ways, that, lying down as after a long day of weariness and labor, we may rise as from a refreshing sleep, disciplined and inspired for a loftier race.

When one seriously reflects on death, it would seem as if he could not reasonably entertain any fear of it, but must regard it as a mere transition from one state of existence to another; a passage which we all must make. And is not he irrational as well as deficient in moral courage and christian faith, who shrinks from meeting, with bold front, what he cannot avoid? But is it the thought of an hereafter that makes men dread death? What dutiful child of a loving Father, can fear a more pitiable condition hereafter than is commonly experienced here? And who even is prepared to say that the quietude of annihilation is not to be preferred to the troubles and perplexities that most experience in this life?

In this venerable gathering place of the dead are congregated the worthies who sat in council over the infant interests of the Plantation; the fathers who reared the first dwellings in the shades of the forest; the mothers who watched over the first born; the young men and maidens who, of all the pale race, first sought these romantic glens and vales, wherein alone to plight their vows. And here are those who have shone as bright stars in the councils of the nation; those who have broken the bread of life for the hungry penitent; as well as countless hosts of humbler souls who loved to tread these hills and shores. And here, too, have the sons and daughters of far-off lands lain down their weary heads with the tears of strangers alone to fall upon their graves.

What are our feelings as we pause among the graves of the earliest tenants of this consecrated spot? A thousand images, these reveling in living beauty, and those dimly discovered by the torch of history or transiently delineated by the flickering glow of tradition, are arrayed before us.

How changed are all things around since their footsteps brushed the dews of these fields and impressed the sands of these shores. A fair and busy city has arisen from the forest shades. The holy pæan of the christian church now sounds where only the wild savage chant was heard. These waters, which to their eyes presented an unbroken field of blue, are now enlivened by the broad white wings that waft rich argosys. The thunders of war have echoed over them and the earthquake has rocked them in their dreamless sleep. One by one their kindred and neighbors were gathered around them, and long have the winds of heaven moaned a dirge over their whole generation. More than two hundred times has the snowy mantle of winter been spread and the sweet garniture of spring been renewed upon their lowly beds.

But all things are not thus changed. We look upon the heavens and they are the same. You evening star shines with the same mild lustre to guide us in our musing walk, that it did to light them along the forest path. The deep music of the ocean harp rolls along these embattled shores in the same mighty strains for our generation that it did for theirs, and the rugged hills and cliffs echo it back as faithfully. And, above all these, the same God who led them through the perils of their lone heritage, conducts our footsteps in the less trying though more dangerous paths of prosperity and among the hazardous refinements of more artificial life.

It is uncertain, as before intimated, at what precise period these few acres were first occupied as a burial place. But it must have been in the early times of the Plantation. For many years, however, the space remained unenclosed, and the graves were dug here and there among the trees. Finally a rude stone wall was erected to prevent the intrusion of straying beasts. And that in good time gave place to a more comely erection.

A century ago the Ground was almost bare of trees. The remnants of the old forest had vanished one by one like vexed ghosts, and little or nothing had been done towards supplying their places. The numerous cherry trees that now adorn the sacred precincts, have appeared within some forty years. And singular as it may seem they sprang from seeds transported hither by the birds; as if those winged watchers would have bowers in which to carol over the dead, or would gently hint to men their duty.

The oldest grave-stone now standing bears the name of "Iohn Clifford," and the date 1698. All the earlier monuments and tablets have long since disappeared; though it is not probable that many of enduring material existed. Simple erections of wood no doubt for many years marked the resting places of loved ones; but these decayed and vanished. Unsculptured stones were reared by other graves, and some simple mounds of earth; and these were removed as more ambitious monuments appeared.

This particular spot was devoted to the purposes of burial more perhaps from the convenience of its location than any other consideration. At that period little was thought of choosing a resting place for the dead where the beauties of nature might attract the thoughtful, or where the mourner's heart might find relief in contemplating the departed as resting in a pleasant place. Yet, whatever may have been the purpose in the selection, the spot chosen was in truth a lovely one. A small pond lay upon the south and west, and many hale old forest trees looked down admiringly upon their gigantic forms mirrored in the placid water. The white lilies unfolded their perfumed leaves and gay birds sailed quietly about. The oak, pine, and cedar reared their stately forms, unconscious that the new race who had come to occupy the land would soon lay them low with as unpitying strokes as those dealt to their own kind found upon the soil. And sweetly the evening dew distilled through fragrant branches and profusely blooming shrubbery, upon the early graves.

True it is that even down to our day, this sacred spot has never been in a condition to boast of much artificial embellishment. But it may long have boasted of what is far better. Beneath these unadorned stones lies as noble dust as that beneath the Roman marble.

And when the earth and sea give up their dead, there will arise from these graves, those with whom warriors and kings, statesmen and philosophers, men whose names stand high on the historic page, would gladly change conditions.

The power of intellectual association has always been recognised, however deeply hidden its channels of operation. The slightest emotion within, or occurrence without, will sometimes reopen vast provinces of thought, recalling every feature of the mental landscape in pristine freshness and beauty. The perfume of a particular flower or a certain strain of music may possess this talismanic power. Some tone in a stranger's voice may call up old loves; some landscape feature, long forgotten scenes.

There are some who possess such original and abstract natures that their outward acts receive tone and coloring essentially, though not entirely, of themselves. But with the great mass of mankind the conceptions are shaped by the outward aspect of nature, the influence of other minds, and the shifting scenes of life.

Sometimes there arise in the common mind, dreamily mingling with the present, long departed phantoms, diverse in their nature and intensity. And thence flow those checkered, indefinite notions that so frequently dance about in fantastic and incomprehensible shapes. But at other times, and in more cultivated minds, the departed return in order and fidelity, illustrating the present and imparting strength for the future.

And how few possess a full realization of the dignity of their higher nature, of the powers of mind. But more especially how few realize the enduring effects, the remote sequences, of their acts and even thoughts. Future ages may be moved by what the most humble soul may execute or conceive. A thought, springing up today, may be acted upon, and go forth, inspiring and setting in motion other minds, expanding and accumulating power, till, in future time, it may turn the world upside down. And that thought may have been born of some rude wayfarer. And may it not be that among those who lie here, awaiting the resurrection, there are those whose conceptions have brought about some of the great things which are the boast of this generation?

When one quits the world, how little can be known of the good or evil he has done. The great account cannot be closed up till time shall cease. And can it even then? Are not the consequences of his acts done here, felt in other souls through all eternity?

In view of these things, what dignity belongs to every man and what responsibility rests upon him. How ought he to live? The faithful soul may take fresh courage for his race; for, however humble here, his name may yet stand high upon the records of a better land. By tender persuasions he may have drawn, by holy examples lighted, other souls in the path of true life. And can he fail of reward?

Just where that little freshly blooming cherry grows, were laid the remains of Deborah Armitage. In 1679 she was, and for many years had been, traveling about Lynn and the neighboring towns, gaining an honest pittance by selling herbs and a few simple medicinal preparations. She was decrepit, and much indebted to her well worn staff, though not exactly the subject of any great suffering. Her apparel was comfortable though by no means exempt from evidences of long service. The bonnet of rusty black, and the dingy brown shawl, which the kind Mrs. Whiting had given her half a score of years before, she continued to wear in grateful remembrance of the donor. And the cloak of coarse woolen cloth reaching to her ankles, with a girdle of leather and an immense hood, which she donned when winter's blasts were howling, was the gift of the young sisters of the parish.

In the woods, Aunt Deborah gathered her sassafras, gold-thread and checkerberry. In her little garden she raised her sage, rue and wormwood. By the roadside she found her catnip and yellow dock. And the meadows supplied her sweet flag root and rosemary. The few bottles of eye-water that she took in her basket were distilled by her own fireside. And the few boxes of salve for wounds and bruises were made by her own hands.

From Monday to Saturday, in sunshine and storm, she traveled hither and thither, diligent in her humble calling. Every one knew her as an honest, pious and simple hearted dame, with tears always ready to flow at a tale of suffering, and hands ever ready to do their utmost in charity. To many a sick bed did she find her way with words of christian comfort which to the trusting soul did more good than her herbs and concoctions. She was never turned from a door, but often bidden to tarry for a meal or lodging; for her presence was deemed a good omen. Yet it turned out that she sometimes made her bed in a barn and supped upon a crust, for she had a delicate fear of intruding on the hospitality of others.

Little children were not afraid to lean upon Aunt Deborah's knee or have her smooth their flaxen heads.

And with delight would they gather around her, seated on their little crickets, to hear her tell how good boys and girls were rewarded and wicked ones punished.

The home of Aunt Deborah was a small rustic cot at the edge of the woods, with a brave little brook working its weedy way in front and an unassuming garden patch in the rear. Some messes of early vegetables and a store of herbs for winter sales were her reward for the few hours of toil that she could devote to her modest husbandry. Along the wall the flaunting leaves of the horseradish and burdock spread; golden saffron heads peered among fantastic weeds; and precious mint struggled bravely among the knotty grass.

From the noon of Saturday to the dawn of Monday Aunt Deborah was never absent from home, save to visit those who were in need, sickness or other adversity, or to attend the services of the sanctuary. And she loved to see the villagers who in their evening walks so often called. The pious had their own zeal inflamed by her warmth, and the careless had their hearts awakened by her gentle warnings. Her tattered and blurred Bible was a fountain head of comfort. And it was delightful to see her earnest struggles to light in other hearts such holy fires as burned in hers. And, we doubt not, eternity will testify that she, unlearned and simple, opened many a sleeping eye, roused many a sluggish soul.

The good minister loved to linger beneath her roof, not because a tankard of her best herb brewing awaited his thirsty lips, nor because when he remained to sup, the whitest cloth that tow could make was spread upon the little round table and the choice cup with its edge of blue and the silver spoon which had come to her as a precious heirloom, were brought forth, but because he might reanimate his own faith by the heavenly glow of hers, and from her meek and unaffected grace learn to guide his own steps. Alone, by night and by day, she passed many hours. But no fears disturbed her trustful spirit. Upon her solitary bed she lay in the still hours of night, fearing no harm, but gratefully contemplating the mercies and promises of her great Protector.

Aunt Deborah, or Aunt Armitage, as she was indiscriminately called, must have been quite aged at the time we mentioned, for it was more than thirty years that she had continued her lowly traffick, selling her herbs and scattering the precious seeds of christian truth and love. Many of the sick were relieved by her, and many of the depraved renewed, in that long time.

The winter of 1680 was one of great severity. The cold set in early, and before Christmas, the streams and ponds were frozen up, not again to be released till the warm fingers of spring touched them. A great body of snow fell, and the ground was not seen for three months. There never had been a better time for getting wood from within and beyond the swamps; a fact made apparent by the enormous piles in many door yards.

But our persevering old friend was not often prevented from pursuing her accustomed rounds. Not unfrequently night overtook her trudging along the crisp and crackling path from Salem Village or Malden, the cutting wind ruthlessly dashing aside her great hood, that it might bestow a rough kiss upon her wrinkled brow. Her long cloak stood her in good stead, as did a pair of thick gray leggins, the gift of Dame Purchis, and a pair of enormous moccasins, manufactured of the uncurried skin of a wild animal, and presented by an old Indian woman whom she had befriended.

About the middle of January, one of the most furious storms of the whole winter occurred. And it came on so suddenly that it overtook many entirely unawares. Several lives were lost, numbers of cattle and sheep were buried, and not a few of the smaller habitations were entirely overwhelmed. For several days, the roads in many places remained impassable. Even the great town sled, with eight yoke of cattle and a score of men with shovels, could not work through. Some of the drifts were so enormous, that the tree-tops rose but little above them, giving the appearance of a succession of milk-white hills studded with straggling shrubbery. People walked from their chamber windows, on snow-shoes. And the principal store in the village was only reached by an archway dug from without.

Aunt Deborah's cottage was almost entirely buried. But the good neighbors assembled with their shovels, as soon as they could, and it was presently exhumed. But on entering, no one was found. At this, however, they were not much surprised, she was so often away. They had no doubt that she was in comfortable quarters and would make her appearance again as soon as the traveling would permit. But a week passed and no one had seen her, though by that time the ways had become pretty well trodden. At the end of another week considerable anxiety began to be felt and inquiries were made in all directions. Nothing satisfactory, however, could be learned, though various reports were abroad, of her having been seen here and there, on this road and that.

The great storm commenced a little before dark, with a northeasterly wind, which, however, was not very violent for some hours. And it was satisfactorily ascertained that Aunt Deborah left the house of Mr. Danforth, in Malden, where she had taken an early supper, a little before it began. She was urged to remain, but chose rather to move along towards home, saying that it would not be dark as there was a large moon, and the storm would not probably be very violent before the turning of the tide, which would be well towards midnight. At any rate, she thought she could safely calculate on reaching the house of Mr. Hawkes, which was a couple of miles west of Lynn village, before there was danger to be apprehended.

But things did not turn out according to her calculation. A hard, cutting snow began to fall profusely soon after she left the house of her kind entertainers, and being obliged to almost directly face the wind, which continued to increase in force, it could not have been long before she found her progress very much impeded and very uncomfortable. The cold being intense, she could hardly have escaped very soon becoming benumbed.

However, be these things as they may, there was found no trace of Aunt Armitage after she had reached the turn in the road which shut her from the view of Mr. Danforth's window. Much anxiety was felt, and many a wearisome search was made. But no trace of her could be found.

And it was not till the warm breath of April melted down the great drift that sloped from a cliff a little off the road, in Mr. Turner's pasture, that Aunt Deborah was found. There she sat, curled up against the rock, as if she had sought shelter, and being overcome by cold and fatigue, had slept. And there, in that inhospitable resting place, her noble spirit fled, leaving its worn-out tenement wrapped in a mighty winding-sheet of snow. Her transition from this life to a better, so far as regards physical pains, may have been easy; though to die in such a lonely spot, and without one loved soul to receive a parting word or watch the closing eye, is always hard. Yet her willing spirit was ever ready for its conflict with the last enemy; and the dark valley had no terrors for her.

Just there, was she laid.

And think you not that her humble walk led to joys which many of the proud worldlings who lie around, realised, as the gates of eternity opened, were more worthy of being striven for than all that the wealth of the whole world could purchase?

There are those who, selfish, untrusting, and mistaking their own characters, may, with some show of consistency, exclaim, as they quit the unsatisfying scenes of life, in the words of Brutus, "O Virtue, I have worshipped thee as a substantial good, but find that thou art an empty name." But no such sorrowful words could have escaped the lips of her of whom we speak; for though she had worshipped virtue all her life without receiving much temporal reward, yet, looking not for the substantial good here, she did not find it an empty name. Though poor, yet was she rich, rich in the godly gift of christian faith and patience. There is a counterfeit patience, that proceeds from unconcern or indolence. But hers was that true patience proceeding from unwavering reliance on the great promise that all will be well with such as persevere to the end; a holy patience, that sustains under all suffering. And hers was that glorious faith that foreshadows a happy issue out of all afflictions.

Freely did this poor old woman give of her hard earned pittance, and never distrust that she was lending to One who would abundantly repay. How often sanctimonious men err regarding their highest duties. One may be punctilious in his attendance on public worship; make long prayers, morning and evening; give freely to pay ministers and build churches; and do divers other most excellent things;—but if he be not charitable, how can he be a Christian? People seem to overlook the great and infallible test of christian character. Men cannot benefit their Maker by their prayers and praises; nor can they benefit Him in any other way; not even by rearing tall steeples, or by offerings and sacrifices, however meritorious all these may be as manifestations of a sense of dependence and need, as stimulants to holy emotions and pious acts, or as evidence of grateful hearts. Everything in the universe, both of mind and matter, are already His; and He is infinitely beyond the reach of all our attempts to do Him good. And hence, does not the sphere of our more active duties lie here among our fellow men and temporal things? Here, we may do beneficial work. Is it not, then, a most solemn truth, that so far as our practical efforts are concerned, pure religion and undefiled consists, first of all things, in doing good to those about us; in visiting the widow and fatherless in their affliction? Our fellow mortals need our help and we can help them; our Maker needs nothing, and before him we have nothing to bestow. Let us, then, have a care that we do not spend so much time and money for mere devotional purposes that we have nothing left for those other eminently important, those practical, christian duties, which must be performed, or nothing will avail.

And even in a mere temporal view, charity is not to be despised. We are all liable, at some period of our lives, to be in adversity. How much, then, does it become us to so bear ourselves, while in prosperity, that when the evil days come there may be those whom we have befriended, to offer their sympathy and aid.

A few paces southeast of the Henchman tomb, yonder, sleeps the dust of the once beautiful and brilliant Verna Humphrey. It was during the earlier part of the pastorate of the good Mr. Whiting — or about the year 1644 — that her eyes first opened upon the scenes of this diversified life.

As the mind of Verna began to unfold it became apparent that treasures much beyond what fall to the common lot had been bestowed upon her. And to the sacred work of the right training of that exalted nature none could be more wakeful than her intelligent father. But how often it is found that in the ways of a mysterious Providence the desires of a fond heart seem not to be blest.

And those secondary graces, too, the charms of person, were with a lavish hand bestowed upon Verna. As her form expanded in early womanhood, an elegance of shape and exquisite chiseling of feature presented such perfection that even the rude wayfarer paused to admire.

Mr. Whiting had taken Verna at an early age into his little class at the parsonage — a class of budding minds which he loved to instruct in those accomplishments which would be most fit to adorn the more elevated society in the land — a class of uncorrupted hearts which he loved to strengthen in the ways of virtue and discipline for the vicissitudes of life. And in many of those young hearts the genial influences of his own nature seemed to infuse themselves, subduing the asperities of temper, and lighting the brow with the sunshine of universal love. How potent is the power that the instructor of youth may exercise for good or evil over those committed to his charge. And how great should be the reward of the faithful and the condemnation of the unfaithful.

We find Verna, at the age of twenty, very much in the character of a young village queen; the admired of all; the object of tender aspiration in many a manly heart; graceful in form; dignified in bearing; affable and engaging in all her ways. Her mental endowment and education were such that she was able to appreciate the lofty in sentiment and character, the beautiful in nature and conception. With the old poets, congregated in the little library of Mr. Whiting, she spent many congenial hours. The vellum quarto of the great Light of Avon, who had then just begun, as it were, to shed his glorious rays upon the world, often reposed upon her lap while in dreamy abstraction she indulged the new and vivid conceptions that stirred the inmost recesses of her soul.

But Verna's love of books was not such as to withdraw her from the delights of social life. She was present at the village gatherings, with ringing laugh and alert step engaging in the sports. And in the more quiet enjoyments of the fireside, her well stored mind, superior conversational powers, and dexterity in adapting herself to those about her, made her everywhere welcome.

And the circle that Verna brightened, extended beyond the limits of her native settlement. Her father was sometimes called to Boston on public affairs or his own private business, which was extensive, and occasionally remained there for several weeks, taking his beloved daughter, to comfort and enliven the hours of absence from his pleasant home. And having those among the gay people of the colonial metropolis with whom he was in social intimacy, it is not surprising that with a father's pride he sometimes led her into scenes and society, which, while most captivating to the young mind, are not always the most free from danger. It was on these occasions that Verna formed acquaintances with some who, though more highly cultivated were not more virtuous than those in the retirement of the humble place of her nativity. She gradually became a frequent visitor in some of the leading families of the colony. And there, in those days, it was not uncommon to meet scions of the titled families of the old world.

But still Verna loved her home with the ardor of a first love. The sparkling beaches, with their spent waves rolling whisperingly at her feet as if struggling to warn of mysteries and dangers beyond; the dark caverns, and battlements and gray towers of rock, where yet the eagle delighted to keep watch and ward; the green fields, pleasant hills, and winding lanes; the humble firesides, where she always found welcome and sympathy; — all were very dear to her heart. But dearest of all were the companions of her childhood and early youth, and the godly man who had labored so faithfully to store her mind with all that was useful and good, and whose pleasant smile and kind word had so often cheered her step as she

K*

climbed the hill of knowledge. And during the hours of absence, in sweet sadness would her mind often revert to the little library where at all times she was welcome to commune with the great and the brilliant of other days and lands whose words of wisdom and true humanity, and glowing conceptions of the beautiful and rare might strengthen her mind and animate her heart. There her beloved Shakspeare dwelt, ready at all times to shed his vivifying influence into her soul; there was smiling Spenser; and the quaint old worthies of the massive tomes who taught of life in its more sombre aspects.

Verna knew not a mother's love. But her father's affection was of that peculiarly deep and tender nature that might be expected to characterise a noble heart, widowed at the birth of its only offspring. Verna's excellent mother had hardly passed the throes that ushered the dear expected one into life, ere the throes of death were upon her. She was deeply mourned. And Mr. Humphrey, shrinking from a possible recurrence of such a scene of trial, never seemed to entertain a thought of forming another union. A family connection, well skilled in household affairs, virtuous and kind, undertook for him the duties of housekeeper and his home continued one of peace and pleasantness.

Mr. Humphrey was a man of means and benevolent heart. His broad acres were well tilled and his barn and store houses never empty. And his doors were never closed against the needy supplicant. As his beloved daughter grew in years, the good man delighted to behold in her the sweet fruits of those lessons of charity which he had so carefully impressed on her uncorrupted heart. The sick and poor were no strangers to her kind offices. And if the prayers of the forlorn, the destitute and degraded, in union with those of the refined, the virtuous and elevated, could have availed, her foot would never have trod a thorny path.

But we cannot dwell on the early history of Verna. Her visits to the metropolis had brought her into such society as was not safe for one so susceptible and confiding and possessing such charms.

During the pleasant days of summer, her acquaintances sometimes came hither to enjoy the beauties of nature, and the charms of her society. Many a woodland ramble and moonlight stroll upon the beaches, diversified the routine of happy days. And it is to be feared that these occasions may have afforded opportunity for the wily to scatter seeds that could produce only a wayward growth.

It was now a few years after the Restoration. And all readers of English history know how rapidly the vices that finally so distinguished the reign of Charles II., and transmitted their enervating effects a long way into the Hanoverian sovereignties, began to prevail. The colonies, it is true, were in a great measure free from the corruptions of the times. But not altogether. Many profligate adventurers came hither from the father land, some from the noble ranks, even, for temporary residence. And not a few of the once happy colonial homes were made desolate by their arts.

Go with us now, for one moment into the still precincts of the parsonage.

It is late at night.

Serene and beautiful the moon rides high in the heavens. And the few stars that are not eclipsed by her brightness, twinkle with a radiance clear and sharp.

A slight breeze comes down from the hills, and the noble pines that stand as sentinels at the gate, shiver and faintly sigh.

Let us enter that snug little library.

The candle burns dimly, for the bent, black wick has long cried in vain for the friendly snuffers. There are persons here; but only two. Mr. Whiting sits upon one side of the table with an open Bible before him. Mr. Humphrey sits upon the other side with his head resting on his hand. And both are weeping. It is most sad to see strong men weep. Children's tears are evanescent, flowing from fountains stirred by a breath and by a breath put to rest. Women's tears freely flow at the common vicissitudes of life, and smiles may presently appear again. Not so with the more enduring spirit of man.

Thus sat the two friends for some minutes. And it would have almost seemed irreverent to disturb the flow of their manly grief. Then the minister arose and with a choked utterance begged his good friend Humphrey not to be so cast down. He reminded him that God in his good providence might soon bring him out of his terrible affliction; that it was not right for a Christian so to distrust and despond; and that though his beloved daughter had suddenly and mysteriously disappeared from his sight, yet, whithersoever she had gone, she was still in her Maker's sight. Then he again read the comforting words at which the Bible was opened, and again offered up one of those fervid and soul-stirring prayers for which he was so eminent, and which gained for him, from the rigid Mather, the expressive title of "Angel of Lynn."

And the sorrowing father returned to his now desolate home much comforted by the sympathy and godly counsel received from his beloved minister. The stars seemed to shed a mournful light upon his path, and the trees to sigh with unwonted sadness.

Dramatic representations have been known ever since the civilization of man. And they probably will continue, under some name, till man again returns to a savage state. Most men are delighted with history. And what is history but a recounting of the great dramas of life; a recalling, before the mind, of the scenes and actors of former days?

The English, though perhaps never betraying an over-fondness for the stage, have always regarded it as an institution of civilization. And the pen of their unapproachable Shakspeare has made the whole world their debtors.

The dramas of the Bard of Avon will be admired so long as men continue sufficiently cultivated to love what is beautiful in the outward world or appreciate what is noble in their own nature. These dramas were all produced between the years 1588 and 1615. And soon after their appearance a more refined taste and fastidious morality began to prevail in stage representations; though it may be asked, in view of this, what the earlier representations must have been.

In the time of Charles I. the theatre appears to have flourished. But when the sturdy Puritans came into power, as might have been expected, it received no quarter. It languished through the whole time of the Commonwealth. But on the Restoration it began to flourish with renewed vigor.

Female actors do not appear to have been known on the English stage before the time of Charles II. That a real woman, and not a boy in woman's apparel, should appear to play the part of Desdemona, Juliet or Ophelia was a new thing. And while it remained new it added immensely to the interest of the theatre. Indeed its attractiveness has not yet ceased. Great inducements were offered for the most beautiful and accomplished to undertake the labors of dramatic life. And the inducements were effectual in numerous instances.

The meed of public commendation is intoxicating. And it was extremely grateful to these adventurous females so soon to become the objects of popular admiration, the recipients of popular applause. And then again, the appearance of the refined and virtuous, for there were many such, had a tendency to elevate the character of the stage itself. But that good effect was, probably, from the nature of the case, only temporary. And it certainly was not an age when much elevation would be looked for in that quarter.

While all but the most provokingly illiberal are ready to admit that there have ever been in the dramatic profession females who did honor to their sex, the general opinion of the world, that it has never been one the best fortified against evil, must be concurred in. The young and uncontaminated female, entering upon the life of an actress, must necessarily give no heed to many of the out-guards that in almost every other sphere remain to warn of danger, and expose herself to influences but poorly calculated to aid the growth of virtue. Herein, perhaps, lies the greatest danger. And it seems to be an inherent one.

In the year 1673, there appeared, unheralded, on the theatrical boards of London, an actress whose personal charms and extraordinary powers of delineation at once elicited the admiration of all. It is not in that sphere, as in many others, that excellence is slow in becoming known. The public eye being constantly on the candidates for favor, the question of merit or demerit is soon determined. In the present case there was but one voice and that loud in praise. Many who had never been accustomed to attend the theatre were at once attracted there — students from their closets, philosophers and divines. Thus was this new and brilliant star of genius eminently honored by those who could appreciate and enjoy the rare in intellectual power and discernment. And thither also were drawn those from the titled ranks; among whom, it is true, were some whose desires were centered in quite other charms than those of mind.

The little coteries that gathered in the green room, too often numbered among them those whose objects were impure and from whose advances the sensitive and virtuous might well shrink. But these were generally from among those whose wealth or position so improperly insured indulgences which would at once be denied to the less favored of fortune. That virtue must be doubly strong, which can withstand covert assaults and pertinacious and gilded appliances under such circumstances as those in which this queen of the drama was placed.

The Merry Monarch himself was sometimes behind the scenes, curious in his disguises, and captivating in the relation of his whimsical adventures. There, too, came Edward Randolph, with manly form and dark curling hair; Pembroke, so affable and kind; the youthful Ellenborough, so witty and polite; to say nothing of others of more burly and boisterous trim; men of wealth, fashion, leisure and taste, but destitute alike of heart and principle. Were not these dangerous associates, though only for now and then an hour, in the green room of a theatre, for one innocent, and by nature confiding and unsuspicious?

The carriage of some young noble was always waiting at the door, when the play closed, to convey the fascinating Star to her lodgings; and in the morning a fresh bouquet was sure to be sent for her acceptance. Upon the off-nights some little party always demanded her presence where wit, wine, and cards were special adjuncts. But unanticipated consequences sometimes flow from wine and cards. And when to them are added the excitements that the smile or frown of a beautiful woman may create, surely perils abound. More than one passage at swords grew out of these occasions.

Our heroine of the stage became more and more the votary of festive life as the season advanced and her circle of acquaintance extended. Her wakeful and brilliant wit, superior education and capacity to trace the sinuous workings of the human mind rendered her most able to rule in such society. Her dark hazel eyes could flash with the fires of defiance or scorn on those whose approach she would check, or melt in child like softness at the advance of such as she would welcome.

The favorite and almost only characters that she personated were those immortal ones drawn by Shakspeare. And while treading the boards, lost in the counterfeit, the applause that rang from the almost frantic crowd, was entirely unheeded by her. She never appeared in what is now known as melo-drame, nor in farce or dance. But in the song that pertained to her lofty part she sang with a voice so modulated to the stately demands of chivalric achievement, the tender accents of love, or the plaintive strains of grief, that a sympathetic cord was touched in every heart.

Gaudy tinsel, patching and painting, she eschewed. Nature's ruddy glow upon the cheek and pure white upon the brow, raven lashes and ample tresses of dark chesnut were all that she required. Her robes were few, but rich, appropriate and becoming.

So passed on the season, full of excitement, full of success.

But did she never, after her professional duties were over, and her admirers dismissed — after her fevered head had tossed upon the pillow till the east was all but gilded by the coming day — did she never then think of a quiet and peaceful retreat, far away among green hills and beside pleasant waters, with tender hearts to feel her cares, honest hearts to guide her erring steps; of hours of sweet and undisturbed repose coming on with the setting sun, and hours of useful activity beginning with the opening day? Did she never think of a quaint and spireless meeting house standing down a grassy lane, where gathered familiar forms, and where familiar faces were upturned to the godly preacher, who loved to speak words of heavenly comfort, and whose lips trembled to utter words of pain even in the sinner's ear? More than all, did she never think of a sequestered burial place, where lay an angel mother, sighed over by swaying trees; or of a tender father, with bowed form, visiting that grave and there, with gushing tears for the dead, mingling those proceeding from more unutterable grief for an erring loved one still in life?

Another season came and this extraordinary young woman again appeared on the theatrical boards, peerless still. But she was more stately and reserved in her daily walk, and less approachable by those who were wont to meet her in a familiar way. So far as professional intercourse was concerned her affability was as conspicuous as ever; but the non-professional visitors of the green room soon perceived that they must seek other objects on which to bestow their attentions and favors. Yet there was one whom she always greeted with a smile of welcome. And he was a wealthy young Earl. It was his blazoned carriage that conveyed her home; and it was company of his approval that she entertained. His means procured the rich jewels that now adorned her person, and the elegances of her enchanted home. True, he was not deemed of the most virtuous class; but he was young, polite, witty and handsome. The customs of the times did not demand fastidiousness in morals, especially among those in his sphere. His sovereign had set an example that most were too ready to follow. And fashion is almost as sure as natural desire to open the door to some species of vice. The reader must be left to draw his own conclusion as to the nature of the intimacy that had become established between the noble Earl and the fascinating Actress.

A beautiful villa stood on the bank of the river, a few miles below London. It was an erection of the time of Elizabeth, and of exquisite loveliness as regarded its own charming self, its immediate surroundings, and the enchanting views afforded from its turrets and balconies. The little park sloped gently to the river, with gravel walks and grassy paths, all finely shaded by noble trees; and fountains sparkled in the sunshine. Stretching far away upon either hand,

and beyond the river, as far as the eye could reach, were cultivated fields and green acclivities, dotted with farm house and copse, all rejoicing in heaven's glorious light.

The villa gardens were full of choice flowers and luscious fruits. And here and there, in some embowered niche, was a statue, of the old mythology.

Within the villa, the elegant rooms were well supplied with books, pictures, and costly ornaments. And a ponderous old harpsicord stood in the hall, inviting the touch of such wandering minstrel, the representative of England's more chivalric days, as might stray within the villa precincts.

But who was the presiding genius in this charming retreat? The same triumphant tragedy queen who a few years before, upon the London stage, so astonished the multitude. Nor was she mistress of the mansion alone, but also of the gay Earl, a part of whose patrimony it was. There now she sits in the gorgeous drawing room that overlooks the calmly flowing river, surrounded by every outward appliance for peace and happiness. A sweet little child leans on her knee, looking up with a face full of trusting love. And she looks down upon that curly head with all the placid joy known in a mother's love for her only born. But a sickening mist comes up between her vision and that sinless idol of her heart; a mist, arising from the fountains of impurity which she herself has stirred. There is a gnawing worm within. Her bosom heaves as unbidden thoughts of the uncontaminated joys of other days arise, days when she was morally fair as that unerring one upon her knee. Again, we behold her seated on a balcony, scanning the glorious scene, and with long drawn sigh, in nature's holy quietude, yearning for that peace which the uncorrupted in heart and innocent in life, alone can know.

In this lovely place, some of the noblest of the realm were at times found. On occasions, it was the resort of certain individuals who would in a private way and for private ends, discuss the great matters of state. The Earl himself held a considerable official position, was ambitious and somewhat given to intrigue. Indeed was there ever a politician who was not an intriguer? He was a favorite of royalty; but even this did not place him above plotting; for there are many who would rather achieve by intrigue what they could more easily attain by open and fair means.

In this retreat, these restless spirits were safe from observation. And like other females, of powerful and aspiring mind, who have in all ages made their influence felt in affairs of state, the reigning spirit of the villa joined in the political debates. And her services to the party whose interests she espoused were of much value, for blandishments will often accomplish what reasoning cannot.

The period to which these occurrences relate was one when the condition of the American colonies was exciting much interest in the mother country. Their commerce was extending; their fisheries were productive; their forests were ready to yield a large increase. And there was a deep and wide spread conviction that they were destined at no very distant day to assume a position in the world important and commanding. Many ambitious and avaricious eyes were directed thither. And many consultations were held at the villa among those whose desires would be satisfied only in the broadest fields of enterprise.

When the accomplished hostess partook in the political discussions relating to those far-off colonies, she astonished all by her accurate knowledge of their history, condition, wants and rights. And she showed herself their uncompromising friend, resolutely opposing every suggestion that might endanger any interest of theirs. Edward Randolph more than once quailed before her flashing eye. His inveterate hostility to the interests of the colonies as well as his base selfishness was apparent even to minds much less keen and wakeful than hers. And king Charles himself, who on one occasion in disguise came beneath her roof, was by his very disguise, for she knew him well, compelled with closed mouth to listen to such an outpouring of bitter truth regarding his administration of American affairs, as had never before greeted his pampered ears.

These were times immediately preceding the dissolution of the colonial charters. And as the old lord keeper of the king's conscience on several occasions found his way there, perhaps some reason other·than mere mistake, negligence or accident, may have existed why in the succeeding reign no record was found of certain judgments adverse to colonial interests, well known to have been passed.

The social delights of this elegant retreat drew together the witty and fashionable. The Earl was lavish in his expenditures, and the rarest entertainments were given. Classic and poetical representations, music and dancing, enlivened the gliding hours; cards and wine furnished their excitements.

But there was a sudden and mournful termination of these things.

With appalling swiftness the arrow of Death laid low the doting Earl. Then quickly upon that gem of the river fell a murky cloud. Not more rapidly does the thunder cloud obscure the sun than did this sad death extinguish the brightness of that radiant home of pleasure.

The heroine was now hardly of an age to make new conquests by personal charms. And it was not easy even in that morally derelict age, for one who had so long stood in a position like hers, to attain a position among those who had never deviated, however eminent her other qualifications might be. The Earl was of a generous nature. But so sudden was his decease that no provision was made for her for whom he really had a most tender attachment, and on whom he had lavished so much. It would hardly be expected that his family connections, who had been to a degree indirectly impoverished by his extravagances, should supply his omission. And so the poor erring one was left in penury. Can there be wonder, then, that she mourned as one without hope?

On a cold but brilliant night in the winter of 1691, there came slowly walking along the road, from Boston, a female traveler, wrapped as well as she might be in a scanty cloak. She had walked all the way from that place, and now, on entering the village of Lynn, seemed so fatigued as to be scarcely able to support herself.

A piercing northwest wind swept over the snow, which sparkled in the moonbeams, and now and then whirled up in eddies so furiously as almost to blind such unfortunate ones as happened to be exposed to its fury. And the little drifts accumulated so fast across the traveled path, that the way became every moment more and more difficult.

The garments of the forlorn traveler to whom we have alluded were entirely insufficient for protection against the severe cold, and of such texture as was worn by those in the most humble condition. Nevertheless, she toiled on, perseveringly, aided by a rude staff that she had picked up by the wayside.

By her side was a little girl, who was quite as thinly clad, and whose chattering teeth and benumbed limbs told of her suffering. But no complaint was uttered by either.

They proceeded in silence, excepting that occasionally the girl, in a tone of the most tender solicitude, would inquire if her mother's strength were still sufficient for their trial. She seemed to have no thought of herself, of the torn shoes from which the little rag covered toes protruded, nor of her tattered bonnet, from which rolled a profusion of glossy tresses, which the wind seemed delighted to whirl about by its cold breath. And as she made her pathetic inquiries, she would turn her drooping eyes upon her parent, while the moonbeam lighted the tears that, in spite of all her efforts, forced their way from the quivering lids. But the mother uttered no response. She could only pause in her weary walk, press that dear one to her heart and sigh.

So the two traveled on. At about midnight they were opposite the house of Jacob Burrill. Here, by a misstep upon the ice, the mother fell, and was so stunned as to become entirely unconscious. The daughter, in wild distress, flew to the neighboring door, arousing the inmates and begging for assistance. No one in distress ever applied at that door in vain. The good man, in a half nude condition, rushed to the relief of the wayfarers. They were, without question or comment instantly taken beneath the hospitable roof. A bright fire soon burned; restoratives were applied; and presently a warm repast invited their attention. They were very hungry, and partook with grateful hearts. The woman had received but slight injury from her fall, and the accident was soon almost forgotten. An hour after found the two safe in a bed of such softness as they had not enjoyed for many a weary month, their prayers having first ascended for blessings on their kind deliverer.

In the morning, they began to prepare for departure. But a few casual inquiries led to a long and earnest consultation. And it seemed a strange Providence that so ordered things that they remained the welcome recipients of Mr. Burrill's bounty till the opening of spring, rendering such small service as they were able to, in return, by the needle, at the spinning-wheel, or in the dairy.

The woman was something beyond the meridian of life. But trouble had given her the marks of one much in advance of that period. Silvery locks skirted her care-worn brow; her cheeks were wan, her form was bent. Yet there was a lustre in her sunken eye, that spoke of a soul yet alive to the realities of life. And her whole appearance indicated that she was one who had fallen from better fortunes. She was so retiring in her habits as to shrink even from friendly visitors, though the little conversation into which she could be drawn, exhibited a mind of intelligence and strength, and a resignation worthy of respect. She made no acquaintances, and appeared desirous only of finishing her earthly journey by some quiet, sequestered path.

The daughter had a gentle spirit, and her habits

seemed as retiring as those of her parent. She was intelligent and pleasing in person; and her modest attire was always tasteful and clean. She loved books and flowers, but seldom seemed inclined to associate with other children.

There were many visitors at the house of Mr. Burrill and not a few kindly seconded the efforts of the good family to cheer the strangers. But their success was by no means commensurate with their endeavors. Village gossips were baffled in their attempts to ascertain the cause of their sorrow, or the reason of their sojourn in the settlement.

When the grass and flowers began to appear, the mother and daughter retired to a quiet little home, far up a green lane, where they purposed dwelling in seclusion, by their own industry supplying their few wants. Mr. Burrill, with his wonted benevolence, assisted them in procuring the few things necessary for their humble home, and was pleased when he saw them quietly settled there, surrounded, as they said, with all they desired. And it was very pleasant to him occasionally to call on them as he came from his field, hard by, to speak a word of cheer. And it would have greatly added to his own happiness, to have seen them smile as if returning to life's enjoyments. But there they lived, the possessors of many blessings, among the chief of which was their cordial and unwavering affection for each other. On the Sabbath, their seats in the meeting house were seldom vacant; and none were more attentive to the long drawn exercises than they. The mother's black veil was seldom lifted excepting now and then to permit the fresh air to play freely on her brow.

The summer waned.

It was a sad thing to behold that mother thus pursuing a sunless path; but much sadder to behold the prematurely fading daughter. The little garden, well stored with choice flowers which had been transplanted from the hill sides by their own hands; the woody acclivity beyond; and the winding lane, furnished the scene of almost their whole exercise out of doors. Occasionally, however, as the shades of evening were gathering, the mother would steal away alone, for a brief space to wander in this burial place. And it was observed that she lingered chiefly at a particular grave, bending over it and deeply sighing, as if exercised by some terrible agony, and finally vanishing, in the dim twilight, like a troubled ghost.

Before the winds of later autumn began to howl, a great affliction descended on that home of love and sadness. The daughter was stricken down by disease incurable. The sorrow that now weighed upon the mother's heart, led to her laying aside, in some degree, the reserve in which she had so enwrapped herself; and she received the few neighbors who came to offer their sympathy and assistance, with many expressions of sincere gratitude.

It was a wild autumn evening and very late. The fast declining daughter lay upon her lowly couch. She had been restless for hours, and now breathed heavily, with an occasional quiver of the whole frame, seeming, in half-dreamy state, to be struggling for something that she could not grasp. Suddenly she waked to full consciousness and convulsively seized the hand that lay upon her pillow. Then with touching earnestness she began to talk of a strange vision she had had; a vision so beautiful and apparently real that she could almost pray for its return. She was in a splendid mansion with brilliant rooms and music and gay company. A shady lawn, with fountains, sloped to a broad river, beyond which fields, and green hills spread out, all glowing in the sunshine. And in the most beautiful room of the mansion her dear mother sat; and she herself, a little child, leaned upon her knee. And there came a man of noble form and pleasant look, who put his arm about her mother's neck, bowed down and kissed her. And upon his knee he took herself, smoothed her curling hair, and said she was his dearest child. He hugged her to his heart and said that he would never suffer even the wind to blow hard upon her, he so loved her.

Scarcely had the little one thus delivered herself, when she sank down again exhausted.

A groaning utterance was just escaping the mother's heaving breast, when there came a fierce knocking at the door. It was opened, and two burly men, boisterous and forbidding in aspect, entered, announcing themselves as officers of the law, come to arrest the woman on the charge of witchcraft. This seemed the bitterest drop in the cup where all was bitterness. All her remaining powers of endurance were summoned; and though she staggered she did not fall. In silence she gave ear to what they had to say. She had been "cried out against," a complaint entered, and now she must be held to answer. As she began to comprehend her new position, a terrible weight fell upon her. She could not speak, but in woe unutterable pointed to the couch whereon her dying daughter lay, as if to beg a respite only till that beloved one were in her winding sheet. And from that couch there came a feeble voice, pleading, in childlike simplicity, against the strange, false accusation. It was a scene of such extreme agony that even the coarsely disciplined hearts of those rude men were deeply touched. Then they withdrew to consult.

And now the mother, with tearless eye, sat down upon the bedside. She spoke not, but gazed fixedly upon that calm face upturned on the pillow. Those gentle, dying eyes opened, full of love and heavenly radiance. Those lips quivered as if words pressed for utterance. Then, by an effort that taxed all her powers, the dying one raised herself, as if in a last attempt to declare something that weighed upon her spirit's wing. But the struggle was too much. She fell back. A slight quiver ran through her fragile form, and —

Another ransomed spirit entered heaven.

At that awful moment, too, the light of the mother's mind went out. With the daughter's spirit it fled away, not again to revisit and illuminate its earthly home.

When the men returned, they even wept at the sorrowful scene. The living one they found quiet and submissive. She uttered not a word, but stood at the bedside, looking down upon her lost treasure, with a vacant gaze, shedding no tear, heaving no sigh.

In the morning the townspeople began to gather. Mr. Burrill and his good wife were there among the first. Mr. Shepard, the minister, also came, and the village doctor, the magistrate, and divers excited women and curious children.

They declared that the woman's heart was broken. And so it was.

Another spring came, and though her health was good, her mind was still a blank. She was constantly wandering about. With venturesome step she would climb the rugged cliff and delve into the glen and rocky pass, as if in quest of something that she longed to find. She would gaze into the river, and trace the woodland stream through swamp and tangled dell, with anxious eye peering into every nook, and with her long staff curiously examining the covert that her foot could not reach. And then she would return, disappointed and restless, on the morrow to renew, with fresh vigor, her unsuccessful search. Occasionally, she would come hither, of a pleasant evening, and gaze intently for a few minutes on the same grave that she had before been accustomed to visit. During her wanderings in the woods, she would sometimes gather flowers and mosses, ferns and green twigs; and when on the sea shore, she would cull glittering pebbles and curious shells. But none of these seemed objects for which she was in search.

One day during the hot summer of 1693, she strayed into the heart of a distant swamp. About nightfall she was seen emerging from the woods with a faltering step, as if extremely fatigued. Presently she sat down on a rock; and those who observed her thought nothing more of it, supposing that she was resting.

In the morning she was found by the rock, swollen and dead. It was supposed that she had been bitten by a rattlesnake; for whenever she discovered one of those venomous reptiles, she would pursue it vigorously, often exposing herself to imminent danger.

On the following day the friendly grave received her weary form.

There, a few paces from that ancient tomb, as we said, sleeps the dust of the once beautiful and brilliant Verna Humphrey — the radiant star that brightened many a home of our fathers in those far off times — the triumphant actress of the London stage — the charmer of the young heart of one of England's noblest blood — the returned wanderer. Yes, returned, with broken spirit and contrite heart, in penury, sorrow and darkness to lay her weary head in this quiet spot. And here for generations she has lain, no more exposed to the temptations and reverses that attended her journey in life.

And that dear offspring of unsanctioned love, all unconscious of its tainted birth, lies by her side, undisturbed by human conflicts or by nature's rage.

And is there no good lesson to be drawn from this simple history of Verna Humphrey?

Somewhere within a short distance of that stained marble shaft, that rises rather ostentatiously beneath the glossy foliage — though the precise spot cannot now be pointed out — must have been laid the dust of the godly Whiting, who for more than forty years was the beloved minister of the flock who gathered in the rude sanctuary reared by the early fathers of the Plantation. And during that long ministry, how many of those who had received holy instruction and comfort from his lips, must have been gathered to welcome his coming. No stone marks the spot where he lies in his serene repose, but his name and his virtues are recorded on tablets more enduring than marble.

You perceive that the venerable man must lie near Verna Humphrey's resting place. And on the resurrection morn, when the tenants of all these graves come forth to meet their Judge, if the day for intercession be not past, and the greater Advocate has not already secured her redemption, she will have an earnest inter-

THE OLD BURYING GROUND. 271

cessor in him who in her spring time of life prayed so fervently and labored so faithfully that she might never stray from the paths of purity and peace.

Just about where yonder irreverently laughing girl is plucking a flower, was buried, in 1685, Manasseh Guatolf. He was born a Jew. Amid the sunny hills of the olive and vine, in luxuriant Spain, did his eyes first open to the scenes of life. Being the offspring of parents conspicuous for their wealth and proud of their Hebrew lineage, no pains were spared to confer upon him a superior education, especially in all the learning calculated to confirm and strengthen him in the ancient faith.

As he grew in years he exhibited talents of a high order, and such as rendered him an object of fear and jealousy to the ecclesiastical side of the government. And it was not long before he felt the iron hand of persecution. He was compelled, by the time he had attained an age to make his influence felt, to flee from his native land. He passed a restless life for a few years, in different places along the coasts of the Mediterranean, and finally journeyed into the Holy Land. At Hebron, the sacred depository of the dust of his great father Abraham, he sat down to rest. But he was soon again upon the wing.

By what turn of fortune he was brought into the western world, we know not. But he appears to have been residing at Boston for a year or two, when he fell in with Mr. Whiting. Both being among the best Hebrew scholars in the country, they frequently met in the higher literary circles. And Mr. Guatolf became so charmed by the benignant character of his new acquaintance, that he formed an attachment strong and enduring. And he presently came to esteem it one of his highest privileges to be near the godly man, making frequent visits to Lynn, and occasionally remaining for several days. He was a rigid adherent to the faith of his fathers; but this did not prevent his perceiving the good and great in those who proudly claimed to be among the chosen of the New Dispensation. Indeed he seems to have been a man of charitable and confiding disposition, having views enlarged by travel and association with mankind under different aspects and in different conditions.

It does not certainly appear at what time Mr. Guatolf became a resident of Lynn, but it must have been a few years before his death. It is not wonderful that Mr. Whiting's influence over him should have eventuated, as it did, in his conversion to the christian faith. By degrees his adherence to the old religion weakened, and finally, on a serene Sabbath morning, in early summer, the venerable pastor had the blessed privilege, before a great congregation, who had assembled from far and near, of baptizing this son of Abraham into the religion of the Nazarene. It was a marked occasion, and much talked of among the good people throughout the colonies.

For many months he pursued his christian walk in the most exemplary manner; and his zeal and devotion may well have put to the blush many who had till then looked upon themselves as foremost in the godly race. He visited the widow and fatherless in their affliction, and kept himself from the contaminations of the world. The fountains of grace that had sprung up within him seemed pure and unfailing. He was constant in attendance on the services of the sanctuary, and took great pains to lead thither others who had been accustomed to range the woods and fields on the Sabbath. And possessing well trained musical powers he delighted to join, with his melodious voice, in the sacred song.

But on the death of Mr. Whiting, which took place in 1679, a cloud seemed to fall on the path of Mr. Guatolf. He deeply mourned the loss of his christian guide and dear friend.

Mr. Shepard succeeded in the pastorate. But his gloomy views of truth and duty, and dismal conceptions concerning the heart of man, his course and destiny, were any thing but congenial to a mind constructed like that of Mr. Guatolf. He seemed to struggle hard to retain the position he had reached. But it was soon manifest, to himself as well as others, that he had begun to lose ground. At times he sought the society of pious people, as if by their zeal to endeavor to reanimate his own. Again, he wandered alone into the fields as if seeking, in solitude, relief for his perplexed and burdened mind.

Some two years passed, and the attachment of Mr. Guatolf for the religion into which he had been baptized, was feeble and still declining. And another year had hardly elapsed when the light had gone out. He had bidden an everlasting adieu to all his christian hope and inspiration. But he did not return to his old Jewish faith. No, he wandered into the frigid wilds of Atheism.

About this time the withering hand of consumption was laid upon him. He was soon confined to his home, and then to his bed. And it was a sorrowful thing to the good people who came to visit him, to find not even one ray of light glimmering in his darkened soul. And so he died; died, denying not only the great High Priest of the christian faith, but also the great Jehovah whom his fathers worshipped. Of all people on earth, one would think, an educated Jew would be the last to die an infidel.

But there lies poor Guatolf, awaiting that resurrection which with his last breath he sternly rejected.

A few yards to the right of the grave of the unhappy Guatolf were laid the remains of Obadiah Turner, one of the most excellent men who labored and prayed for the success of the Plantation, while it was yet in infancy. Time has long since smoothed down the swell of the ground that marked his resting place, for he has occupied that lowly bed for more than a century and three quarters. He was a modest, pious and active man; and his genial mind was constantly, as it were, dispensing sunshine upon the path of those who journeyed in his company. All these creditable things appear from the few records which yet remain; but had we as full accounts of him as we have of many of his cotemporaries, we doubt not he would stand in a most eminent light. In the earlier part of our volume this meritorious pioneer has been prominently in view. And we need now only add that as he laid down trusting in a merciful Redeemer, we doubt not that he will arise to enjoy the recompense of a good and faithful servant. He went down into the dark valley, clothed in the panoply of christian faith, and with that holy hope and trust, that takes away the sting of death.

It is pleasant to endeavor something that may extend the memory of one so worthy, as there are enough to sound the praises of the merely liberal worldling. But what is the value of the life of one who makes mammon his deity, who spends his days in gathering that which will, when he is gone, be squandered by prodigals who only ridicule him for his groveling labor and care, compared with the life of one like him of whom we speak?

And O, how immeasurably more to be desired is a departure like his, than a departure like that of the wretched Guatolf. There they lie, almost side by side, awaiting that resurrection which the one rejoiced in contemplating and the other sneered at as nothing but an idle name.

Not far from the northeasterly corner of the enclosure, where those flowering locust shrubs are growing, was anciently a reception tomb; that is, a tomb in which bodies were deposited until such times as the graves which were finally to receive them could more conveniently be digged. Deep snows or frosts in winter, and various causes at other seasons rendered this a desirable arrangement. There was no fear of body-snatchers in those days; nor was there any thing else to create an apprehension that the sanctity of the grave would be invaded.

This sacred depository, the receiving tomb, was never very strongly fastened; indeed it was closed up by merely shutting the flap doors, which fell obliquely together, in the manner of old fashioned cellar doors, their own weight making them sufficiently secure.

It was on the afternoon of a sultry day in August, 1697, that the remains of Elizabeth Melrose were deposited in this tomb. The solemn burial service of the Episcopal church had been read as she was consigned to her mother earth, for she belonged to one of the few church families then in the vicinity. And her funeral had been attended by a very large concourse, as she was greatly beloved for her kind heart, bright mind and charming person.

As the pale corpse lay exposed at the entrance of the tomb, the red light of the declining sun struggled through the foliage as if striving once more to kiss the blanched cheek and warm back into life the inanimate form. The coffin lid was open; and as the mourners filed silently by, to take a last look, she seemed in a sweet repose that it were sacrilege to disturb. The flowers and evergreen twigs that adorned her fair brow and spotless robe, drank in the tears that profusely fell, as if they were distillations of early dew.

The sun went down; the coffin was closed; and she was left for her long sleep.

That night a terrific thunder storm swept over the settlement. About ten o'clock it was at its height. The peals were appalling, the flashes almost continuous. Rain descended in equatorial violence, and the wind filled the air with whirling leaves and branches wrested from the groaning trees.

It was at about that hour that a townsman who had been caught abroad in the tempest, was indescribably terrified by suddenly beholding, amid the war of elements, a few rods before him, and crossing the road that ran just north of the Burying Ground, a thin, white form. It apparently moved from somewhere among the graves; but whither it went, his fears prevented his observing. He doubted not that he had beheld a genuine ghost, and his hasty step was instinctively turned towards the minister's.

At nearly the same time, the inmates of the house of Mr. Downing, who were the nearest neighbors, were startled by a noise at the outer door, it seeming as if some one had pushed or fallen against it. And they thought that they likewise heard a feeble cry. The good master of the household instantly threw up the ponderous wooden latch, and the door swung wide open. Upon the rough stone step, drenched, trembling and speechless, lay a fragile form. It was wrapped in the white robe of the grave, and faded flowers drooped upon the brow.

The good wife and daughter sprang at the summons of the husband and father. And that apparently supernatural claimant of their hospitality was soon upon a comfortable bed, the recipient of every restorative appliance that the most willing hearts and ready hands could command.

That strange visitor was Elizabeth Melrose. She had been prematurely consigned to the tomb, but amid the war of elements had waked and made her escape from its grim portals.

She appears to have been in a trance, so much resembling death, that no one imagined that the fatal arrow had not sped. Whether the tremendous electric discharges had the effect to awaken her, or whether she was roused by some other means, it is not easy to determine. But her own account was that she suddenly awoke, as from a sleep, in a remarkable condition of physical strength and self-possession. She was immediately aware of her situation. But having power to raise the lid of her coffin, which had not been closely shut, and which was constructed like most coffins in those days, with the lid running the whole length, she had little difficulty in releasing herself from her fearful prison. From the tomb itself she soon escaped, for the lightning disclosed the passage, and the door had been left partially unclosed, having swung against a stone that had fallen from the adjacent bank.

One can hardly conceive that a slender girl should have possessed such courage and strength in so awful a situation. But it affords another instance of the extraordinary capabilities of both the human mind and body in an extremity. In the ordinary walks of life a realization of the full extent of our own powers is very seldom forced upon us.

There, near that little enclosed spot of sacred earth, where rest one household's dead, were, in 1671, deposited the remains of Ephraim Newhall, a man of commanding virtues and an excellent teacher of youth. Diligently did he labor in his vocation, and unceasing were his endeavors to prepare those under his charge not only for success in this life, but also for the higher christian walk, which surely leads to life eternal. Possessing such means as by economy were sufficient to ensure a livelihood, he refused all compensation for his services. He said that what he had was given for his support, while laboring for the good of those around him, and he should be guilty of the heinous sin of covetousness by demanding what would be equivalent to a double compensation. He had received a classical education, and had a mind capable of appreciating the beautiful and noble. A small volume of touching poetry emanated from his pen, all sweetly tinged by pious and manly sentiment.

Would that such exemplars were more common.

The evening of the twentieth of November, 1665, was damp and comfortless to those abroad. The trees were almost entirely denuded of their leaves, the few that remained being dry and shriveled, and seeming to tremble with impatience to leave their parent stems. And now and then, in spite of every filial tie, some would leap off and dance away upon the wind. The darkness set in early and was very great, for there was no moon and the clouds rolled heavily up from the north.

It was perhaps eight o'clock, when four stalwart men, bearing upon their shoulders a bier whereon was a coffin, without pall or other covering, entered the Burying Ground, preceded by the lame sexton, carrying a flaming torch of pitch. Half a dozen townsmen followed. And the discordant music of a battalion of wild geese that had been overtaken by the night, accompanied that strange march.

The sexton limped along, at the head of the group, leading the way among the trees toward the southerly wall; and there, among briars and rank vegetation, paused. Hanging his torch upon a dead branch, without uttering a word, he pointed to a newly digged grave. The bearers lowered the burden from their shoulders and placed it on the ground near the grave.

For a few moments they all stood still as if each were waiting for the action of the others. The wind sighed mournfully, and the trees tossed their lank limbs wildly about, like giant ghosts at their revels. The red light streamed from the torch, which flared and smoked, imparting an unearthly glow to the forms around, and throwing a spectral radiance upon the rude coffin, the yawning grave, the gray old trunks, and far off among the brambles and shivering ferns.

They stood in silence. No sob nor other mourning utterance was heard, save the sighing of the trees and lonely weeping of a little rill. But they did not loiter long. The old sexton again pointed to the grave and then to a coil of rope that he had hung near his torch. They took the rope and by it lowered the coffin to its last resting place.

Then the old man began hastily to shovel the earth upon it, as if anxious to have it in the shortest possible time buried from the sight of man. Rapidly the earth rattled down, and presently the grave was filled. Then those strong men trod and stamped upon it till all was even with the adjoining surface. Now a long sharpened stake was brought and held upright upon the centre of the grave. Then, by the most vigorous arm, a huge sledge was swung, and as the sturdy strokes fell upon its head, it sank rapidly. Presently a dull sound was heard, for the point had reached the coffin. Another vigorous blow, and there was a stifled crash; another and another; and then the stake head had sunk even with the earth.

The work was done. And the strange company slowly and silently retired, preceded again by the limping sexton, bearing his torch, which by this time began to burn dimly and flicker.

This was the burial of Alden Howland, the Suicide.

It is the holy Sabbath eve.

The breeze has lulled away, and the delicate foliage of early summer scarcely stirs. All nature seems sinking into repose, as the sun withdraws his last beams from spire and tree top. A few visitors linger in this consecrated spot, scanning the records on the stones. They speak only in whispers. Here are children, too. They step lightly on the graves, many as short as they, and their shout and laugh are hushed. And see that old man, with gray locks, seated upon yon cold granite slab, with head bowed down and lips moving, as if he were muttering some complaint or prayer. He seems like one who has outlived kindred and friends and come hither to ponder on his loneliness and perchance commune with their spirits, craving intercession for release from the burden of a cheerless life.

What hour or place more meet for serious thought?

Around us lie the godly men and women of olden time, who went down into the dark valley without fear, protected and sustained by christian faith and hope. Here repose the noble fathers who with strong hands and generous hearts shielded and succored the humble and weak. Here lies the soldier who bled for our liberties; the glowing soul who labored and persevered, through perils and wrongs, that he might secure the rights that we enjoy.

Here lie the learned, the honorable, the liberal. And here, too, lie the young, the beautiful, the pure; closed eyes that once sparkled with joy; pale lips that once curled with mirth; cold hands that once clasped other hands with friendship's warmth; pulseless hearts that once beat with the inspirations of love and sunny hope.

Here they lie, undisturbed by the hum of business that so constantly floats around them, and all unenvious of those who are most successful in the race for worldly good. Their ears are closed to the sound of the church-going bell or the jubilant parade; their eyes to the gaudy and cunning things of man's device, the lovely and magnificent of nature's handiwork. The cricket chirps upon their lowly bed; and there the busy ant constructs her nest, and the spider spreads his web.

But, you say, there is a darker view. And so there is. Here also lie the drunkard, the libertine, the profane scoffer, the surly miser, the oppressor of the poor. And it is true that the grass grows as freshly and the flowers bloom as sweetly over them as over the most worthy who lie here. And when the snowy mantle of winter comes, it falls white and pure upon all alike. But there is beyond this another truth, which all along we have endeavored to keep in view; a truth that should startle every unawakened heart. And that truth is, that from all these graves the dead must come forth. Yes, on that great day of everlasting doom, this motley host must rise, and wheel into the judgment court. And then and there, in the vivid light that illuminates the most secret recess of every heart, will the true condition of each soul appear. Then how will men's judgments of their fellow men be changed. And how forcibly shall we all perceive the vanity of the life that has closed, the reality of that which is opening.

THE OLD TUNNEL MEETING HOUSE.

> "Hail, honored fane! Though not in thee
> Were gorgeous nave and aisle;
> Yet was thy rude simplicity
> More loved than marble pile."

For something like a century and a half immediately preceding the unpretentious year 1828, observant travelers who journeyed from the metropolis of New England by the great eastern road, could not have failed to notice, on passing through the westerly part of Lynn, a large, quaint structure, standing conspicuously on the open Common. On making inquiry, they would have been informed that this was the OLD TUNNEL MEETING HOUSE. The term "old" being used as a sort of jolly adjective rather than as indicative of age.

This memorable edifice was erected in 1682. And for generations it remained a gathering place of the most unalloyed of the puritanical stamp.

To modern eyes it would appear a strange specimen of architecture both within and without. It was square upon the ground, and the roof ran up in the centre, surmounted by a belfry, much like an inverted tunnel; and hence the classic sobriquet by which it was for such a long period distinguished.

The Old Tunnel Dedication Day, was, of course, an occasion of great parade. The weather was propitious and everything assumed a holiday trim. A large number of the clergy were present, and lay delegates from far and near.

There was the Reverend John Rogers, of Ipswich, a descendant of the Smithfield martyr, whose head, though at that time he was not much above fifty, was adorned with silver locks, and whose bearing was lofty and austere. He was unquestionably a man of learning, for the next year he was installed president of Harvard College, though his death occurring immediately after, no opportunity was afforded for his friends to relate pleasant fictions or his enemies to relate unpleasant truths about him in his new sphere.

Then there was the Reverend Mr. Richardson of Newbury, another of the learned and sedate old puritanical preachers.

There, likewise, was the Reverend Joseph Gerrish, of Wenham, the "curious, orthodox and profound" divine, as well as "curious, orthodox and profound" lover of good living; his countenance beaming with intelligence and quiet humor. The discriminating John Dunton says in his journal, that he was "devout without moroseness or starts of holy frenzy and enthusiasm," and "primitive without the occasional colors of whining or cant." And he gratefully adds that when he called on Mr. Gerrish he was entertained with a noble dinner. A judicious offering to the stomach is wonderfully effective in securing a good opinion. And it is worthy of remark that when any one has a favor to ask his best time to make application is when the one from whom he would receive it has lately risen from a fat table. Hunger is one of the worst advocates a man can possibly have. The animal condition is a much better index than most people realise. There is little to be feared even from a tiger if his stomach is in a proper state.

It is, of course, unnecessary to mention that Mr. Shepard, the minister of the parish, was present, proud of his new house and of the goodly company assembled to do honor to its dedication. But though he dispensed with the outer layer of his stern and frigid habit he was careful by no means to compromise his dignity. Has not the reader observed, that of all people on earth, a minister with a new meeting house is the most proud? We once alluded to this curious fact, in conversation with a clerical friend. He admitted it, but claimed that the pride was felt for the honor done to the Lord. This was satisfactory, and led to the conclusion that the fair lady, when she proudly flaunts her silks, may be merely intending honor to the silk-worm.

The dedication services occupied a good portion of the day, and were conducted in a manner harmonious and profitable. The singers performed their onerous duty in a temper remarkably free from discontent and bickering, which was perhaps in a measure attributable to the soothing influence of the German viol, which, so far as our knowledge extends, was then, for the first time, introduced into a house of worship, in the place.

But the Dedication Dinner was declared to be the crowning glory of the day. And as we have at hand a long letter, written by one who was present, giving, in graphic terms, an account of the affair, we cannot do better than avail ourselves of it, and transcribe as follows:

"Y^e Deddication Dinner was had in ye great barne of Mr Hoode, which by reason of its goodly size was deemed ye most fit place. It was neatly adorned with green bows & other hangings & made very faire to look upon, ye wreaths being mostly wrought by ye young folk, they meeting together, both maids and young men and having a merry time in doing ye pleasant worke. Y^e rough stalls & unhewed posts being gayly begirt, and all ye corners & cubbies being clean swept and well aired, it truly did appear a meet banquetting hall. Y^e scaffoldes too, from which ye provinder had been removed, were swept clean as broome could make them. And they too had comely decorations.

"Some seats were put up on ye scaffoldes, whereon might sit such of ye antient women as would see ye doings; also maids and children. And thereon I did descry, on looking up, as I sat at meate, some dames with knitting worke; showing good ensample for industry to ye younger ones about them. But most that I did see thereon were maidens & children, being all in their best attire and with smiling faces. Y^e white capps of ye old folk, looked neat and tidy and ye hair of ye maids being some in braides and some in curls, was glossy & beautyful to look upon.

"Y^e great floor was all held for ye company which was to partake of ye feast of fat things, none others being admitted there save them that were to wait upon ye same. Y^e kine that were wont to be there, were forced to keep holiday in ye field. And ye fowles, save such as were kept for service on ye table, were likewise made to pass ye time without, tho they would sometimes make endeavor to get back to roost upon ye beam that ran above ye table; which was not permitted seeing what harm might come to them that sat beneath.

"But while ye company were busy with their knives

and forks, a lusty one did steal his way to ye beam, where, mayhap, he might have perched till ye feast was thro had it not happened in this wise: A savory dish had just been put smoking upon ye table, and Mr Rogers was helping himself therefrom with ye great horn spoon, when lo, ye whole was spoiled by ye unmannerly doing of ye fowl above, who must needs just then scratch down an aboundance of dirty litter, making ye soup look well peppered. Some did much laugh at ye comical turn. And thereupon ye cock must needs crow and look down upon us seemingly well pleased with his dirty doing.

"Mr Shepard's face did turn very red; and without speaking he catched up an apple and hurled it at ye misbehaving bird. But he thereby made ye bad matter worse, for ye fruit being well aimed, it hit ye legs of ye fowl and brought him floundering and flapping right down upon ye table, scattering gravy, sauce, & divers other unclean things upon our garments and in our faces. But tho this did not well please some, yet with most it was a happening that made great merryment.

"Dainty meats were on ye table in great plenty, as bear stake, deer meat, rabbit & fowle both wilde and from y° barn yard. Luscious puddings we likewise had in aboundance, mostly apple and berry, but some of corn meal, with small bits of sewet baked therein; also pyes & tarts. And we had some pleasant fruits, as apples, nuts & wild grapes. And to crown all, we had plenty of good cydar & ye inspiring Barbadoes drink.

"Mr Shepard and most of ye ministers were grave & prudent at table, discoursing much upon ye great points of ye deddication sermon, & in silence labouring upon ye food before them. But I will not risque to say on which they dwelt with most relish, ye discourse or dinner. Most of ye young members of ye Council & Committee would fain make a jolly time of it.

"Mr Gerrish, ye Wenham minister, tho prudent in his meats & drinks, was yet in right merry mood. And he did once grievously scandalize Mr Shepard, who, on suddenly looking up from his dish, did spy him, as he thot winking in an unbecoming way to one of ye pretty damsels on ye scaffolde. And thereupon bidding ye godly Mr Rogers to labor with him aside for his misbehaviour, it turned out that ye winking was occasioned by some of ye hay seeds that were blowing about, lodging in his eye; whereat Mr Shepard felt greatly releaved.

"Y^e aged Obadiah Turner sat next to Mr Gerrish at table, he being one of ye building committee, & much thot of for his many good doings in ye space of his long life. Being some deaf, he must fain keep his gray head curiously bobbing round, lest he should lose some of the good sayings which were uttered by ye company. He was temperate in his drinks & in his meats, but brim full of merry thots. He was too old, he said, to make much discourse, or he would relate many wonderful things of ye antient days of ye Plantation, ye Collony, ye old people here & of our blessed church. And one asking him how it came about that he so well remembered so many curious things which every body declared he did, of ye old times, he said that for many years, he every day writ down all wonderful things that happened, & had now in his front room desk, enow records to make a faire booke.

"Master Rogers & Master Shepard held some talk in Latin, a part whereof seemed to concern Timothy

Alden, who sat about ye middle of ye table. He was a man of middle age, and of ye Malden church. He had not been soe prudent in using ye good things as others had. I did discern many spots of gravy and blotches of sauce upon his garments which I did not think ye fowle spattered there. His speach grew thick & his eyes heavy, and ye company were much pained to hear him of a sudden break out with parts of a mawdlin song. But presently one inviting him to walk out and view Goodman Boardman his wonderful calfe, he did go. And as they walked adown ye lane, arm in arm, we did hear parts of ye song, brot back on ye wind, growing less & less as ye distance grew.

"Y^e new Meeting House was much discoursed upon at ye table. And most thot it as comely a house of worship as can be found in ye whole Collony, save only three or four.

"Mr Richardson, ye Newberry minister, in a very loud voice & stately mien, proclaimed that tho ye house was a noble temple, it yet was but a fit casket for ye godly jewel of Lynn to shine in. Whereupon a most lusty crow was set up by ye same old cock that had been on ye beam. He now appeared poised on ye upper window sill looking down upon us with great seeming sauciness. Y^e crow, being in approval, as it appeared, of ye pleasant speach of Mr Richardson, did greatly amuse ye whole company. They shouted & clapped their hands in great glee.

"And when ye uproare about ye old rooster was ended, Mr Shepard arose and with profound obeisance to right and left, in great modesty sayd that ye lustre of ye jewel, he feared, would be much dimmed in ye brighter glow of some other that might from time to time shine in ye same casket, and he looked smilingly on Mr Rogers, as if in him beholding such a jewel. And thereupon ye cock crew again, & flapping his wings put astir much dust and litter, which fell upon ye table. Many of ye company now hurled apples at ye misbehaveing fowle, but they not being good of aim, only two came within half a score of inches of his perch. He then stretched out his neck, and looking down upon us, made a strange whirring noise, as if he would deride us, as well as he could with his unmanageable voyce, and flew out upon ye ground, seemingly in great disgust.

"Mr Gerrish was in such merry mood that he kept ye end of ye table whereby he sat in right jovial humour. Some did loudly laugh & clap their hands. But in ye middest of ye merryment, a strange disaster did happen unto him. Not haveing his thots about him, he endeavoured ye dangerous performance of gaping & laughing at ye same time, which he must now feel is not so easy or safe a thing. In doing this, he set his jaws open in such wise that it was beyond all his power to bring them together again. His agonie was very great, and his joyful laugh soon turned to grievous groaning. Y^e women on ye scaffoldes became much distressed for him. And ye pretty daughter of my neighbour John Armitage, leaning over for to look did lose her poise, & would have broke her bones by falling to ye floor, had not ye strong arms of one by catched her.

"We did our utmost to stay ye anguish of Mr Gerrish, but could make out little till Mr Rogers, who knoweth somewhat of anatomy, did bid ye sufferer to sit down on ye floor; which being done Mr Rogers took ye head atween his legs, turning ye face as much upward as possible, and then gave a powerful blow &

sudden press which brot ye jaws again into working order. But Master Gerrish did not gape or laugh much more, on that occasion, you may be sure; neither did he talk much, for that matter.

"No other weighty mishap occurred, save that one of ye Salem delegates, in boastfully essaying to crack a walnut atween his teeth, did crack instead of ye nut a most useful double tooth, & was thereby forced to appear at ye evening meeting with a bandaged face.

"There was much sound discourse at table on ye affairs of our church and ye churches about us; of their difficultys & tryals; how they become from time to time exercised & distracted by wolves getting in amongst ye flocks, so many constantly comeing here from abroad, of unsound doctrine & ungodly lives. Such, comeing and preaching their pestigious doctrines, shock all godly people and make nothing but mischief amongst us. And we greatly fear that in years to come ye wicked seeds that they sowe may spring up, and if not choak to deadly effect, yet greatly obstruct ye growth of true religion in ye land. Much to this purpose was talked over by ye ministers and delegates present.

"Obadiah Turner did make bold to reply that all goodness was not confined to ye old ways. In some new things there might be truth and comfort, and for his part, he was moved to look into new pretentions before proclaiming them to be of ye Devil, & see if there be not some good that might be picked out; saying that he did not beleave that ye Devil ever yet had entire possession of a human heart; & saying, too, that there be them in our midst who would fain do God's work in judging of ye hearts of men; which he did not deem meet. And he asked where our blessed

Christianity would have been had every body keeped their skirts clear of it while it was a new thing. Some wondered at heareing ye good old man talk in that wise; but all listened with good heed to his short speech.

"Much likewise was said about ye affairs of ye Collony, & what they across ye water may be doing for and against us. It is undenyable that we have reason to fear that matters will not long go so smoothely with us as they have gone, for we have learned that divers scandalous sayings have been uttered against us to ears in high places. King Charles we do not think loves us overmuch, tho we be loyal subjects, and in ye late terrible war did our utmost to extend & make firm and sure his rule in these parts.

"And on these political matters Mr Turner did likewise have a short say, warmly affirming that ye people of this goodly land will one day become a mighty people & will then pay back ye wrongs committed on their weakness. Ye whole table clapped heartily at his sayings. And one whom modesty would have me hold nameless here, called on all present to drink to ye health and long life of Master Turner. It was done with much good will, by some in ye use of cyder, and by others in ye use of stronger drink. Whereupon Mr Turner replied, that as to ye long life he had already had that, & as to ye health, God had much blessed him thro ye many years that he had lived, and he hoped that for ye little part remaining, no heavy pains were in store for him.

"Master Gerrish did move to much laughter by a short speach, of great wit, about women folk. This was before ye happening of ye terrible accident to his jaws. And it was greatly relished by ye faire ones on y⁰ scaffoldes as well as by us below. And I did behold many sparkling eyes peeping over & many thanks descending upon his head in y⁰ shape of bits of evergreen.

"Master Shepard would fain give us some discourse in Latin. But so many not knowing that tongue it made little stir, tho y⁰ Doctor from Cambridge took it upon him to talk much of it, saying that it was very brave and learned.

"Some songs were sung, mostly concearning old Englande and things there; none of y⁰ songs being unseemly in such a company & on such an occasion. Divers psalms and hymns were likewise sung, y⁰ women upon y⁰ scaffoldes joining in with us below.

"Most of y⁰ company were at times much exercised with laughter, which hath been deemed healthful. And so I think it is, in moderation. But too much is weakening as hath been sayd; the which seemeth true, for one or two of y⁰ lay bretheren on this occasion, who did laugh most roisterly, became so weakened that their heads must needs loll from side to side in great looseness.

"We also had riddles and blind sayings put for to guess out, & many other cleaver things to make y⁰ time pass pleasantly.

"And on y⁰ whole we did find much profit as well as pastime in y⁰ occasion, being right well pleased with what our ears did hear and our appetites did find. So noble and savoury a banquet was never before spread in this now famous town. So said Master Turner; & so all said.

"God be praised."

And so ends the contemporaneous account of the great Dedication Dinner. As the shades of evening gathered the friends from abroad retired as guests to the hospitable homes of the villagers. In many families, the capacious brick oven had been put in requisition, and the suppers that smoked upon the tables on that evening, might well induce those who had been partakers of the public feast, to mourn for their lost appetites.

An evening meeting was held at the new meeting house, which was attended by the clergy and many other grave people. Mr. Gerrish preached one of his most luminous doctrinal discourses. And from his solemn manner one might have imagined that not a merry word had passed his lips nor a smile illuminated his countenance in a month's time. There was still a little stiffness in his jaws, but not sufficient to prevent his usual clearness of utterance.

The young folk assembled at a dedication ball in the little hall over the room which was formerly occupied as the store of Dexter and Laighton. Some of the delegates and others from abroad had brought their daughters, sisters and sweethearts. And what entertainment could be more agreeable to these, than a moderate and modest indulgence in the fascinating mazes of the dance? They had a merry time; and as it afterward appeared such impressions were made as finally resulted in the transplanting into Lynn of two or three of the most beautiful flowers that the neighboring settlements afforded. And the gay company were not at all overawed nor surprised on beholding, after the services at the meeting house were over, half a score or more of sober visaged men and women enter and seat themselves on the bench that ran along the side of the hall, and remain, complacently gazing on the happy scene, till the festivities closed.

One may be pardoned for feeling a little amused at some of the inconsistences exhibited in the foregoing details. But they are characteristic of human nature. It may perhaps be said that the old settlers in some respects set their standard for the regulation of conduct higher than human nature would bear; and in their attempts to climb the height, became subject to many slips and backward slides. Numerous instances might be referred to in which there certainly was no marked unity between their precepts and practices.

To speak again of dancing: they denounced that as one of the Devil's most cunning traps by which to ensnare the youthful soul; but yet there is abundant evidence that they regarded the dedication or ordination ball as a proper adjunct. Perhaps the most godly people attended, and so made it what it ought to be; thus taking a different course from some modern good people who never try to improve the world by example, but delight to stand afar off and fire gospel blunderbusses that echo about men's ears, attract attention and may once in a while damage some redout of the evil one.

Those worthy fathers had fled from religious persecution and the slavery of the old world; but once in power here, they deemed it meet to deny to those who could not conscientiously come into full communion with them some of the dearest rights of citizenship. And while preaching temperance in all things and liberty and equality for all men there appear to have been those among them who were without a protest shipping Indian prisoners of war to Barbadoes, to be sold into slavery for return cargoes of rum. And the Old Tunnel itself had its "nigger pew," as it was popularly called — a close board erection, high up from the gallery, in the extreme northeast corner of the house. And there the poor cuffys had to sit, shut up like lepers, unseeing and unseen, while their grave masters — for there was negro slavery in the Bay State in those days — sat in the airy courts below, listening to the glorious gospel of liberty and equality.

The sin of incontinence was, by these pious men, deemed of the blackest dye; but the agreeable custom of "bundling" by no means shocked them; and the blooming fruits of the institution who so frequently appeared at the baptismal font, even in the Old Tunnel, attested to its popularity.

But some might call such apparent inconsistences by another name. Human nature is perverse and inclined to rebel against rigid exaction. The strictness demanded may have led some to revolt, and recede towards the opposite extreme; forming, as it were, a separate party in the midst of another. And each party may have pursued a course consistent with itself. This, however, is simply saying, in another way, that the righteous may have been consistent in their pretentions and the unrighteous in theirs. And no one will dispute that. But the fact still remains that many of the good settlers entertained the antagonisms in their own individual breasts.

And now, in drawing our volume to a close, we propose introducing a few sketches of the jewels that shone in the Old Tunnel during its earlier days, though some of the brighter ones, who have shed their lustre in other parts of our volume, will not be recalled. And these sketches we shall intersperse with occasional brief details of occurrences that seem worthy of notice. As before remarked, however, it is not a part of our plan to treat of persons or events pertaining to times subsequent to 1699, excepting in cases where it may appear incidentally necessary.

We have a disposition to present the bright side of things. Though in our progress we have not shrunk from presenting the dark side when duty seemed to require. There is an old adage that it is better to rejoice than weep. And Providence has ordered that in the world there shall be much more to excite pleasurable than sad sensations; thus plainly indicating that the former are more approved than the latter. And we have endeavored, under these views, to deliver ourselves in an agreeable way. So if the reader should in our pages discover anything that seems like pleasantry he will please consider it as dictated by principle, rather than as a spontaneous breach of that gravity which nature has always striven to force upon us.

We commenced our task in an agreeable frame of mind, induced by the modest determination to be satisfied if by this Book we should be so fortunate as to contribute sufficient to sweeten what would equal one life time. And now let us see what sort of a calculation may reasonably be made.

In every year of one's life there will ordinarily be three hundred and fifty days, during each of which eight hours will be spared from sleep and other necessary and recreative demands. And hence there will be in every year twenty eight hundred hours thus spared. And in sixty years, which are quite as many as can be calculated on aside from those of infancy and sickness, there will be one hundred and sixty eight thousand hours to be provided for. Now we trust that every person who reads this volume will find ten hours of his precious life pleasantly and not unprofita-

M*

bly occupied. And in the same modest way we trust that seventeen thousand individuals will read the volume. Not that there will be that number of copies published, at least of the first edition; for if but three thousand are published and each of these is read by six persons, we shall have eighteen thousand readings, which, multiplied by ten, the number of hours devoted by each reader, gives us one hundred and eighty thousand hours, which is indeed twelve thousand hours more than our estimate requires. As regards the quality and intensity of the enjoyment to be derived from a perusal of our volume, we have not sufficient boldness to speak. And we beg the reader not to conclude that these abstruse calculations have been entered into for an ostentatious display of mathematical acquirements, but because by them some other hitherto unprofitable steward may be incited to attempt something for the increase of the common stock from which the happiness of the world is in general derived. In almost all cases difficulties lessen as we meet them. And viewing or meeting an obstacle in detail wonderfully reduces its formidableness. A century is no great of an affair, disposed of by hours.

There is, however, another thought connected with this matter of time. How can one individual know what the exact conception of another is as to time? In other words, reader, how can you determine that an hour as marked by the clock, does not appear full five times as long to you as it does to me? That it may possibly be so, is shown by the fact that in a dream one may in five minutes go through scenes that in real life he could not go through in ten hours if in twenty. This proves that it is not the absolute duration but our conception of it. Two men make an appointment to meet in one hour. They do meet at the given time, for both understand what the period outwardly and arbitrarily marked as an hour is; but in the mean time they may have lived, so to speak, essentially different periods, as determined by their mental conceptions. This is evidently true from the fact, long since stated and by every man's experience confirmed, that as we grow older the years appear to decrease in length. It has been satisfactorily established that to one of the age of ten, a year seems just as long as four years will seem to the same individual at the age of forty.

And further, who can say that as regards the lower animals, the conceptions of time may not be very different in different species, or even in different individuals of the same species? Who is competent to show that what we call the fleeting life of a butterfly may not be to him as long as three score and ten years are to a man?

Soon after noting down these reflections we happened to take in hand a volume of the Spectator, and presently came across some speculations similar to one or two of them. The first impulse was to ruthlessly strike out what we had written, both because the old moralist expressed himself much more felicitously, and because ours might seem like imitations. But on second thought we concluded to do no such thing; for however much a line or two might appear like imitation, we could boldly challenge both word and thought as our own and truthfully declare that we had not read the others till ours were in black and white; though perhaps we ought to blush in acknowledging such unacquaintance with so approved a model in English literature. Instead therefore of molesting the lines we even took comfort from the circumstance that our speculations had for once run in so high a channel as those of the wise and virtuous Spectator of old.

The occurrence, however, gave rise to still other reflections. No doubt writers have often been charged with the really heinous offence of plagiarism when they were not guilty. The same idea might spring up in several minds; and one might give expression to it without knowing that another had anticipated him, when in fact such was the case. It is only when the phraseology or something else renders guilt morally certain that the offensive charge can be justified. We recently observed in a southern publication a somewhat singular explanation given in a defence against a charge of plagiarism. It was, that years before, the passage on which the charge rested had been attentively read and deeply impressed upon the mind; and had been made use of without once realizing that it was merely an offspring of the memory and not otherwise of the mind. And this explanation was accepted as sufficient. It may be observed, that intelligent writers often quote, without designating as quotations, phrases and even more extended passages, that are presumed to be so well known as to leave no one in error as to their origin. It seems as if none but a critic in a high fever would object to this. It is simply relying on the intelligence of the reader instead of occupying space by references or disfiguring the page by inverted commas and apostrophes.

There is a curious conceit that we remember to have come across in an old writer, to the effect that a certain number of ideas were originally created for the use of the whole race, and that these have been circulating ever since, sometimes turning up in one brain, in one shape, and then in another brain in another shape, but always essentially the same. Perhaps, however, it might be better to say that it was originally ordained that the human brain should be capable of working in just so many different ways; thus being able to produce just so many different thoughts or ideas and when in different brains similar or identical action takes place corresponding thoughts are produced. If anything like this is true, the power of action must be almost without limit; sufficient for the production of more erratic and airy wanderers than the solar system could accommodate.

It would cost us too much self-denial not to add that there was one passage in the volume of the Spectator alluded to from which we drew considerable comforting assurance. The very unassuming author thought that twenty would be a "modest computation" of those who would peruse each of his papers. Now we had put down the number of our readers at only six. We do not recall this to appear more modest than he, but for the opportunity to add that if the reader should consider ours, in quality, as standing, in regard to the Spectator as six to twenty, we should be ready to declare ourselves abundantly satisfied.

One does not half understand a man by reading a grave and stately biography of him. And the biographer who treats only of his Subject's most dignified traits leaves his work half done. Glimpses of his every day life, of his loves and hates, his labors and recreations, are needed for a proper understanding. We would know what kind of meat he prefers for his dinner, whether he loves plum broth and veal pie, as well as what books he has on his library shelves, or what studies occupy his attention. It is interesting to learn whether he walks erect and is of perfect form, or stoops in his gait, is bandy-legged, or splay-footed; whether he wears an old hat and red waistcoat, or is a dandy with curled hair and white kids. If he twitches and jerks and touches the posts as he walks the street, we like to be told of it. Whether the little girls get kisses and the little boys cuffs when he meets them, or beggars get pennies or curses it is always interesting to know.

Boswell, who certainly was not deserving of martyrdom for his intellectual eminence, produced a wonderfully interesting biography of that giant in intellect and ill manners, about whom he so long revolved as an obsequious satellite — a biography which will interest mankind for ages to come. But if in place of that gossiping author, one of the lofty sort had undertaken the work the popular recollection of both subject and writer would by this time have reached the verge of oblivion.

The letters of great men usually furnish most acceptable reading, for in them are generally found genuine breathings of the spirit. And in preparing the biographical sketches in this volume, we have many times had occasion to lament the impossibility of procuring more letters and scraps of writing whereby to enrich our pages. But most of the worthies were little accustomed to the use of the pen beyond what the common affairs of life demanded. We have gathered what materials we could from contemporaneous sources and endeavored, in an impartial way, to digest them for the reader's benefit.

Such considerations as appear in the foregoing, induce us to believe that the following passages from an old letter which seems to have been the production of one Samuel Walton would prove highly acceptable. Whether the writer was of the same line with piscatory Izaak, we cannot say, though the genius of the two seems to have been developed much in the same direction. We consider the letter a treasure, giving, as it does, a graphic view of one or two characteristics of Mr. Shepard, the first minister of the Old Tunnel, which we have nowhere else seen alluded to:

"The minister, Mr Shepard, tho in no wise giuen to saying or doeing any but grave things, yet hath some loves that be not of the studie or the pulpitt. And amoung his loves he doth reckon eals. He will sometimes try the sport of catching the same. And I would fain tell of a time we had on the ryver of Saugust, of a cold day, with our speares.

"Mr Shepard did say to me, in ye morning, 'Samuel,' sayd he, 'I do beleave in eals, and am minded to go to the ryver this afternoon and speare for some, not haveing had a dish of the dainty things since ye last week, of a Tewsday; and, Samuel, I would have you go with me.'

"'Well, Master Shepard,' quoth I, 'it would suit me well to go, and I will call for you in good time, with my hand sled & speare.'

"'So do, so do, Samuel,' sayd he, 'and I must depend upon you, as you come along, to call at Mr Purchis's house, & get the loan of his speare, as I haue none. And I will be ready with an axe wherewith to cut the holes in the ice, against your comeing with the sled. And the Dame will likewise make ready for us a bite of something whereby to stay our stomacks. And if you have a mind, Samuel, you may bring along your little red keg, for mine hath sacrament wine in it, and I will put a little something in yᵉ same to warm our stomacks withal. For it is best, Samuel,' sayd he, giveing his eye a little turn, 'to go prepared to meet mishaps.'

"'Of a truth, Master Shepard,' quoth I, 'you are ever mindful of yᵉ wants of body as well as soul. The keg shall be there.'

"Presently after dinner I did as Mʳ Shepard had bid me, calling at Mʳ Purchis's for the speare and being at the house betimes. Yᵉ minister was already in his warm mufflers, red leggins and big bootes. So we soon got on our way to the ryver, I dragging the sled and he bearing yᵉ two speares on his shoulder, they not riding well on the sled. We held much grave discourse on the road, about the Deuil & his late dooings hereabout by witchcraftes and other diabolical contrivances, and yᵉ defeats put on him by God's power thro his servants the godly ministers.

"Getting upon the ryver, we straightway set about our work, the time being short before sunsetting. Our holes in yᵉ ice being cut, 'Now,' quoth I to Master Shepard, 'stir about, stir about, for the air is mighty chill; and I dare promise we shall have a goodly mess and be ready for home afore night cometh on.'

"Some lusty prey soon fell to vs, whereat we took encouragement & did not note yᵉ time till nigh the going down of the sun. The cold grew to be very great, insomuch that when we wetted our garments they presently froze stiff. And to our great discomfort the wind from the northeaste, began to blow hard and the snow to fly. By a mishap, when cutting a fresh hole, yᵉ axe slipped from my benumbed hand and went to the bottom, greatly to our grief, for the loss of it was more than the gains by all the eals that we could hope to catch. But it was a prouidence that Mr Shepard well sayd we should bear with patience.

"It getting dark apace, I gathered the eals into the box vpon the sled, & advertised Master Shepard that it was high time to think of moveing; wherevpon he withdrew his speare from ye hole, and being about to step to the sled, came nigh to breaking his back by a forward pitch, not being able to move his feet.

"'Mercie on us!' quoth he 'why, Samuel, my feet are both froze hard to the ice.'

"I was much terrifyed, and sayd, 'Master Shepard, I fear that you did not stir about, as I bid you, when we began to speare. Did you not take note that while speareing I walked around the hole and keeped my feet astir, for ye new water drawing up with the poles doth put one in great hazard of froezing down. I be not so forward as to hope to instruct mine own minister in what doth pertain to ye holy ordinances or in ye learning of ye schools; but I do think that in spearing eals I may show more science than some having greater godliness.'

"'Samuel,' quoth he, 'you did indeed bid me stir about, but I thot your meaning was to stir the speare, about, & that I uerily did, mvch to the weariness of my arms, which have suffered great pains with the ceaseless stirring. But we must not parley, Samuel, for I am beginning to greatly suffer.'

"The axe being gon I knew not what to do. With the speare I could do nothing, ye prongs bending so badly. And while casting about for some other means, quoth Mr Shepard,

"'Come hither, Samuel, and stand with your back towards me, & near. You are shorter than I, and by putting my hands vpon your shoulders, and gaining as they say a purchase for the strongest muscles, I may peradventure strain my bootes from the ice or myself from the bootes, tho they are mightie tight about the ankle.'

"'Well thot of,' quoth I, and stood as he did bid me. But I came nigh being crushed by ye force he put vpon me, in the tryals to free himself; yet he could do nothing.

"'Samuel,' cryed he, 'this is indeed a bad business, and I know not what is to come of it. But no time is to be lost, for the darkness is already vpon us; and besides, ye snow is falling fast & ye cold is very great. Haste you to the nearest habitation and crave succor. Bring a kettle of hot water, an axe, or some means whereby I may be discharged from this vile imprisonment. And, Samuel, bring likewise a little something warming to take within, for that brought in the keg hath long since been exhausted.'

"I essayed to do as he would have me, when lo, much to my distress I found that I too had been imprudent in too long standing still, & was myself a prisoner, being frozen down as strong as Master Shepard. Casting about as to what had best be done, we could fix on nothing. And all ye time ye bad matter getting worse, our hearts did begin to fail us.

"'Samuel,' again cryed Mr Shepard, after some thot, 'we have nothing left, as I see, to depend on, save our lungs. We must set up a halloing, such as shall be heard by some wayfarer, if such should happen to be upon the road; or, if there be no traueller abroad, then we must make ovrselues heard as far off as yonder habitations at the foot of the hill, or even to ye tavern beyond. And, Samuel, we must do it speedily, or every thimble full of marrow in our bones will be chilled, and we shall be buryed vp in ye snow which begins to drift so around vs.'

"'Had we not better,' quoth I, 'sing a psalm together, for by so doeing we may make a chord, as it were twisting our voyces together and thereby making a louder alarrum. And by the means of a psalm we may likewise be crying for earthly help and praiseing God at ye same time, which we should always do.'

"'Well thot of,' returned he, 'well thot of. Samuel, there is always some good thing turning up in your mind; but if there be any of those high keyed songs of the world's people that might be heard farder off or catch the ear quicker than a psalm or hymn, strike out vpon one, and I doubt not that God will overlook our prophanity in our extremity.'

"'I think, Master Shepard,' said I, 'that we should neuer do wrong, be the extremity what it may. And I make bold to exhort to the use of a psalm, in the first place.'

"'Well, well, Samuel,' quoth he, 'a psalm it shall be; and we must quickly strike the same or it will be all ouer with vs. Begin, Samuel, begin; and have a care that the pitch is high.'

"'Nay, nay, Master Shepard,' returned I, 'but you know better than I ye psalm best suited to our condition and peril.'

"''Sdeath, Samuel,' he replyed, with some quickness, 'we must lose no time in parleying.' And thereupon he put his hands vpon his hipps, and commenced in a mighty voyce ye most comforting words of the psalm set to ye enspiring tune of Goodhope. And we did sing with all our might, haveing greater care for noise than musick.

"Presently we did hear one vp ye lane, calling loudly

for alarrum, declaring that he heard ye wilde beasts crying down from the woods, and bidding all come forth with musquets for to shoot them. Then great fear did come vpon vs lest we should be fired vpon thro the darkness and shot for wild beasts. So we stopped our song and Mr Shepard cryed in plain words of great lamentation and with a lusty voyce. And presently to our great releaf and the saveing of our poor, frail bodys some were made to hear our cryes and understand our distresses. They speedily came to our rescue; and all declared that we were just freezing and that in a few minutes all would have been ouer with vs. Not being able to walk, they carryed us in a tender manner to ye tavern, where we were well warmed within and swaddled and doctored. But we have greatly suffered euer since.

"I haue fears that ovr disasters be in some way the work of the old serpent the Devil, for eals be somewhat in likeness of ye serpent kind. And henceforth I will no more meddle with what may be children or imps of ye great tempter. And Mr Shepard hath declared that he no longer beleaves in eals.

"God be praised for so preserving vs. Amen."

———

Among the refugees from European oppression who came to North America after the establishment of the earlier colonies, there were none more interesting than the Huguenots. After the revocation of the edict of Nantz many a tearful eye was turned hopefully towards America, and many of these poor French Protestants fled to our shores and established themselves in little colonies. But the emigration flowed chiefly to the south of New England. New York, Virginia, and Carolina received them kindly. In some instances special laws were made for their naturalization. And as they were in very reduced circumstances, large donations, public and private, were cheerfully bestowed on them. Their taxes, for public purposes, were very generally remitted. And in various ways they were most kindly dealt with till they were able to supply their own wants.

What kind of reception these friendless refugees would have met with had they, to any extent, sought shelter among the puritan settlements it is not now possible to determine. But judging by the course pursued toward others the presumption cannot be regarded as favorable.

The little lodgment that the Huguenots made in what is now the town of Oxford, in Worcester county, appears to have been their only one hereabout. And though the English do not seem to have ever assumed a decidedly hostile attitude towards this inconsiderable colony, they yet do not appear to have offered them aid or comfort. Alone they heroically met the assaults of the Indians, and endured the keenest privations and sternest perils. But they finally dwindled away and disappeared, without having received help, sympathy, or even christian recognition.

It was as true of the Huguenots as of any people that the earth ever bore, that they forsook their loved firesides and homes for Religion's sake. By that one fatal stroke of malign power, the revocation by Louis the fourteenth of the gracious edict of Henry the fourth, more than fifty thousand were forced to flee, stripped of their possessions, and urged on by the dread apprehension of the scaffold, the dagger and the faggot. Numbers turned their eyes to lands beyond the western wave. True, a wilderness lay before them;

but behind them loomed the red fires of St. Bartholomew's.

It is refreshing to find that among the churchmen of New York and Virginia, if nowhere else on the American shores, the poor Huguenots found a peaceful retreat. And in after years their noble blood that flowed down through the veins of Jay, Laurens, Boudinot, and a host of others whose names have become illustrious in American history, abundantly repaid for all the benevolent efforts that were put forth to save them in the day of peril.

On a chill, drizzly Sunday afternoon, in November, just before the hour for the commencement of the services at the Old Tunnel, there approached along the road that wound up the middle of the open Common, a stranger, of such appearance as to attract the attention of the loungers about the porches and horse sheds. He was a gentleman, seemingly about fifty years of age, tall, erect, and of fine proportions. His hair was slightly lined with gray, and dark mustaches curled upon his lip. His whole bearing was singularly dignified and commanding. But his highly intellectual countenance bore the impress of care and sorrow. He wore, buttoned closely to his throat, a coat cut in French military style, but without any decorations indicative of the soldier's profession.

Leaning upon one arm of this stranger was a lady of middle age and extremely prepossessing appearance. Her fine form and features attracted many admiring eyes. But her countenance, like his, seemed clouded by sorrow and anxiety.

Upon his other side tripped a beautiful girl of some seventeen summers. She carried in her hand a bouquet of late autumn flowers that she had evidently gathered on her way across the Common. She wore a fashionably trimmed French bonnet, and had the appearance of one tenderly bred. Occasionally she would almost pause in her walk, to bestow upon her parents, for such the others seemed to be, a look so full of confiding love, and withal so tinged with the sorrow that appeared common to them all, that the coldest heart might well have been touched.

On reaching the seat to which they were shown, the three strangers knelt, in silent prayer, in accordance with the ancient and beautiful custom which prevailed in all branches of the christian church, from the earliest days till the time when the Puritans commenced their purifications. They knelt — and while on their knees, a sudden break in the clouds illumined the whole house; the warm sunbeams streaming through the little diamond panes and falling in inexpressible beauty upon the bowed heads. The old Romans would have deemed this a happy omen, and such strange worshipers in some way favored of heaven. But our unimaginative fathers probably considered it only as a special interposition to enable them the more clearly to discern an idolatrous act.

The services closed, and the congregation retired, many of them stopping to lounge in the porches and about the doors, to exchange salutations and discuss the news and gossip of the week. The strangers passed quietly out, and were suffered to go their way without receiving any courteous recognition, or even the slightest notice beyond being rudely stared at. But if the villagers said nothing to them they said enough about them and their "church fashions."

Some days passed and it was ascertained that these

strangers were a family of French Protestants who had fled from a happy and luxurious home with the small means that in their hasty retreat they were able to secure. Something had attracted them to this particular spot, and they came with the intention of making arrangements for the purchase of land and the establishment of a colony.

It appeared that the gentleman's name was Boudinot. He was able to converse pretty freely in the English language, and immediately set about the business for which he came. He was not long in paying his respects to Mr. Shepard and the chief men of the parish, for the purpose of making known his plans and interesting them in behalf of himself and his fellow sufferers. But he found them as cold as stones. They seemed to possess an extraordinary apprehension of everything evolved by a French mind; talked of the poverty of the land; and expressed in very decided terms their dread of having the seeds of spiritual thorns scattered in their beautifully tilled portion of the garden of the Lord.

On the day following the third formal conference of M. Boudinot with Mr. Shepard and the other chief men, there was a great training on the extensive and convenient area in which the Meeting House was centered. An array of booths, in which were sold fruit, cakes, beer, cider, and all sorts of muddling drinks, graced the sides of the sanctuary. And the legitimate effects of these were soon apparent. Some got drunk and had fights. Some danced, with lewd girls, in the back apartments of the booths, to the music of cracked fiddles. Some laughed at the tricks of the buffoons and speeches of the mock orators. And some soberly watched the evolutions of the soldiers or quietly pro-menaced with their wives, daughters or sweethearts, mourning, at every spare moment, over such depravity.

The troops assembled from far and near. And they made an imposing display, each individual being arrayed very much according to his own fancy. Here was a coat of dingy red, and there a jacket of pea-green; here full yellow leather breeches and there gray tights and red leggins; here an unshapely bear skin cap of enormous dimensions and ferocious aspect, such as might excite the envy of the most uncivilized Russian, and there a cap of squirrel or racoon skin, with tail erect for a plume — to say nothing of others, of indescribable material and fashion, decorated, perhaps, by an eagle feather or a contribution from the tail of goose or gobbler or even the more lowly inhabitant of the barn yard.

On reviewing them, one might have imagined that they had adopted the tactics of the valiant Chinese, and depended upon their extraordinary appearance to frighten invaders from their territories; or designed such a display as would be pretty sure to render their Indian foes stupid from admiration.

We are sorry to believe, by the way, that the hostility towards the Indians, in many instances, received a decidedly religious coloring. Too many seem to have thought that it was doing God service to destroy the red men. And under such circumstances, many who would otherwise have been least courageous were zealous to meet the dangers of the field, finding it much easier to bring their minds to fight for a passport to heaven than to gain it by repentance and amendment. Such has always been the case, both before and since the sanguinary lustre of the Crusades beamed upon the world.

N

But we would certainly say nothing disparagingly of the courage of the colonial soldiery. The parade in question appears to have been a sort of military fancy show — a dress parade, to use a more refined term. When they took the field for real service, they went forth uniformly accoutred in homely regimentals but with hearts undaunted by the prospect of a winter's march through snowy wilds, to meet cunning and relentless foes; and with hearts all aglow for their homes and their religion.

The troops, on the bloodless occasion in question, performed a variety of extraordinary evolutions. But unfortunately, the commander who was somewhat new in his position, was inclined to pay his respects to the liquor booths rather too often. So about the middle of the afternoon, while going through an exercise similar to the graceful one of whipping-the-snake, he got the whole line inextricably entangled. He was extremely mortified at his misadventure before such a crowd of spectators, many of whom were from abroad; some, of superior military rank. The poor man was in very great perplexity. He strode round, ordering and countermanding, sweating and swearing, till he was well nigh exhausted. The sober minded felt great pain for him. And those disposed to make merry over the mishaps of others — there being a few such in the world even in those days — gave the reins to their risibility. And presently by the excitement of some and goadings of others matters seemed to be fast passing from the comic to the tragic. Loud hootings began to be heard. And here and there strong arms were raised, in gyrations demonstrative of anything but peaceful intent.

At this juncture M. Boudinot suddenly appeared at

the side of the distressed commander. His dark eye glowed as if some new inspiration were upon him, and he drew himself up in such a singularly soldierlike and commanding attitude as to instantly attract the attention of those about him. Without any apologies or hesitancy he immediately began, in a clear, full voice, to issue orders to the entangled troops, who still continued in vain manœuvring, like some gigantic snake, wounded and desperate. Instant obedience followed his commands, every soldier seeming as if bound by some irresistible impulse to obey. Only a few simple orders had been given, when, to the astonishment of all, the coils and kinks in the ranks were resolved, and all was restored to order. Once wheeled into line, the panting soldiers looked upon each other in amazement, and then upon their new commander in awe, and finally set up such a shout as would, had it been all wind, have shaken the very belfry from the Meeting House.

M. Boudinot entered with great spirit into the remaining exercises. He took the sword from the unresisting hand of the commander and marched and drilled the men in a manner that excited the greatest admiration. Under his skillful orders the troops performed intricate evolutions with an ease and exactness that astonished themselves as well as others. They began suddenly to look upon their legions as highly accomplished in the military art, and were not much surprised when in his terse speech at the time of dismissal he declared that after a little further discipline they would be fit for an imperial review.

When M. Boudinot returned his sword to the commander, that then cloudy-minded and abashed functionary curiously examined it from point to hilt, as if in search for the hiding place of the talismanic power so recently developed. But being disappointed in finding it still the same old sword, he attempted no further exploits, but dismissed the troops forthwith. A number of platoons of volunteers, were, however, immediately formed, and with two drums and a fife escorted M. Boudinot to his quarters — the dingy little village tavern. And there they left him with a round of cheers which brought his wife and daughter in fright to the scene.

This exhibition of military skill in M. Boudinot, instantly turned the tide. It now set tumultuously in his favor, and in twenty four hours overwhelmed every objection to his idolatry in kneeling in the Meeting House and even to his French brogue. He was now looked upon as one able to render essential service in the day of peril. Mr. Shepard declared that it would be rejecting an offering of Providence to decline receiving one so evidently appointed to be a protector. A meeting was immediately held, and it was by acclamation decided to bestow much more than he had previously asked. And various other christian-like and honorable acts were resolved on. Indeed it is difficult to determine what they would not have done for him had it been proposed as a condition on which he would remain.

But within forty eight hours after the setting of the sun that rejoiced in beholding that remarkable parade of the brave colonial soldiery, M. Boudinot, with his sorrowing little family had departed from Lynn, never again to set foot upon her soil. They went to Virginia, where favorable terms for settling were readily obtained and where they were soon joined by others who had fled from distracted France. The daughter soon married a wealthy young planter. And some of the present leading southern families sprang from the union. A grandchild of hers was a colonel in the army of the Revolution. And one of the most able senators, in the present congress of the United States, is accustomed to boast of his descent from her.

Among the noblest efforts of our forefathers were those directed towards the founding of educational institutions that would enable all classes to receive such instruction as would be necessary for success in life.

The establishment of the free schools of New England seems to have been the offspring of a new order of thought. The idea had prevailed that the masses, if educated, could not be governed by the so called divinely constituted authorities. And there was much worldly wisdom in the idea. For as soon as the masses should become enlightened they might doubt the divine authority.

When, however, the New England immigration commenced, this old opinion began to decay, and the conception that men might possibly possess power to govern themselves, began to prevail. And following closely on that there seems to have been another, not at first clearly defined, but easily traceable, to wit, that here, in this newly reclaimed heritage, great experiments in the art of self-government were destined at no very distant day to be undertaken. And preparatory to such important events, a certain amount, at least, of education would be necessary. One of the first things set about, then, was the establishment of elementary schools. And it is not perhaps too much to say, that these early conceptions were the springs to which are to be traced, in an eminent degree, our national happiness and renown.

At first, the clergy labored much in the educational field. Indeed, they may, in a general sense, be spoken of as the first teachers. And great honor is due them for their zeal and efficiency. They were not accustomed to plead the inability of the youthful mind to bear the burden of study, in excuse for their own indolence.

The Third Plantation was always able to boast of as efficacious means for the instruction of her youth, as any of her sister plantations. And in our highly favored time, as appears by the annual reports of the committees, the schools within the borders of her charter-blessed child are quite unsurpassed by any under the canopy of heaven. Indeed, do not the state educational reports show that the common schools throughout the commonwealth are immeasurably superior to anything that the sun has discovered in any other place since the time when he commenced his daily search into the hidden things of earth. Greece and Rome being now in the rear, it may be interesting to imagine what we shall arrive at in a couple of centuries more. As before remarked, it is a blessed thing to have a good opinion of ourselves. But if in making known such opinion it is just as convenient to avoid odious comparisons and unnecessary detractions, it is not objectionable to do so.

Blessings on those good old fathers for planting those educational institutions which have produced such glorious fruit.

Amariah Turnbody — a singular and unbecoming name, by the way, and one which it is perhaps fortunate that he did not have the luck to transmit — swayed the scholastic sceptre for a time in the little rustic gathering place for dirty faces and dull heads, that stood on a small conical knoll, some ten inches beyond the reach of the most extended shadow that the ambitious Old Tunnel could throw by the aid of spire and setting sun. And he was an active and consequential personage among the worshipers in that endeared fane.

Master Turnbody possessed an active brain; a brain extremely fertile of ideas, such as they were. But unfortunately there was a degree of discord among them that a colony of cats and dogs might emulate. In their disunion all strength of character was lost; for we suppose the converse of the popular maxim must be admitted, and that in disunion there is weakness. Any way, he was by their means reduced to a simply eccentric character.

He no doubt had sufficient book learning for his position, for he had gone up the ladder as far as the Latin rundle. He had a genius for poetry, and wrote out, in rhyme, some of the harder lessons, fancying that in that form they could be more easily learned and remembered. And no doubt he was right, for jingle is more attractive to people in general than solidity. But with his singularities were coupled some of the most excellent qualities that a teacher of youth can possess. He was pious, good-tempered and industrious.

It is quite characteristic of schoolmasters to philosophise and theorise. And Mr. Turnbody was not singular in this respect. Among other conceptions a little out of the common order were his theories regarding the lower animals. He believed that all animals had a way of expressing their sentiments, and that it was within the bounds of possibility, at least, for man to discover the means by which the thoughts, so to speak, of beasts, birds and fishes, could be ascertained. This is an interesting conceit, well worthy of a Turnbody, and one that no reasoning can prove false. A man is always safe from exposure in whatever absurdity he supports, provided he has the sagacity to locate his entrenchments beyond the reach of human reason.

Mr. Turnbody was much pleased by the conviction that he himself had grasped certain leading principles that lay at the foundation of this curious knowledge. And, acting upon this, he is represented to have really shown wonderful skill in judging of the desires and purposes of individuals of the lower races. He seems, certainly, to say the least, to have established an excellent understanding with some specimens, if it be true, as stated, that he was one afternoon seen going down the middle road of the Common, with a cow, an old ram, a dog, a goose, and an enormous rat, following close upon his heels, each heedless of the others, but all anxious to gain his attention, and, perhaps, as the poet says, to share the good man's smile.

These views of Mr. Turnbody were brought forcibly to the mind of the writer, by a curious occurrence witnessed an hour or two before commencing this very page. And perhaps they would not have been alluded to at all, had it not been for the occurrence. A brief account of what we refer to may interest the reader.

Geese have never been famed for their intellectual endowments, though that opportune and eloquent expression of their rational fears, on a certain occasion, at Rome, might support some claim. But let the common opinion go. This very morning, while leisurely pursuing our way across the open fields, our attention was arrested by two large flocks of those feathered trumpeters, coming over the hills on their migratory journey southward. They appeared at points quite distant from each other. But both parties were belching forth with unrestrained voice, as if in warlike defiance or important negotiation. In the rear of each flock, as is common in these flights, were a number of laggers; and these evidently impeded the progress of the squadrons, which seemed anxious to press on, as a storm was vigorously pursuing. Whether these laggers were lame or lazy, it was not easy to determine; nor was it of much consequence, as, according to the proverb, Providence provides for both. And besides, in this case, as in many others, lameness and laziness would be equally detrimental to the other party. Presently the two flocks began to converge. And as they rapidly approached each other their vociferations became more and more alarming, till it seemed as if a most destructive collision were about to take place. They met. But no symptom of anger was manifested. After a little manœuvring, the laggers of both flocks formed into a battalion by themselves, and took a more inland course, while the two large bodies separately bore away on their old courses, no longer impeded by those that had weighed upon their skirts. How Mr. Turnbody would have interpreted this management we cannot say; but it seemed to us very much like a sagacious arrangement to get rid of dead weights in a way that would be effectual and at the same time not repugnant to tender consciences. And we are furthermore delighted to record the incident as supporting the comforting proverb just alluded to.

Few things tended more to elevate Mr. Turnbody

in the estimation of the good people than his activity and usefulness in the sacred precincts of the Meeting House. If the minister were indisposed, he was at hand to read a chapter and expound, or make a prayer. And he usually took it upon himself to line the hymns and mark time; which latter he did with a grace that all the attempts of Father Kemp fail to reach. He was always ready to assist the ladies, young and old, from their pillions, and to show strangers to seats. Indeed there was no useful work about the sanctuary that came amiss to his ready hand, from the pulpit exercises to the snuffing of the tallow candles that during the evening meetings flared and dispensed rivulets of grease over the tin candlesticks and thence upon the heads of the worshipers. On one occasion, however, he came near becoming a martyr to his officiousness.

The Old Tunnel was so constructed that the bell rope came down in the centre of the middle aisle. And the bell ringer was of course one of the most conspicuous objects. There he stood in the dignity of his great office, bowing to the measured strokes that called together old and young, grave and gay. And as they filed by him to their seats, carefully did the fair ladies gather their robes around them and give ample berth to his rib-breaking elbows.

Had the good dames of that day worn to meeting dresses as much extended as do the ladies of our time, the poor old sexton would have been sorely put to it for room. But they did not appear in the house of worship in full dress. They labored under the belief that He in whose special presence they gathered had no particular regard for fine dresses, and left it for modern worshipers to discover that He is pleased to assume the office of inspector of garments; for it is not allowable to say that any visit the sanctuary to be seen of men.

But to return to the occasion on which Mr. Turnbody met with the disaster that came so near extinguishing him.

One Saturday the sexton went out on a fishing excursion, and by some mishap, chargeable to wind or tide, was unable to get back in season for his Sunday morning duties. The hour had nearly arrived for the commencement of the services, and the bell had not yet sent its solemn summons abroad. Many had assembled and were waiting in wonder at the silence that reigned in the belfry. Mr. Turnbody was there; and after fidgeting about and several times going out to look up the street towards the sexton's house, he spat on his hands and boldly seized the rope, which, as just remarked, came down in the centre of the house, in view of the whole congregation. He gave one or two lusty tugs, and presently some glorious peals announced to the world without that there was a new acquisition within.

But Mr. Turnbody did not fully understand the art and mystery of scientific bell ringing, and had not been made aware of any danger. He neglected to let the rope properly slip, and before he realized any particular necessity for caution found himself half way up to the roof, still grasping the rope as tightly as if his life depended on the tenacity. He gave a terrific shriek. But in a moment, the reversal of the motion of the wheel brought him down to the floor again with such violence that it is astonishing that half the bones in his body were not broken. He lay gasping. Men and women rushed to his assistance.

He was presently restored to consciousness, and to the great relief of all found to be but little hurt. A vacation of two weeks was sufficient to restore him.

We cannot help thinking that Mr. Turnbody's ascent afforded about as ludicrous a sight as was ever witnessed within the walls of the Old Tunnel. Up he went, like a fish fairly caught, his knees twitching towards his chin, and the broad tails of his light blue coat flaring out mischievously as if determined to bring into view sundry invidious rents in the unmentionable garment beneath, which was of brown velvet, and fitted so closely as to endanger the circulation. He did not, however, believe in what he termed the "devil drawn whimsey" of the circulation of the blood, which Harvey had many years before made known, and which he and a certain traveling doctor had disputed about, all the way, at the funeral of Obadiah Turner.

At school, master Turnbody was fond of awarding to this and that pupil, imagined to possess a resemblance in character, the name of some personage of historical renown. And he was accustomed to frequently remind them of the virtues they should imitate and the vices they should shun, as developed in their prototypes. He had a Socrates, a Mark Anthony, and a Cromwell; a Xantippe, a Cleopatra, and a Mary Stuart. And it would have surprised him, had he been permitted to live as long as they, to have seen how strangely, as trees, they departed from their supposed bent as twigs. He would have seen his Socrates in the stocks for stealing Mark Anthony's chickens. Cromwell he would have beheld a love-cracked pauper. In the slattern wife of a wood-chopper he would have discovered his Cleopatra. And as to his Xantippe, he would have found her a pious, and sympathising nurse of the sick, renowned for her patience and kindness. But notwithstanding all these, he was quite as good a prophet as people usually are who attempt to discover the adult in the child. And it should be remembered that in his day the glorious light of phrenology had not been shed abroad.

At the time Mr. Turnbody taught here, and for more than a hundred years afterward, the people spent money grudgingly for the outward appliances of education. The school-houses were mean and inconvenient; the benches rough and uncomfortable; and too often the floors were damp and filthy. Brooms could not be afforded, though a couple of quarts of rum would have bought, of some strolling Indian, enough of those made of stripped birch, to serve for a whole year. Once or twice a month, however, the scholars were despatched to the woods for hemlock boughs wherewith to sweep. And these expeditions were occasions of rare fun to the boys, though tearing through the briars and shinning up the rough trunks were death to their linsey-woolseys. And when they marched home with their woodland spoils it surely appeared as if great Birnam wood had again started for Dunsinane, but mistaking the road had arrived at Lynn.

The venerable Ezekiel Oldpath was a teacher here for some years onward from 1691. His bald head was conspicuous every Sabbath, near the northwest corner of the Old Tunnel. He was well qualified for the duties of teacher, both by education and natural temper. And he had taught in Boston, at intervals, for some twenty five years, during the earlier part of his life. At other intervals he had been agent for fishing companies, attended to surveying, acted as scrivener, and so forth. His first appearance in Lynn was in the capacity of surveyor. And he was so charmed with the place that he determined to take up his residence within her borders.

Master Oldpath's sterling sense placed him above most of the prejudices and jealousies of the times, and his urbanity and prudence had an excellent influence on the restless spirits around him.

He was one of the most active and judicious in operating against the hallucinations and villanies of the witchcraft eruption of 1692; and to his exertion, in a great degree is to be attributed the fact that it prevailed to a small extent within these precincts, while neighboring places were absolutely distracted. He warmly controverted the views of Chief Justice Stoughton in a correspondence with that dignitary. And in concert with the wise Saltonstall he rendered essential service in saving innocent lives. President Mather and his redoubtable son Cotton came out several times to confer with him and endeavor to induce him to look at the mysterious matters through their spectacles. But they found him as immovable as the everlasting rock under the lee of which his modest habitation nestled.

There stood his little school-house, exposed to the rough kisses of the cutting wind as it swept down from the northern hills, forming a central point for the eddying snows to dance about. The shivering little ones came gathering from miles around, and eagerly snatching their motley caps from their heads, unveiled their purple faces to meet the ruddy glow upon the hearth. Then would the good man lay aside the wonted dignity and distance of the school-room, to assist in restoring the benumbed limbs, ere he called his little subjects to duty. And the duties of the day, in his school, always commenced with the Lord's Prayer, repeated in concert. Then followed the reading of the Litany, every pupil audibly joining in the responses, or the Psalter, in its daily order. True, this did not well please some of the more rigid anti-churchmen. He was labored with on the subject, but declared that though himself no churchman, he yet would not dispense with those exercises so long as he taught; for he deemed their influence of more value to the young mind than all the other exercises put together. He never did yield, and on his death bed recommended a continuance of the custom. And we do not believe that the school would have been damaged had it been continued even to this day of worldly wisdom.

Master Oldpath took great pains, while lecturing his pupils, to impress upon their minds such things as would prove most useful in life. He had a respectable class in surveying, and on many a pleasant afternoon did he lead them forth, if not to show how fields were won, to show how they were surveyed. But above all, he labored assiduously to instill into their minds the great principles of moral rectitude and living piety.

As a naturalist, Master Oldpath was famed throughout the colony. In his surveying expeditions he had good opportunity to indulge in his loved studies and to collect specimens. And a capacious unfinished room in his house contained a really valuable museum. The great Linnæus was not then born. But Ezekiel was able, by his own experience and the assistance of a few others, to perfect a system of botanical classification, quite ingenious and easy of application. And it is a matter of much regret that the many useful facts he collected regarding the natural history of this region have not been handed down to us through the medium of more perfect records. Printing was not so common and cheap then as it now is. The art preservative is a blessed art, though not very discriminating; for while it preserves one page of value, it preserves forty that had better pass into oblivion.

It was always pleasing to Master Oldpath to have his neighbors and fellow-townsmen, as well as strangers from abroad, examine his collection. And many a pleasant impromptu lecture did he give to the parties who took him by surprise as he sat in his curiosity room, arrayed in his calico gown, velvet slippers and little black skull-cap. And often of a moonlight evening has the timid knock of youth summoned him to the agreeable office of entertaining lovers who had strolled up the balmy lane perhaps with a bouquet or curious pebble, brought as a simple propitiatory offering; and his blessing was sure to go with them as they turned upon their homeward path unseen among the whispering trees to kiss and talk of love.

The brilliant skies and balmy breezes often called Mr. Oldpath forth upon long pleasure excursions to the forest or seashore, though he usually took his surveying implements with him, as if in compromise with a practical conscience. And he made many observations and determined many facts, useful and curious. It may be mentioned that he appears to have been the first to remark that the gorgeous coloring of our forests in autumn is not produced by frosts, but by the ripening of the foliage. And it is remarkable that many, even at this day, remain ignorant of the fact. Observation shows that trees do not change color all at one time any more than fruits all ripen at one time.

The white birch and swamp maple, for instance, often put on their beautiful yellow and scarlet, in August; and even, to a small extent, in a dry, warm season, as early as July. Irving, Bryant and others of the most charming American writers, would not have adopted the error and assisted so much to fix it in the popular mind had they been as observant of such things as Master Oldpath.

Soon after the ripening of the foliage the heavy frosts come. These loosen the leaves and they soon fall. Then, if we have it at all, comes the Indian summer. That lovely interval afforded a study of peculiar interest to Mr. Oldpath. It was as difficult for him to keep within doors during the half dozen days of its continuance, as for an astronomer to remain housed during an eclipse. He long endeavored to ascertain the natural causes of such a delectable elemental condition. But he was unsuccessful, and frankly acknowledged that the red man's explanation was as reasonable as any he could give; namely, that it was a period when a breath from the hunting grounds of heaven was permitted to sweep down to earth. Nor has any more rational explanation been given, to this day.

Master Oldpath died with the scholastic harness on. He was suddenly seized by the grip of the fell destroyer while on his way from school, of a summer noon, and after a painful struggle of forty hours yielded up his breath. His last flickering thought seemed to be of the precious little souls under his charge. And his last words were: "Come, come my children we must prepare to hasten home apace. How suddenly doth night come upon us. Let us pray."

Mr. Shepard preached a long funeral discourse over

his remains, containing many stately periods and much sound doctrine. His text was: I. Kings, iv. 33: "And he spake of trees, from the cedar tree that is in Lebanon, even unto the hyssop that springeth out of the wall; he spake also of beasts, and of fowl, and of creeping things, and of fishes."

Many learned and good people from abroad came to his funeral. And the Old Tunnel bell never sounded in more mournful notes than while they were bearing him to his final resting place in the Old Burying Ground.

It is refreshing to dwell on a character like that of Master Oldpath; so unselfish, and so serene amid the agitations and conflicts of the restless world. And from a walk like his most useful lessons may be drawn. We may perceive that better and surer paths to happiness exist than those which end in the vanity fair of wealth. The meanest creature of earth, air or sea, was an object of interest to him. The noble oak upon the hill top and the lowly fern in the vale afforded him hours of pleasant study. The modest violet and creeping moss which were heedlessly trodden under foot by other men were to him more beautiful than the most luxurious carpet of man's fashioning. With a holy satisfaction did he contemplate all the works of nature, discerning the hand of the great Original as well in the whirling thunder storm that ravished the landscape as in the serenity of a summer twilight.

It is unquestionably true that many of the teachers of the first sons and daughters of our favored land were profoundly learned. And it is also true that they kept constantly in view a more exalted object than is common with teachers at this day. In that less complicated condition of society comparatively little of the diffusive kind of education, if it may be so termed, could be brought into action. The ordinary business transactions were simple, and that active curiosity which now leads so many to endeavor to pry into the mysteries of every conceivable department of knowledge, without any definite object in view, was not deemed so worthy of encouragement as efforts of a more practical nature.

Many of the first teachers, as before remarked, were of the clergy. And no one requires to be informed of the fact that they were a learned race. A high toned classic coloring often pervaded their discourses; and the fancied dignity imparted by the scholastic displays, in writing and in speech, would now appear as bordering on the ludicrous. And the English hierarchy, being able to withstand their valorous assaults with the ponderous artillery of Latin, Greek, and Hebrew, may well have continued to claim invulnerability. And again, being of the most rigid order, they naturally inclined to look anxiously to the spiritual condition of those under their charge. And this was sanctioned and urged by the universal temper of the community. So long as those elementary principles which would be required in the ordinary transactions of life were firmly fixed in the mind, mere intellectual attainment was regarded as of secondary importance. There were but few books and proportionately little book study. A comparatively large number, were, however, put to the study of Latin, and without the aid of English grammars, obtained a good knowledge of their own tongue. Latin was, at that period, an almost necessary study to all who would make any pretension to learning. Not only were phrases in that language common in books on almost every subject, and interspersed in the legal forms, but the Sunday sermons were enriched by them.

Some are inclined to imagine, in view of the limited variety of school books then in use, that but little was taught. But the fact is that the accomplished and industrious teachers were a sort of embodiment of classic and scientific knowledge, and through the engaging and effective medium of familiar lectures and conversations, imparted, in history, geography, and the natural sciences, instruction to as great an extent as was demanded or deemed expedient.

But, as remarked, the early teachers kept in view a more exalted object than is in our day required, expected, or perhaps we may even say desired, of common school teachers. It was with them but a small part of duty, to fit those under their charge, to be merely successful members of society; to qualify them for the mere business of life, or to pass through life with the mere characteristics of intelligence. Their better efforts were directed to the nobler purpose of firmly planting in the virgin soil of the uncorrupted heart, a vigorous growth of those exalted virtues which would bring forth the fruits of sterling principle and unswerving integrity; so that when the youth went forth into the world, every act, whether in business, politics, or any other department of the social economy, might rest on the sanctified basis of truth and justice. And was it not this, that made the institutions they planted so enduring? Was it not this that imparted to them that solid, immutable character which has enabled them to withstand all the conflicts that have from time to time agitated society, and which have turned other, and at times more prosperous institutions, upside down?

And what was the reward claimed by those faithful old teachers for thus training the first children that made merry these streets? The annual stipend of a few pounds currency or perhaps a few measures of grain or a few pounds of meat from each family. But could that have been called a reward? Most certainly not. It was but the means of sustaining life. Their reward was of a far more exalted and enduring kind.

We find the somewhat eccentric Doctor Jotham Tyndale a worshiper at the Old Tunnel during the last ten years of the seventeenth century. He sat near the centre of the house.

In stature, Dr. Tyndale was singularly diminutive, being hardly five feet high, and by no means corpulent. And his physiognomy was such as a stranger would at once determine belonged to one remarkable for something, though he might be puzzled to say what. His chin was bony and tapering, his nose long, sharp, and a little hooked. There was a redundancy of ivory in his mouth, and his lips were very accommodating for the display of the same.

In personal descriptions it is always expected that the forehead shall come under notice, because it has been ascertained — by the gas light of phrenology, we believe — that the higher faculties reside there. But here we are at fault; for the Doctor's hair had such a propensity to retreat upward, and the plain from the brow to the crown was so regularly inclined, that it was impossible to determine where the frontal territory ended and the summit level began. And besides, his hair was always strained back to such a degree that one would have supposed it difficult for him to shut his eyes, and there bound into a cue, by an eel skin. And this cue was a distinguishing feature, one in which he took an almost childish pride, and one which finally came near being the death of him; such a judgment often overtaking the worshiper of an idol. The appendage projected almost horizontally and was knotted at the end in most picturesque style.

We are aware that cues, wigs, hair powders, and so forth, were not much in vogue at that time, but there are always some whose genius travels ahead of their age. And Dr. Tyndale possessed a rampant genius. Such things, however, were known at that period. Hair powders were used in England a hundred years before, by the opera singers. And we read that wigs of all colors were in use in the good old days of Queen Bess. We also catch glimpses of cues all along from the period of the Reformation; to say nothing of the old painting in which St. Peter figures with one. Yet it appears that the greatest enormities of the kind did not have their turn till Queen Anne's time.

Dr. Tyndale appeared a little vain in the matter of dress. He wore yellow breeches tied at the knees by tasty red ribbons, and a bob-tailed green coat, which he always kept buttoned so tightly that the loops broke out in rebellion against the strain put upon them. An enormous white collar fell over the green one of his coat, resembling an ancient lady's vandyke. Long scarlet stockings and leather shoes, with the toes turned up like skate-irons, and kept well black-balled, adorned his nether extremities. And jauntily upon his head sat a round topped hat, with which the sportive winds were continually playing pranks.

As to the parentage of Dr. Tyndale we are able to state very little. Whether he could trace his genealogy in a direct line to William Tyndale the celebrated reformer and martyr who had the honor of producing the first English version of the New Testament, we do not know, but presume he could; for any one can trace his pedigree to just about the point he desires. The pretty family trees that we sometimes see modestly fruiting in parlors prove this. But we do not mean to insinuate that the Doctor ever undertook to so trace his lineage; probably he did not; for doctors, as all know, are remarkable for their modesty.

Many people seem to think that all who go through the same course of study must turn out equal in scholarship. And judging Dr. Tyndale by this rule he was very learned for he went through, at Harvard college, the same course with the most eminent men in the colony. But judging by a rule that takes capacity into account, we might be forced to a different conclusion regarding his accomplishments. We do not mean, however, to intimate that he was not worthy of high respect; for though not among the most prominent in his profession, he was yet above the average.

The Doctor was very active, traveling hither and thither on his errands of mercy with great rapidity, sometimes on horseback with saddle-bags of medicines, and sometimes on foot with a knapsack of the same strapped to his back. His practice was extensive, at least so far as territory was concerned, and various. He was, of course, both surgeon and physician. And he even turned his hand to farriery when occasion required, though in this latter branch he had so many rivals among the farmers who were ambitious to be ranked as professional men, that he could not shine with any great brilliancy.

Few of Dr. Tyndale's patients had reason to complain of his neglecting them. Indeed what physician can be charged with neglecting patients; at least those of the paying class? Sympathy for those in affliction, if not a positive sense of duty, prompted him to more than ordinary care and attention. He had a feeling heart, soothing manners, and a high appreciation of fees. His medicines were prescribed in large quantities, as was the custom of the times. And by his good nature and pleasant talkativeness, he did much to keep the spirits up while the drugs went down. He trotted the sick children on his knee, and told them pretty stories of good boys and girls who loved to take the sweet medicines that he brought. And the older folk gulped down rivulets of his nauseous concoctions, made palatable by an infusion of what is metaphorically a product of the good wife's leach tub. None had a happier way of flattering than he, and none had a higher appreciation of its effects.

One of the most remarkable cures ever effected in the human system occurred in the practice of Dr. Tyndale; and by omitting an account of it we should leave even this brief notice greatly defective.

Aaron Rhodes lay very sick of a painful disease, the nature of which does not precisely appear, though from the accounts we judge it to have been some sort of a bronchial abscess. It had rapidly enlarged and there was imminent danger of suffocation. The Doctor perceived that unless the internal gathering were speedily broken death must ensue. But how to break it was a question that all his ingenuity could not solve. The crisis was fast approaching, and the worthy man was very greatly exercised not only in regard to his professional reputation, for it really seemed as if there were no imperative necessity for the man's dying, but also from grateful esteem for the patient, who had befriended him in various ways. He was constant in his attendance, and manifested his anxiety, now by gazing down the afflicted throat; now by walking the floor at a nervous pace, with his head down and his cue pointing up and shivering under his agitation; and then by pausing to rub and press the patient externally, in the neighborhood of the gathering. But all his efforts seemed incompetent to avert a fatal termination.

Late on a Sunday evening, we find the sick chamber presenting this tableau: The sufferer lies upon the bed, with an uneasy struggling for breath. The Doctor sits in an arm chair, before the fire, with his legs stretched out and affectionately crossed. His beloved cue projects back, over the little table that stands behind his chair, with its array of medicine cups and phials forming a body-guard to the tallow candle, the radiance of which would be greatly augmented by the friendly offices of the snuffers that glisten in their little lackered tray upon the mantle. The prim nurse sits nodding on one side of the fire, and upon the other, curled on the cushion of the easy chair, reposes the gray house cat, occasionally arousing for a moment to gape and stretch and then returning to her sleep. Almost perfect silence reigns. There is no wind without, and the fire does not crackle, for the Rhodes family burn peat. The hard breathing of the patient alone is heard. The Doctor himself soon begins to feel drowsy and nod. And nod follows nod in accelerated succession. Finally, there comes one backward bow, so forcible as to bob the end of the cue directly into the flame of the candle. And thereupon, O horror and mystery, there comes such a terrific explosion as almost shakes his little head from his shoulders. The darling cue is blown all to pieces and sent flying in singed tufts into every corner of the room.

The Doctor bounded across the chamber with the agility of a shot kangaroo, his elbow dashing through the window and his head bending the metal sash. Then he skipped up and down, shrieking and with his hands working his head every way as if endeavoring to be sure that it were still in the place where it grew. The nurse and cat, by a process that neither of them attempted to explain found themselves in a safe position beneath the bed.

But how fared the sick man? He had eminent cause to rejoice under the fulfillment of the good old aphorism that every wind blows good to some one. How shall we express our joy for him? When the strange explosion took place, he happened to be lying with his eyes fixed upon the fated cue as it curiously bobbed back and forth, seemingly at some tantalizing game with the candle. And it appeared to him, as he lay there watching, so much as if the candle when it got a chance to retaliate for some teasing movement of the cue, had given a snap that resulted in more than it intended, that he could not restrain a burst of immoderate laughter. And that laughter saved his life. And many a hearty laugh, before and since, has done as much good. It broke the abscess; and after a little strangling from the escaping contents, he was relieved and at once beyond danger. And he continued to moderately indulge in the healthful exercise till his complete recovery; and indeed to the end of his life, whenever the scene of that night came to mind; the Doctor himself not refusing occasionally to join in his cachinnation, as they talked the matter over. These occasions, however, were liable to end in sadness, for the Doctor's hand would instinctively stray to the barren waste where once flourished the object of his idolatry whose loss had been mourned over with a bitterness not exceeded in intensity by any dispensation from his saddle-bags.

But the cause of the destructive explosion was a profound and alarming mystery for some time. There seemed no possible way to account for it. If it should prove that the Doctor's head were something like a charged bomb-shell and liable to explode at any time, it would be dangerous to have him about. But still there was no authority for his restraint. People, however, immediately began to appear shy of meeting him, and some of his patients forthwith sent word that they felt so much better that he need not come again till sent for. And the calls for his errands of mercy and profit became alarmingly infrequent.

The extraordinary occurrence was of course soon known far and near. And it was interesting to listen to the many theories that were propounded in elucidation. The one suggested by Mr. Shepard seemed the most scientific, proceeding on the supposition that thunder and lightning might exist in the human head, in a dormant condition. And indeed it must be a stupid head that has not some electricity in it. But people were not then so scientific as they now are, for Franklin was not born. Had they possessed the knowledge that soon after electrified the world it is not unlikely that they would have insisted, for the security of human life, that Dr. Tyndale should wear a lightning rod down his back.

But the mystery was finally solved. The Doctor and his good wife were one evening sitting at the supper table, partaking of their frugal meal and pleasantly talking over the events of the day. Presently something recalled with special force to their minds that unexplained catastrophe the memory of which had continued to hang like a dead weight upon them. All of a sudden the Dame dropped her spoon, which was just then drawing near to her mouth, laden with luscious pau-pie. Her eyes protruded, her countenance assumed a strange expression, and she began to struggle in the attempt to articulate something. The Doctor sprang towards her, thinking that she was choked. But she soon recovered herself and pushing him aside told him to sit down and she would unburden herself. The good man had before experienced what she was pleased to call unburdening herself and did not anticipate much comfort. Nevertheless, he meekly seated himself with open ears.

Dame Tyndale now began by asking the Doctor if he did not remember bidding her, while she was dressing his cue, on the fatal day, to give it a good powdering. He replied that he did so bid her, for he expected to go to Boston to a doctors' meeting. She then looked him straight in the eye for something like two minutes. Her gaze was reciprocated. And it would have rejoiced any philosopher to observe the dawn and radiation of intelligence as they appeared on those serene countenances, marking as they did, with great strength and beauty, the distinctions between man and the graven image. The talismanic word powder had power to explode the whole mystery.

The worthy Dame had never before that day powdered the Doctor's cue, and when called to the duty had no conception that the dredging-box instead of the powder-horn should be resorted to for material. In her simplicity she had managed to work into the cue such a quantity of gunpowder as would have probably blown his head to atoms had not a considerable portion worked itself out during the day.

Through that comical agency, however, the cure of Mr. Rhodes was effected. And had Dr. Tyndale possessed the sagacity of some of the profession, without their honesty, he would probably have taken advantage of the accident, and insisted that the whole was a plan of his own to effect the cure. In that case he might have been canonized for his wit if not for his skill.

Those accustomed to worship in our modern sanctuaries, with richly carpeted floors and cushioned seats, can hardly form a just conception of the discomforts, as they would appear to be, to which the worshipers in the Old Tunnel were exposed. Bare floors below and bare rafters above met the gaze of those who assembled there. The wild winds of winter whistled and squealed at the rattling windows, and often succeeded in the mischievous enterprise of powdering the worshipers' heads with snow. Within, there was no fire to set at naught their chilling effects; and warm must have been the hearts that could keep beating through the long drawn discourses. The heavy galleries hung gloomily upon three sides; and the cheerful sun found it hard work to illuminate much of the hallowed space.

Above the lofty pulpit hung the ponderous sounding board, capacious enough to concentrate the vocal eccentricities of the most airy rhetorician; and on which, as Amy Martin declared from information derived from the old lame man who carried the book with blood-red leaves, the witches held an adjourned meeting during a dreadfully tempestuous night in the ever memorable year 1692, they being driven from the swamp in which their meetings were usually held, by a great overflow of water. Considerable alarm was excited by this information, coming through so authentic a channel. Diligent inquiry and search took place. But the most certain evidence of the sacrilege having been committed consisted in sundry small indentations apparently burned into the edge of the board. These were thought to have been made by the fingers of the witches as they were clambering up. But Master Oldpath succeeded in convincing the most considerate that they were produced by the sexton, who the year before undertook to destroy a colony of wasps that had taken up their quarters in a crevice above, with a blazing pine knot attached to a pole; through which cruel act he came near burning down the house itself.

And by this incident we are reminded to present a few facts connected with the great Witchcraft outbreak. Take whatever view we may of the strange excitements of that memorable year — 1692 — they cannot be regarded by the reflective mind in any other light than as extraordinary and eminently suggestive.

Upon a gloomy Sunday afternoon in the year just named, the Old Tunnel worshipers were meekly listening to one of Mr. Shepard's elaborate discourses, when, as he was just arriving at the "improvement," the whole congregation were startled by furious exclamations from a girl named Nanny Sealand.

"Whist! whist! whew!" she exclaimed, jumping upon the seat and throwing her arms about in a violent manner; "Whist! dost not see upon the window by the pulpit the shadow of Goody Bassett, beckoning to Nabby Collins, in the corner there? And dost not see the book she hath, with blood-red leaves and black boards?"

At this, Nabby Collins, who was an ignorant, nervous girl of some seventeen winters, sprang up, shaking and twitching as if an earthquake and a whirlwind were experimenting on her, both at the same time, and wildly snapped out:

"Ay, ay, at the dogwood swamp it is! There's the meeting. You told me so before. O, I'll be there. Red bread to eat and red drink! Devil's sacrament! I'll be there, when the black dog comes to show the way. He'll scratch at the back door and howl on the stepping-stone. O, whist, whist, minister! You've said enow, and lost your text! See there, see there! a black cat sits on the beam above, nursing a red-winged mouse. O, stop, minister!"

And by the time she had uttered her incoherent exclamations her excitement had become frightful, and she fell down in a spasm. Presently recovering, she trotted, on all fours, with great speed, toward the door. But those about her having by this time in some degree regained their self-possession, restrained her from making her way out.

"Great God preserve us," ejaculated Mr. Shepard, "from witchcrafts and other of the Devil's doings! It verily seemeth that the vitals of God's people hereabout are straightway to be torn out by satanic claws!" And he uttered a heavy groan, piteously expressive of deep apprehension.

Without the "improvement," the services were brought to a close. And most of the people lingered about the doors for some time, with gloomy countenances, discussing the prognostics of the approaching storm. But Master Oldpath was there and endeavored his utmost to suggest to the minds of those about him such common sense views as might do something towards turning the tide of the excitement that he knew must ensue. Perceiving Mr. Shepard's great perplexity he urged him to at least do nothing to increase the apprehension that the Devil was about to commence a desperate foray upon this happy Israel. "For," said he, "if these in truth be the Devil's doings, God's people will best show themselves by not owning that he hath such power. If pious folk come to think that they may at any time be snatched from God's hand by the Devil, it might seem that the Devil hath the strongest arm. But for my part, I do not believe that Satan hath much to do in these matters. They come by frenzy of mind and roguery." And the sensible old man said many things to the distressed crowd, calculated to allay their fears. That very evening, too, he visited the afflicted girls and gave much wholesome advice to those who had them in charge.

Perhaps a few of the older persons now living, may remember having in their boyhood seen, firmly nailed to the northwest corner-board of the Old Tunnel, as high up as the gallery window, a clumsy horseshoe. It was almost as conspicuous as is the revolutionary cannon ball that still so uniquely adorns the front of Brattle street meeting house in Boston. That horseshoe was said to have been nailed there by the sexton — whether at the instance of the watchful Shepard it does not appear — some time during the week succeeding the events just detailed. And it remained for more than a hundred years. The reader cannot be ignorant of the fact that horseshoes were early discovered to possess the power of keeping witches and other evil spirits at bay. In this age of conceited wisdom, however, they have rather fallen into disuse for that purpose.

As may well be supposed, the excitement spread and things soon began to wear a threatening aspect. No time was to be lost in parleying, and Mr. Oldpath, with a couple of others of like way of thinking, formed themselves into a kind of examining and advisory committee, assuming the duty of inquiring into alleged cases of witchcraft as they might occur, expressing opinions of them and giving advice. They had not, of course, any power or inclination to interfere with the jurisdiction of the courts, nor indeed to act in any manner on formal complaints. But by judicious management in their circumscribed sphere, great good was accomplished; calamities and distresses of divers kinds were averted, and no doubt innocent lives saved.

Some strange cases came before them.

Jediah Breed, a drinking, but otherwise fair sort of a laboring man, stated that on the Friday evening before, he was seated in Rachel Moulton's back room, about dusk; that he had been hard at work during the day, cutting and splitting wood and was now resting and waiting for his supper. While he was thus waiting, and Rachel was frying the meat, there came down the chimney what appeared to be a very large squirrel, having a head like that of a monkey. The animal sat himself on the edge of the frying-pan, and seizing a piece of meat, began to eat it, apparently with the most ravenous appetite, regardless of its fiery heat or the flames around him. The astonished chopper very much wondered at what he saw, not only because of the animal's power to endure heat, but also because squirrels were never known to take such food. Rachel took no notice of the intruder, though she stood by the fire. And upon his expressing astonishment at her blindness, she declared that there was nothing there and that no meat was missing; that four pieces were put in, and four remained.

Jeddy told the committee, when they came to examine upon the point, that he greatly wondered at Rachel's denying that she saw the animal, for he was at that very moment before her eyes; and he could, moreover, hear his teeth snap as he bit the meat. But he did not count the pieces remaining in the pan; nor did he know how many were put in at first.

He further stated that as Rachel was spreading the dishes on the table the animal leaped upon her shoulder, and he, being greatly terrified, seized a birch stick that lay at hand and endeavored to give the intruder a smart blow. But he was too quick for him and dodged he knew not whither. And he saw him no more. But Rachel was greatly offended, declaring that she saw no squirrel nor felt anything but the blow, which she deemed insulting, and such as none but a drunken man would inflict on a lone woman. It was not, however, till they were seated at the table that the conviction was forced upon him that Rachel was an entertainer of evil spirits. From the appearance of the upper portion of her dress he was convinced that the imp, having eaten his supper in the guise of a squirrel, had gone to rest in her bosom.

The good sense of Mr. Oldpath and his associates at once discovered that the wonders described by the besotted wood-chopper originated in a sudden attack of what is now known as a merry sort of delirium tremens. He was closely questioned regarding his recent drinking habits and obliged to own up to much that he would rather have concealed. Finally, Mr. Oldpath turned upon him with such a lecture as he was very glad to hear the conclusion of, and ended by advising him, with marked emphasis, to say no more about the affair, or he might get to the stocks for drunkenness and the whipping-post for assaulting Rachel.

And he prudently took the advice.

Ruth Chase, a young woman who lived with Eli Chadwell, witnessed some occurrences that came near producing very great excitement. The committee called on her to learn her story, and found her quite ready to communicate the facts on which her dreadful suspicion rested; which suspicion was that she had seen the veritable black man, the Devil himself. It was early on a Monday morning. She had jumped from her bed and drawn aside the window curtain, to determine the aspect of the weather, as it was the family washing day. The first object that caught her attention was a tall, muscular black man — though when closely questioned she would not affirm that he was black, as it occasionally seemed as if he wore a short black veil — coming out of the woods at a quick pace. He had on a long gray jacket with huge buttons, and ample breeches with eel-skin knots, as they appeared to be, at the knees. On his head was a three-cornered hat. She could not distinguish his feet, but an hour or two after went out and examined the ground and could find nothing but cloven tracks. These, however, she admitted, on a rigid cross-examination, might have been made by the cows as they came from pasture the night before, though they seemed more rounded than cow tracks. In his mouth was a long clay pipe, from which he now and then blew sparks, which flew about like little blue stars, convincing her that there was brimstone in the atmosphere. He had a bundle under his arm, done up in a red handkerchief. And from the shape of the bundle she thought it was a big book — the book of witch records. She had heard that the witches held a meeting the night before, it being Sunday, in the North Swamp, and supposed he had been there with the records. He went up by Mr. Tarbox's barn and struck three blows on the weather-board with his crooked walking stick. Presently Goodwife Tarbox came to the door, and they talked together for a few minutes. He then handed her something from the bundle, and disappeared. She verily believed that he gave her the book to sign, or some bread that was left at the witches' sacrament held in the swamp. In closing, Ruth reluctantly admitted that she had a little grudge against Dame Tarbox on account of a difficulty regarding a clothes-line.

During this recital, Mr. Oldpath himself seemed possessed in some unnatural way, insomuch that his associates began to fear that he was suddenly becoming a victim of the black art. He jerked round, and eyed the narrator with a most comical scrutiny. Then his eyes glistened, and he seemed much put to it to restrain a violent explosion of some kind or other.

But Ruth having ended, he sat quietly for a few moments as if ruminating on the remarkable affair. And then the explosion came, sure enough; it was terrific; but no damage was done as the element was laughter. The others, though they loved to see him in such a joyful exercise, could not join with him, for they did not know what he was laughing at. And they began to be more and more alarmed at the accumulating evidence that he was bewitched or getting beside himself in some way. At length he gained power to vociferate:

"Ruth Chase, if your eyes had been rightly open you would have seen no wonders. You ought to have known that it was me, yes, me, Ezekiel Oldpath, whom you took to be the Devil. Look, now, see if I may not pass current for a white man, and if my feet would make cloven tracks? look, look!" and up went an enormous hide-shodden foot to the table top. "On that morn I took my kine to pasture at an early hour, and did indulge myself with a pipe by the way. Seeing mushrooms plentiful I did gather some into my red handkerchief, and on my way home, spying Goodwife Tarbox in her doorway, gave her not only a pleasant morning salutation but some of the dainties. As to what you say about striking the barn I know nothing save that while near there I descried what I took to be a weazel and struck at him with my walking staff. One of the flaps of my hat got loose two or three times and fell forward in a way somewhat detrimental to my eyes; and you must have made the black veil out of that poor cloth."

It is easy to understand what the conclusion of that examination must have been.

Increase Carnes, a middle aged man who lived on the same street with Mr. Shepard — Petticoat Lane, as it was afterward called — and whose bushy head certainly did not contain an unusually large amount of sense, was sorely vexed, on several occasions, by unseen assailants. He was present at the meeting house at the time Nanny Sealand made her strange demonstrations, and was observed to exhibit considorable excitement. He started up from his seat in the western gallery, and after describing certain mystic figures, in the air, with his arms, violently thrust his hands into his pockets, and hastened out of meeting, grunting and groaning by the way.

The particular transactions which he detailed to Mr. Oldpath and his associates, took place at his shop. He was a shoemaker, and worked in a rough little structure that stood near the site of the present City Hall. On Tuesday evening he went to his work, after supper, as usual. It was very dark, and the sleet, driven by a northeast wind, was almost blinding. The first thing he did after entering the shop, was to grope round for his tinder-box and matches. And while doing so, he was several times startled by what he imagined to be whisperings and suppressed laughter. And he thought his fingers were now and then snapped at by sharp teeth. They were also badly pricked, as if awls had been thrust into them; and he showed several fresh wounds in confirmation of his statement.

Having found his tinder-box, he was much put to it to strike a light, for the tinder had become damp; whereat he much wondered, as it was carefully covered. However, he finally caught the faintest spark, which he was leaning over and carefully nursing with his breath, when a leather scrap, coming with great force, hit the box and overturned the whole into the shop tub. He was terribly frightened; but being encouraged by hearing the footsteps of some one passing the shop, and momentarily expecting a neighbor for a job of work which he had finished just before going to supper, he gathered courage to search for the tinder-box of a shopmate. This he found, and presently had his candle lighted, and a fire blazing in the little fireplace in the corner. But his wood was green and he could not induce it long to lend its virtuous aid in cheering up the dirty domain. He punched the hissing sticks, laid up the brands and blew upon them as well as he could through his almost toothless gums. But all to little purpose. In ten minutes the last spark seceded and the brave little tallow-dip was all that remained to war against the cold and darkness. He placed it in a wooden socket, and by his crane-like fixture swung it out in front of his seat, into a position to shed most light upon his work.

Having made these preparations, Carnes took off his jacket and sat down to work. He continued to hear occasional whispering and tittering, and began more and more to fear that some sort of witchcraft was brewing. Nevertheless, he determined to tough it out, at least till the expected neighbor called, for he had some pride in the matter, having been taunted as a coward. But he could not avoid peering about the shop, as well as he was able to by the aid of his dim light, as he now and then fancied that he heard rustling or squeaking noises. In the back part of the shop was a small space divided off by a barricade of fire-wood, a heap of scraps, and a couple of cider barrels. But he could not muster courage to venture an exploration in that suspicious territory. As he sat busily at work, however, his heart began gradually to revive. And hearing persons occasionally pass near the window, he finally gained such heart as to whistle a psalm tune and mentally bid defiance to the whole army of devils.

How long he remained in this comfortable state, whistling and working, it did not appear, but all of a sudden, a gust of wind, coming, as it appeared to him, from the roof, instantly extinguished his candle, and left him in total darkness. At the same time he heard a horrible scratching and scrambling about the cider barrels. And then he seemed verily to become the sport of a legion of merciless devils. The leather scraps flew about his head as if driven by a furious whirlwind, hitting him on every exposed part with a force that made him dance in agony. Then he was seized by the arms and shoulders and twitched about in a manner that almost forced his joints asunder, his unseen tormentors laughing all the while as if greatly enjoying the sport. He was so terrified that he had no power either to resist or make an outcry, and had but slight expectation of surviving the assault.

As a sort of closing operation, he was forced down again upon his seat, and there compelled to undergo a kind of rough shampooing. Paste and wax were worked into his hair, scraps crowded down his back, and, worst of all, dirty water from the shop tub was poured down his throat by the clam-shell full. There is, indeed, no knowing how the violence would have ended had not the expected neighbor arrived. The moment that the door latch was raised, his tormentors ceased their operations and disappeared.

The neighbor fortunately had a lantern. Carnes was found in a deplorable condition. But he was not cut or bruised. His hair and beard, however, were completely matted with wax and paste. Under repeated assurances that he was not wounded, and had only, from appearances, been the victim of some of the younger devils who were out on a frolic, he revived, and was soon able to go home, under convoy.

Early the next day, Carnes was for starting off in great haste to make formal complaint to the court against a decrepit old woman living on Nahant street, called Patty Allen, as being the witch who sent the evil spirits upon him. She had from some cause become obnoxious to her neighbors, and was almost friendless. Being of violent temper she was prodigal of threats, and during an altercation with Carnes, a day or two before, had warned him to look out for a shower of something, but of what, he could not understand, as she just then slammed the door in his face; but he thought it might have been a shower of scraps. At all events, such a shower had come, and he naturally connected the threat with the event.

Mr. Oldpath happened to fall in with Carnes just as he was starting on his errand to the judicial dignitaries, and was so struck by his appearance that he paused to ask what disaster he had met with. The poor fellow was bare-headed, though the morning was chilly, for he was afraid to put his hat on lest he should never get it off again; and his countenance wore a most rueful expression. Mr. Oldpath listened to his story, and finally convinced him that the better way would be for the committee first to investigate the matter, as thereby the witchcraft might perhaps the more surely be fixed upon the old woman.

No time was lost in getting the committee together, and the examination was held in the shop where the dark doings took place. Gideon Spinney, an aged man who resided in the neighborhood, hearing of what was going on, hastened to the shop, and found the three Solomons in great perplexity. The testimony had all been given in, and they saw no rational means by which to explain away the convictions of the recipient of the supposed satanic favors. But Mr. Spinney, as soon as he had got breath and attended to his nose, suggested that he was able to state some things that might throw light on the affair, and went on to say that the evening before, at about the time Carnes judged the assault to have taken place, he was passing along the road, and as he approached the shop saw a young rogue making his egress from the back window, followed by two others. Whether they observed him or not he was uncertain; but they immediately dodged over the stone wall. He was near to them at one time, but attempted no pursuit, knowing that they could easily outrun him. He however overheard one of them say, "By Jericho, ha' n't we had fun with the mouldy old coward. Let him jaw my lame mammy agin and call her a witch. If he does, there will be another shower of scraps, like as not, and mayhap thunder too. He 'll have to comb his old pate and wash his face now, if so be 't his monthly scrubbin' time ha' n't come round. I hope, though, we ha' n't hurt his old carcase much."

The ancient manuscript from which the foregoing is derived, is too much defaced at its conclusion to admit of being deciphered. But it can easily be imagined how the case terminated.

Mr. Oldpath and his associates continued on their way, examining into the alleged cases of witchcraft as they occurred in the neighborhood. And they found, at every step, so much that was explicable on natural principles, so much that was clearly the fruit of apprehensive and strongly imaginative minds, and so much that was chargeable to downright roguery, that they were more and more encouraged to proceed. And to their judicious action is perhaps to be attributed the freedom of the place from the grosser features of the "lively demonstrations of hell," as Mather called them.

It is thought that Mr. Oldpath had great influence in opening the eyes of Judge Sewall, as he visited him several times; and on the occasion of the general fast, made memorable as that on which the Judge stood in penitential attitude before the congregation at the Old South meeting house in Boston, while his expurgatory paper was read, no one pronounced a louder or more heart-felt amen than he.

The Mathers, and Chief Justice Stoughton found in our worthy townsman a resolute defender of the unfortunate, and soon learned the expediency of not unnecessarily coming in collision with him. But it would be unfair to assume that Mr. Oldpath was entirely exempt from the belief that such a thing as Witchcraft may have existed. That would be, as it were, to unchristianize him, considering the universal belief of the christian world at that period. Yet, whatever his belief may have been, it is certain that he was zealous in searching out the abominable cheats, and ceaseless in his efforts to allay the excitement. Nor would it be fair to assume that even a majority of the cases could be explained as easily as those we have given. Some seemed entirely inexplicable on any known principle. And it was a note-worthy remark of a late eminent jurist that had he been upon the bench he could not have avoided pressing a conviction on the evidence presented in several cases.

Many attempts have been made to designate a sufficient cause, aside from any thing supernatural, for this extraordinary outbreak, known, the world over, as the New England, or the Salem, Witchcraft — the Witchcraft of 1692. The peculiarly trying situation of the colonists, at the period immediately preceding, has been much dwelt upon, as having been influential in preparing the public mind for such an excitement. That certainly was a most dark period in our history. The broad land was still, to a great extent, overshadowed by the ancient forest. The Indians had been engaged in a desperate effort to rid the land of the pale faced intruders. And to their wily and ruthless warfare had been added French bravery and skill. That dreadful conflict known as Philip's war, commenced in 1675. The red men fought with a desperation that could only characterize the death struggles of a brave, proud nation; a nation which indeed passed away over blood-stained snows and amid the glare of blazing habitations. Six hundred of the flower of the colonial soldiery fell; six hundred dwellings were consumed. But the disasters of the "swamp fight," sealed the fate of the red men. There was no one left, worthy to bear the mantle of the heroic Philip. In 1690 the French and Indian war raged. And the ferocity of the leading parties was not mitigated by their mutual professions of being followers of the Prince of Peace. The political affairs of the colonists, too, had for a long time worn a gloomy aspect. The colonial charters were annulled in 1684. And in 1686, Sir Edmond Andros commenced his oppressive administration.

They were indeed trying times. And the poor colonists might almost have been justified in the imagination, that having been so long exposed to the rough usages of men, without being subdued, they were now to have some experience under the tender mercies of devils. But yet, viewing the matter in the serious light that it deserves, one would hardly think that political or warlike agitations had much to do with opening the way for such an excitement as Witchcraft; particularly as the occult shadow brooded over regions where such agitations were not known. It would, indeed, seem as if such disturbances in temporal affairs might have a tendency to divert the mind from those views of spiritual affairs that appear necessary to produce such an excitement. Our whole country is at this moment laboring under an agitation most terrific. The flag of secession is unfurled; the lurid clouds of civil war have burst; hundreds of thousands of those who one year since recognised each other as of the same happy brotherhood are now arrayed in opposing warlike ranks. A season of unspeakable peril and distress has suddenly overtaken the glorious Union formed under our common father, the sainted Washington. God alone knows what will follow this upheaving; but happy should we be if we could rationally fear no greater calamities than those of 1692. We are reminded of our remark on page 121, and must say that the ship has reached the breakers rather sooner than anticipated.

Does it not appear more likely that the "Delusion" had its origin in the favorite conceit of our ancestors that their shining piety had moved the evil one to make special efforts for their destruction?

Some intelligent minds, however, will contend that the Witchcraft manifestations, call them ultramundane or not, were such manifestations as may take place as strictly in accordance with some law as any event in the natural world. The law may be past finding out, but our ignorance cannot prevent its operation. The earth, in its progress in space, may pass through a region of meteors, astonishing and alarming the inhabitants. And so, they reason, may be the course in spiritual things;—at certain points spirits may be discerned, and their influence felt; and we may be called to experience many things, startling, wonderful and apparently supernatural, but yet the results of immutable hidden laws.

When the Witchcraft spell broke, the minds of the people underwent a reaction quite as remarkable as any thing connected with the strange affair. It is a sad subject, but presents features worthy of the grave consideration of christian and philosopher. In almost every age there is an eruption that astonishes and terrifies the world. But in not many cases are we forced to turn to the supernatural in forming an estimate regarding them, for men's passions and evil tendencies are sufficient. The progress toward these eruptions may often be traced. Sometimes it is slow, almost imperceptible; and sometimes it is like the raging of the prairie fire.

Glance, for instance, at the infidelity of France; watch the working of the sweet poison thrown into the body politic in the first half of the eighteenth century; see how like a subtile disease it fixes upon the vitals; how by cunning and varied appliances it ultimately reaches every class, circulates in every vein; and then, moulded by the ambitious for selfish and depraved ends, and urged on by calm, inflexible energy, like that of a Buffon or a Condillac; by allurements like those of a Rosseau or a Voltaire; by daring, ferocious impiety like that of a Diderot, see it burst forth in such a whirlwind as overwhelms with fierce destruction, peace on earth, trust and hope in heaven. Then were the sunny banks of the Loire made pestilent by the dissolving remains, and the waters made red and warm by the gushing blood of innocence. Then the ghosts of the betrayed and sacrificed wandered among the smouldering ruins of fallen temples and altars, and wept for desecrated household fanes. And this was just one century after the distractions in New England.

Was there not something quite as unaccountable and quite as horrible in the French Reign of Terror as in the New England Witchcraft? And are there not eminently useful lessons to be drawn from moral earthquakes such as these? By watching the gathering elements fearful dangers may often be averted.

—

In the third range from the pulpit, in the Old Tunnel, was the seat of the venerable Deacon Mudget. He was always seasonably at his post, though he lived nearly two miles distant. It was said — and greatly to his praise — that he was never known to close his eyes during the services, however protracted or soporific they might be. And he was noted for his determined opposition to everything wearing the semblance of indecorum within the sacred precincts. Indeed he seems to have been a sort of high church Puritan. It is the excellent trait just alluded to that we wish to illustrate, and shall at once proceed to relate an occurrence which in its time made considerable stir.

We have already had occasion in these pages to celebrate the proverbial peacefulness and good behavior of church choirs. But all rules admit of exceptions. And it would not be remarkable if once in a century or two, members of a choir should be betrayed into some slight exhibition of jealousy, ill-nature, or other small indiscretion.

The choir at the Old Tunnel had unwarily slidden into the reprehensible practice of taking sweetmeats and fruit to meeting, wherewith to regale themselves while resting from their arduous labors, secure, as they thought themselves to be, from the observation of those below, behind the gallery breastwork. But Deacon Mudget was not unapprised of their wrong-doings. And his massive mind was for one whole Saturday night, while watching with Aaron Rhodes, deeply exercised in devising means to remedy the evil. So lost was he, about midnight, in his reflections, that he stirred the sick man's dose with the snuffers instead of the spoon, and did not discover his error till the patient began to strangle with the greasy motes. But he finally hit upon a plan sure to attain his object.

Near the meeting house was a tree of delicious pippins, just then in their prime, on which the members of the choir had not unfrequently committed depredations. And as the Deacon went to meeting, the next day, he just balanced his pocket with one or two of the apples — the great good to be accomplished probably in his mind outweighing the small sin of the appropriation. With the fruit in his pocket he entered the house and took his seat among the singers. They were astonished to see him there though he was known to be a good singer. He was a little eccentric, they were well aware, but none doubted that he had come among them for a good purpose. Soon after the sermon commenced, however, they were taken all aback on seeing him draw a pippin from his pocket, pare, and begin to cut it into small slices, now and then, with unflickering gravity, bestowing a morsel upon his own expectant palate.

Presently he generously handed to all the others, pieces to satisfy their watering mouths. And thereupon every pair of jaws in the choir were in motion. But the first breath had hardly been drawn when it became difficult to draw another. The facial contortions on every side were extraordinary if not exactly picturesque. The poor singers writhed and rocked from side to side, their mouths frothing and their eyes rolling in fine frenzy. Every one but the Deacon was evidently suffering some horrible agony. He, good man, sat calm as a summer morning, champing his pippin, with eyes reverently directed pulpitward. Soon, however, the agony of the choristers reached such an unendurable pitch that they simultaneously started from their seats, hawking, spitting, strangling, retching, and, in more than one instance, even taking the step beyond.

The minister stopped short, and the whole meeting was in an uproar. If the witchcraft excitement had not subsided long before this, they would at once have concluded that the Devil had concocted the mischief. Finally, things reached such a pass that the Deacon felt himself called upon to explain. He came to the front of the gallery and with a sort of fugitive gravity playing upon his countenance, went on to say that he had long mourned over the undevotional habits of the singers, and to the end that he might renew their sense of duty, had procured a quantity of dragon root, which he had distributed among them leading them to suppose that it was apple. And he hoped that the lesson they had received would have the desired effect. Probably the reader knows what dragon root is. But if he does not, he may be informed that it is a root so intensely pungent, that, if gathered at a particular season and from a particular location, cayenne pepper is more soothing to the palate. The worthy Deacon had, with monstrous cunning, made the distribution in such a sleight-of-hand way that no one suspected his pious fraud.

The good man immediately left the company of the

P

singers, or even the sanctity of the place might not have saved him from broken bones. But the very ludicrousness of the thing had a tendency to restore some of the sufferers to good humor.

The matter seemed to pass off without such manifestations of resentment as might naturally have been expected. Nevertheless, it turned out that on a dark night, some time after, there was a great outcry in the road that passed by the house in which the leader of the choir lived. And by a strange coincidence, that very evening there happened to be assembled there all the female members of the choir; while, by another coincidence, quite as remarkable, all the male members happened to be absent.

When the outcry took place, as if by a single impulse, all the girls rushed to the windows. And instead of manifesting terror, as womankind ordinarily would, at what was evidently a most riotous proceeding, they vigorously clapped their hands and actually screamed with laughter.

The rioters had in their midst a venerable looking individual, mounted on a substantial cedar rail. He seemed very much frightened, expostulated, remonstrated and begged for quarter, in a voice greatly resembling that of Deacon Mudget.

Among the first pews set up in the Old Tunnel — for they were not all set up at the same time — was that of Henry Jetson. It was a little west of the centre of the house, well toward the pulpit, and quite convenient for his deaf mother. No pew was more constantly occupied or more attractive. It was handsomely fitted up in the style of the times. But the chief attraction was Nora Humphrey, a ward of Mr.

Jetson. Her beautiful face and tasty attire drew the attention of many worshipers; for at that time, the devotions of some were liable to be diverted, as they even now are, from the Invisible to the visible, especially when the latter appears in the shape of a beautiful woman.

Nora was not a native of Lynn; nor did she long reside here. She was from England; but had spent some years, before coming here, with relatives in Boston. She was of a good family and had been disciplined in all that rendered a young lady in those times accomplished. And as she possessed a mind that readily accommodated itself to life's vicissitudes and sought for happiness in every position, with a deep love for the beautiful and romantic in nature, she found her situation here especially congenial. We well remember hearing a virtuous grandam speak of her grandmother's relating how the bright-eyed, laughing girl, with rosy cheeks, and dark curling hair flowing from beneath her fashionably trimmed French bonnet, was accustomed to trip into the western door of the sacred edifice, by the side of the good Mr. Jetson. But we had always supposed that much fiction was woven with the traditions, till confirmation of their truth, in the main, was found among the old writings before alluded to, which furnish so much of the more local portion of this history..

It will not be wondered at that Nora soon possessed more than the friendship of youth of the other sex. Yes, it appears that in more than one bosom she had kindled a spark which a gracious smile would have roused to a flame.

Among the most devoted of her admirers was Charles Wilson, a youth of much promise. And he appeared to stand foremost in her regard. He was her companion in the evening walk, her gallant at the social gathering. And as months passed without any occurrence to disturb their close intimacy, it was considered by the village gossips as settled that the day was not distant when a union would take place.

As things were thus proceeding, Lucy Wilson, a twin and very dear sister of Charles, upon a pleasant evening unexpectedly called on Nora. She found her seated alone, near an open window, absorbed in the perusal of a letter.

Of the interview between these two young ladies, which proved so sad a prelude, we have found an account embodied in a letter written by Lucy herself to a female friend who appears to have been visiting in a distant part of the colony. And from this letter we extract as follows:

"Presently, as Nora perceived me, she sprang from her seat, and in a right merry tone bade me welcome, exclaiming, in joyful words, that she had good news; that the letter which she held in her hand had been brought by the Indian Runner who received it at the ship which had that morning arrived at Boston. She said that it was from her betrothed, and urged her to prepare speedily to depart for Old England, for he would presently come to America, and return with her as his bride to settle on his Lincolnshire estates.

"At this I was greatly astonished and disturbed, never having heard that she even had a lover any where abroad. But recovering myself, and fancying that she might be only essaying a merry jest, I did assure her that thus jesting was not seemly, and was little relished by brother Charles; for he had many times gravely chidden me for my foolish gayety with

William Tarbell. But she, observing my concern, assured me that she spake but the plain truth; that she indeed had been betrothed ever since she first came hither.

"A sense of the great disappointment that I saw was in store for my dear brother, falling heavily upon me, I replied, with emotion that I could not restrain, that if she indeed spake the truth, and were espoused to one away, her retrospect should be any thing but pleasant; for she had deceived my brother, deceived me, deceived us all.

"With sobs and strong protestations she declared her innocence of all intention to deceive. Thoughtless, she said she might have been, but not wicked. And she fell upon my bosom weeping as if her poor little heart would break. She begged that I would forgive her great error, which now arose like a dark mountain before her opening eyes. And she entreated me, in words bespeaking great agony, to intercede with Charles, that he also might forgive. And to God, she said, she would that night fervently pray for remission. My heart was stirred with pity, notwithstanding her grievous wrong; and I endeavored to speak words of comfort. She now clearly saw her error, she said, though while the favored recipient of his courtesies she had been involved, as it were, in a pleasant mist that soothed her soul and veiled her eyes. I was, indeed, cut to the very heart, and could only withdraw in silence, bestowing my last kiss upon her fair forehead. And on my way homeward I held sad communion with my own heavy heart, seeking for the best means by which to make known to my dear brother the sorrowful news."

Without making further extracts we may add that

the unpleasant facts soon became known to every village gossip. And the beautiful Nora was much censured. She, however, while suffering many painful hours, persisted in the declaration that she never intended to deceive. And no doubt it was so. Her offence proceeded from thoughtlessness.

The Indian Runner who had brought the letter from the ship, seemed in some mysterious way to consider himself implicated in the affair. He had been much attached to the Jetson family, particularly to Nora, who had received from his hand many a nosegay of rare forest flowers, and given him some coveted return from her store of trinkets. But this occurrence seemed to make a strange impression on him. He made several visits to a young laborer in the service of Mr. Jetson, whom he in true Indian style designated as Pitchy Sam, and held serious talks with him, in the wood yard or corn field. At the close of the last interview, he exclaimed with an energy of voice uncommon for an Indian:

"Ugh, ugh! Pitchy Sam! Me say she be wicked! she ought to die!"

A short time passed, and the youth to whom Nora was affianced arrived in Boston. It was soon arranged that the nuptials should be celebrated in that town, and that the wedded pair should take passage in a vessel presently to sail on her return voyage.

The day came that was to be the last of Nora's residence in Lynn. The night came that was to be the last whose shades would darken around her pillow in her loved rural retreat. She had taken an affectionate farewell of those friends who had for the last time come to pay their respects, and was now alone in her chamber. For one moment she buried her face in the vase of wild flowers upon her table, which had been tendered as the last gift of the Indian Runner, who had visited the house at nightfall. Then she knelt and offered up a fervent prayer, in which, we may be sure, the name of the heart-stricken Wilson was not forgotten. And then on her pillow she sought repose from her alternate feelings of happy anticipation of the future and involuntary pain for the past.

The morning sun, whose first rays were wont to awaken Nora, fell unheeded by her on her couch. Amazed that with a long journey and a great event in prospect, she had not risen as early as her accustomed hour, her friends entered the chamber. A swollen and lifeless form was all that remained of the bright and beautiful one whom they had so much loved. On her bosom lay the hideous coils of a venomous reptile, his fangs still piercing her inanimate cheek.

"She ought to die!" portentous words from Indian lips! The last request which the Indian Runner made of Nora was that he might be permitted, with his own hand, to place upon the table in her room the flowers he had brought, saying that with that delicate act a medicine man had connected a charm. Unsuspectingly, his request, though odd, was granted.

The people of Lynn never saw him after that fatal night.

The remains of Nora were deposited in the Old Burying Ground, not far from the southeasterly corner. There is no mark by which to distinguish the grave. The beautifully wrought stone, placed there by the sorrowing youth who had come to claim her as his bride, and which bore the single word "Nora," has long since disappeared; neither is there any swell in the ground, for time levels all things. For many years the summer verdure thereabout was trodden down, for it was a spot to which the village maid in her evening rambles would resort to drop a tear to the loved and beautiful; a tear to her whose verdant resting place has now been refreshed by the dews of more than a century and a half.

And a few paces southward from Nora's grave is the spot where was lain the weary head of Charles Wilson. The blighting of the affections of his warm heart, the clouding of his sunny hopes, soon brought him to a bed of sickness. And hardly had the white mantle of winter been spread upon her grave when he was released from all his earthly sorrows and conflicts.

The lesson involved in this brief relation should not be unheeded by the youth of either sex. The tender affections can seldom be trifled with in safety, notwithstanding all the scoffing and philosophizing of the cold of heart.

If it be unpardonable cruelty in a young man, when he becomes aware that the affections of a youthful being of the other sex, have, in the ever deepening ardor of the female temperament, been directed toward him as the object around which they would fondly entwine, feeling in his embrace a safeguard against the storms that sweep across the path of life — if it be unpardonable cruelty in him, we say, to encourage the more closely drawing of those tendrils, with the guilty design of ruthlessly sundering them, or with the perhaps equally reprehensible view to some undefinable present gratification — is it not also unpardonable cruelty in a case where the sexes stand in a reversed position?

Are there frigid worldlings who would sneer at occurrences like this, as if they resulted from some ignoble principle of our common nature? Go to, unsanctified ones! Are not you in love — some with sordid wealth, some with childish honors? And are your idols more worthy of true and holy love than the sentient and glowing images of your Maker?

Near one of the windows on the south side of the Old Tunnel, sat Dame Ramsdell, the light of her mildewed and strangely furrowed countenance, always, excepting by favor of a point blank front view, entirely hidden, if not literally under a bushel, certainly under a bonnet of such dimensions as to be quite competent to contain an equal measure. This bonnet was manufactured by her own industrious hand from rushes gathered in the meadows. And she was otherwise attired in an ample dress of tow cloth, the manufacture of the same industrious hand. A capacious pocket dangled by her side, often crammed with sweetmeats for good children and herbs and ointments for sick men and women. She had a formidable staff, on which she relied for support in her walks, and as a weapon of offence in punching giggling girls who made themselves merry over her infirmities and unfashionable appearance.

This worthy dame became eminent among women, for divers reasons. First, she had been the smartest spinner and weaver in the place. Her old wheel whistled, night and day, and the amount of raw material that came in at its whistling and went out in the shape of cloth, might have put to blush a Rhode Island water mill. Second, she was greatly skilled in the use of herbs. Her capacious garret was a vast depository of spoils from the fields and woods, and her very person was redolent of herby perfumes.

Third, she was the mother of more children than any dame who had lived in the place from the beginning of the settlement. These she found useful as safety valves for a naturally warm temper, as models on which to display her manufactures, and as subjects on which to experiment with her herby concoctions.

Again, she had bestowed on this appreciative community the inestimable gift of Zephaniah Ramsdell, who, before his third decade was passed had grown to be the pride of men and pet of women. Even in his very early days Zephaniah made such an appearance as indicated that he possessed a rare genius. When he accompanied his mother to meeting he was dressed exactly like a very old man, having a broad brimmed hat, breeches, with eel-skin knots at the knees, and enormous shoe buckles. Upon his nose, for his eyesight was a little imperfect, were mounted a pair of huge, round-glassed spectacles, which an ingenious neighbor had manufactured for him, by setting a couple of cheap burning-glasses in a leather frame, after grinding down their convexity and polishing them as well as he could.

By the time Zephaniah was a dozen years old, his genius was so developed as to excite a strong interest in the observant Dr. Tyndale. He insisted that there should not be, in this case, another of those mournful wastes of gifts so common in the community; that the youth should be put to study. And he offered his own services in directing the toddling feet toward that spring of which the poet advised to drink deep or taste not. The lad was soon persuaded to grapple manfully with the terrors of the Latin grammar. And such success attended his struggles that he was speedily prepared to knock with confidence for admission at the front door of blessed Harvard. He entered, and for some months sustained the virtuous pride of his mother by his rapid progress.

There are some things beside true love that never do run smooth; and Zephaniah was destined to become practically acquainted with the fact before his second collegiate year closed. He was one day sternly called to account, by the venerable president, for having taken a neighboring damsel on a sleigh ride. Not being able to give such an excuse for his breach of a salutary regulation as the worthy functionary could appreciate, he was forthwith ordered to lay aside his loose garments and prepare for a whipping such as would afford a fair offset for the enjoyment of his ride. Thus measured, he knew the punishment would be terrible. But he submissively disrobed, and endured the flagellation till he began to fear that his wounds would get beyond the restorative power of even his mother's most choice ointment. He then ventured, in a modest way, to remonstrate against any further infliction. But his remonstrance was as little heeded as if it had been directed to the plaster bust that adorned the shelf above their heads. The blows continued to fall thick and heavy. And there is no knowing to what the zeal for discipline might have led had not a desperate blow from the sledge-like fist of the now enraged Zephaniah knocked the classic head of his superior through the window.

This indignity could not be atoned for. Zephaniah was expelled in disgrace, and trudged home on a cold winter night with his back burdened by academic chattels and his heart burdened by regrets and embryo plans. He sat himself down again in his quiet home, and assisted his mother in her multifarious occupations; became a little misanthropic and dreamy; took long, solitary walks in the woods and on the sea-shore; wrote poetry, of course; and, in short, pursued the same track that a genius usually does under such difficulties. We have come across a number of poetic scraps apparently from his pen; and must say that in our poor judgment his proud mother was not far from right in her declaration that he was an "oncommon rhymer." We have a suspicion that the motto in our title-page was composed by him, as well as such of the other mottos as are in the same style.

Dr. Tyndale's interest in Zephaniah continued. He was pleased to often have him at his house. And it was finally arranged that he should enter as a student of medicine.

Zephaniah made commendable progress in his studies and became more and more a favorite with his patron.

One pleasant day a professional brother rode out from Watertown, to visit the Doctor, and brought his daughter, a blooming lass, with him. Zephaniah was invited over to sup with the strangers. And who, of all people on earth, should those strangers turn out to be, but the very girl who was his companion on that unfortunate sleigh ride, and her father. The two young folk were soon engaged in animated conversation and the tender hearted maiden gave all but tearful attention to the recital of the mishaps that had followed their contraband enjoyment. While expressing many regrets for the suffering he had endured she took occasion also to express much admiration of his bold spirit and heroic action in the dark hour of the flagellation. And in some mysterious way this interview proved initiatory to an intimacy that occasionally drew him to her father's house.

Whether the cunning Dr. Tyndale had any hand in managing the affair, we cannot ascertain; but are able to add that Zephaniah and Mary were presently affianced, and when he had concluded his studies, and Mary's father had completed arrangements for retiring from practice, they were married. The happy bridegroom entered at once into an extensive practice, beside having every present need supplied from the ample means of his generous father-in-law.

So, after all, the flagellation did not turn out to be so very disastrous an affair.

And herein is presented another instance in proof of what has been so often said — that few can discover in the boy, what the man will be. Few, indeed, have the discernment of a Tyndale. Zephaniah himself could not have foreseen his good fortune, even by the aid of those unique spectacles that formed such a dignified addition to his youthful visage.

It appears to have been rather a common thing, during a long period, for individuals to sketch down the Sunday sermons, or portions of them, as they were delivered. An expert had little difficulty in doing this, as the manner of delivery was usually very slow and the enunciation distinct. The manuscripts were then lent around among those who were too infirm or lazy to attend meeting, and thus became effective aids to the pulpit. Not that the preachers of those days did not have itching eyes to behold their brilliant thoughts in print — so different were they from the modest clerical brethren of this day — but printing was too expensive a luxury to be indulged in on any but extraordinary occasions. There were no parish or Sunday school libraries, and few books of religious instruction, in circulation; and the contents of those few were so familiar that these sermons possessed a delightful freshness.

Most of the specimens that we have discovered, have, however, proved more or less defective. And some are so purely doctrinal as to be of comparatively little interest. But from one, which we find in so neat and light a hand as to induce us to think it was written out by a female, perhaps after having been taken down by some one else in rougher style, we must be allowed to make a few extracts, as exhibiting something of their manner of imparting ghostly instruction, and also as affording aid to the reader in his pious reflections. We regret being unable to ascertain who preached this sermon. It certainly is not exactly in Mr. Shepard's vein, though it seems to have been delivered at the Old Tunnel during the early part of his pastorate. Joseph Whiting, a son of the beloved Samuel who so long ministered to the society, was settled as assistant to Mr. Shepard, some two years before the Old Tunnel was built, though the connection continued only a short time. And it seems to us that the style of this sermon much resembles his. But by whomsoever it was preached, few will deny the value of the godly hints that even these few extracts contain.

It should not be forgotten, however, that a great many of the sermons of those times were in a style very different from this. A good deal of the doctrinal preaching was harsh and repulsive; and the controversial, for the most part, exhibited a spirit very different from what modern worshipers would call meek and gentle. With the single remark that, considering the ancient mode of delivery, the discourse would probably have occupied full an hour and a half, we proceed to the extracts:

. . . . "Behold, how beautiful, in this delicious spring time, appear the blossoming trees. They stand forth arrayed in more than kingly robes. And great is the promise of a most generous bestowment of fruit in due season. But, alas, how often do the fairest promises fail. Yea, little indeed can we discern from the blossoming what the fruit will be. Without constant care and watchfulness, the insidious worm may early begin his deadly work. The fiery blight, the nipping frost, the parching drought, may come and blast the brightest hopes. And so is it with the fair promises of youth. Without constant care and watchfulness, the world, the flesh, and the Devil, by snares, allurements, and damnable artifices, may corrupt and destroy all that is beautiful and innocent. Therefore do I fervently exhort all to watch and pray. Watch against the stratagems of the old enemy; pray for godly purpose and strength."

. . . . "Ah, how many before me are wont to esteem themselves shining pitchers of silver in the tabernacle of the Lord, full of precious wine. But I declare unto you that in the sight of God ye are all lustreless pewter pots, battered and unseemly, full of unwholesome and bitter water."

. . . . "Praise is very pleasant to the human ear, and multitudes are so greedy therefor that they will even bestow it on themselves without stint. But one is enlisted in a far less worthy service while praising himself than while striving to do so well as to command the praise of others. By rightly directed efforts all may secure the sweet meed of praise; but, alas, how many strive to magnify themselves in the eyes of their fellow men by ways that proclaim that they would use virtue only as a stepping stone to the good graces of those about them, not loving its own precious self. False ambition; vain strife! We should all do our best with the talents bestowed upon us. He who possesseth but few talents and diligently employeth them, is more worthy of praise than he who hath many talents and doth exercise them but in part, even though by that part he accomplisheth more than the other. Yea, I say unto you, one talent, rightly and diligently employed, telleth more for the glory of its possessor than do ten talents for the sluggard. And then again of praise; what profiteth it if the whole world laud and magnify thine acts if they be not acts that thy heavenly father will approve?"

.... "In religion, as in all things else, zeal may be likened unto fire, blind and unknowing of itself. If directed by a true love to God and man, and by well tempered judgment, it will lead to the holiest accomplishments. But if not so directed, in fierce rage it will but consume and destroy."

.... "Go forth into the fields. And there, away from the angry strife and vain babblings of men, and amid the beautiful exhibitions of God's handiwork, meditate. Meditate upon thine own weakness and dependence; upon the good providence of God, thy duty to thy fellow men and to thine own soul. Meditate aright, and let thy meditations rule thine acts. So shalt thou bring peace to thy soul, chasten thine aspirations, and make thyself of more devout, unselfish spirit. Ah, yes! the balmy air will impart vigor to thy body, and the nobler determination strength to thy soul. Go forth, then, in the gray morn, the silent eve, and amid the glorious works of nature, meditate and enjoy."

. . . . " Christian, beware how thou enterest the boundless wilderness of the law, for therein grow many thorns and briars that plague and damnify. The very air is full of temptation, and few indeed can escape without having his christian garment torn and bedraggled. Just though thy cause may be, desperately uncertain is its end. Yea, one pound, safe in the pocket, is better than three in the law."

. . . . " Examine thine own ways. Dost thou therein find cause to despise thyself? If thou dost, then be assured that others will despise thee. But and if thou wouldest stand well in the eyes of others, take heed that thou doest nothing that seemeth wrong in thine own eyes."

. . . . " What is more unseemly than the pretentious discourse of some even godly men. One saith, I hold the true doctrine, come ye to my faith, or stumble in darkness. But how knoweth he that he is in the true faith? He diligently searcheth the scriptures, perchance; but can he say that his poor, weak mind is sufficient to compass the whole meaning? He treateth the Word as if it were a thing of man's device, and not a thing standing distinct from man and proceeding from the Infinite. And should he not remember that his neighbor, haply as wise and prayerful as himself, hath, by like diligent search, come to a different stand? Ought he not, then, the rather, modestly to say, such or such seemeth to me the true doctrine? But and if he doth not even get his doctrine from his own search, but taketh that of the household of faith in which he was nurtured, he but receiveth it at second hand; and if they that taught him err, where is his remedy? Alas, how often is God's holy word made foolishness by man's interpretation."

Near the southern entrance of the Old Tunnel was the seat of Francis Reddan. What little hair he had was very white. He was also lame, and blind of one eye. As he came in, his broken jaw would work as if he fancied himself delivering an exhortation, though not a sound issued from his lips. But as all had heard of the terrible conflicts that occasioned his infirmities, not a symptom of mirth agitated even the most thoughtless breast.

Mr. Reddan was pious, intelligent, and greatly respected for his unwavering neighborly-kindness. He was a native of England, and born in the neighborhood of the renowned Hampden. Breathing a free air, and associating with unsubdued spirits, he was, while still a mere boy, famous for his stern opposition to every thing that savored of tyranny. At an early age, he suddenly left his father's house, joined the parliamentary army, and soon gained from his discriminating commander such acknowledgments as made him known among the valiant hosts as a brave and trusty youth.

At the battle of Worcester he received his first wound, which was very severe, and was the occasion of that erratic working of the jaw just alluded to. But this grievous experience by no means quenched his ardor for battling in the cause his conscience approved. He continued to render good service to the Commonwealth till his bravery could no longer avail.

After the Restoration, when so many who had been active in the cause of the Commonwealth, emigrated to America, he came hither. He intended to have pitched his tent farther south; and it was a disastrous event that brought him to Lynn. When the vessel in which he came over neared the land, they found themselves off the entrance of Massachusetts Bay. A violent storm arose, and it soon seemed as if the emigrant-soldier, after having escaped so many perils by land, was at once to be destroyed by a peril of the sea. The vessel was driven furiously into and about the Bay, and finally stranded on Lynn Beach, which has since become extensively known as the scene of several of the most terrible shipwrecks that ever took place on the Atlantic coast.

It was a dark and dreadful night of storm when the vessel was wrecked. The sea raged with such fury, and the cold was so intense, that it is wonderful any soul on board survived. Only two, however, were lost. The others, by various means, reached the land, and were well cared for by the townsfolk. The bodies of the two who were drowned, were recovered, and buried from the meeting house, with all the solemnities that could characterize the last rites over dear friends.

Mr. Reddan was so much injured as to be compelled to remain housed for several weeks. And the kindness he experienced from those on whose hospitality he had been thus suddenly thrown, made such a favorable impression on him that immediately on his recovery he announced his determination to remain here.

He married Anne Johnson, and settled on a small farm, near Saugus river.

While Goff and Whalley, the regicides, were in the vicinity of Boston, Mr. Reddan is supposed to have rendered them essential service by warning of approaching danger. And at the time Goff so mysteriously appeared in Lynn, as related in our sketch of Oliver Purchis, he had been on the alert, for several days. It is, moreover, believed that the midnight flight of the regicide from the house of Mr. Purchis was to the house of Mr. Reddan.

The great King Philip war again aroused the martial spirit of Mr. Reddan. And we find him in the field bearing himself with the same bravery and experiencing the same rough fortune that characterized his earlier soldiership. He was at the massacre of Bloody Brook, in Deerfield, in September, 1675, having joined Lathrop's command. And he was one of the very few who escaped the disastrous Indian ambuscade.

After fighting heroically, for some time, Mr. Reddan was borne down and trodden into the bog. Presently a ferocious enemy discovered him in his helpless condition, and proceeded to raise his head on a stump in preparation for the scalping-knife. The implement had already been drawn across the forehead, when a youthful fellow-soldier, perceiving his peril, sent a ball through the heart of the savage, who fell head foremost into a muddy pool.

Thus rescued, Mr. Reddan remained a while, gathering strength, till able to crawl to a place of safety. And before many days he found means to reach his home. But he was not restored sufficiently to take the field again during that war.

Let us now take a look into the Old Tunnel. It is a pleasant Sunday afternoon, a year or two after the erection of the honored edifice. There sits the worthy Mr. Reddan, with head erect, by no means ashamed of the scars that disfigure his countenance, his loose jaw laboring in the most grotesque manner, as his wandering thoughts are called in, for the duties of the sacred place.

And nestling close by his side, is his beloved and really beautiful daughter Cora. She is dressed in a pretty gown of English stuff, rather gaily trimmed, with a silk sash, knotted at the side. The dress fits her graceful person most charmingly, and altogether she presents a picture of rare loveliness. There she sits, with a quiet air, her serene blue eyes seldom roving from the godly teacher in the pulpit, excepting at short intervals to scan the scarred countenance of her revered parent. And at those affecting intervals such as sit near may often observe a tear course down her fair cheek, for she knows of what perilous events those scars are mementos.

Mr. Reddan loved his fair Cora with the ardor of a widowed heart, for her mother had been taken away years before, and he seemed to have little left beside her, for the affections of his declining years to cling around. And she was worthy of his love. They were always at meeting together, and in their long walks home, through the quiet green lanes, he endeavored to impress most fully upon her susceptible mind the great truths to which they had been listening. His long months of mourning had softened his heart and opened new channels of reflection. And he now felt the warmest sympathies and recognized the loftiest duties of the Christian. He seemed to be enjoying a pleasant rest, after his many years of toil and danger. His means were now ample for his moderate wants, and with a thankful heart he looked upon himself as highly blessed. Enjoying, also, the esteem of his neighbors, and the consciousness of having performed many worthy deeds, might he not feel at ease?

But the scenes of life are constantly changing; and no sooner does one begin to congratulate himself on the prospect of repose than he is again upon the wing. The beautiful Cora, on a certain evening had spent an hour, in the best room, in company with her neighbor Richard Lewis. This meeting was not unknown to her father, for from him she concealed nothing. And who could stand higher in his regard than Mr. Lewis? for it was his quick sight and ready arm that saved him from the ruthless scalping-knife on the bloody day at Deerfield.

Presently Richard sought Mr. Reddan, and asked him in. Cora sat quietly at her knitting work, as he entered. Yet, a close observer might have discovered that she breathed quicker, and that her cheeks were more glowing than usual. But Richard had faced too many perils to lose his self-possession on such an occasion, and with an unfaltering voice asked the good father if Cora might be his bride.

"I knew full well," he replied, with emotion, "that it would come to this at last. Well, well, Richard, she may be thine. I would not obstruct the things that be ordained, though nature will have it that I had far rather the scalping-knife should have done its deadly work than lose this sunbeam from my house."

He then took their hands and affectionately pressed them together in his own, while his tears fell fast. Then he silently withdrew. And Richard and Cora stood some moments, as it were transfixed by their emotions, before they were enfolded in each other's arms.

The betrothment of Cora and Richard had a strange effect on Mr. Reddan. The whole current of his mind seemed to change, and he began to lose all interest in the affairs of life. Even the religious meeting had less and less attraction for him. His former serenity was changed for a settled moodiness. And thus he continued, till, upon a fair autumn day, he was found dead in the woods, with his hand still grasping the gun which had evidently been the instrument of his death. He was out hunting, and his death may have been the result of accident. But there were those who believed he had taken his own life. It is a harrowing thought. But if it were so, how few can comprehend the intensity of the affection he had for Cora; an affection which took captive reason itself and left him the blind victim of a fearful impulse.

One of the strangest scenes that ever happened at the Old Tunnel took place on a dark evening in that year so pregnant of mysteries, 1692. It was a very uncomfortable time for those abroad. A high wind came down with a triumphant whistle from the northeast, the sleet was cutting, and the cold benumbing. Nevertheless, there was a numerous gathering, from all the region round about. They had assembled to hear the famous Cotton Mather discourse on the doings of the invisible tormentors who were then beginning their lively warfare against God's holy people.

All sorts of vehicles were standing in the lee of the building, and the poor horses snorted and shook their heads, as if remonstrating against the cruelty of their masters in leaving them thus exposed. And upon the windward side, the gusts drove the hail and big drops against the windows, with a fury that indicated a determination to try the strength of the diminutive diamond panes, or even, perhaps, to compass the greater mischief of carrying away the little belfry, and thus leaving the edifice a noseless Tunnel.

Within the sanctuary, the tallow candles flared, as the blast swept over them, and spitefully dispensed their unctious droppings in a manner indicating that in that place at least there was no respect for persons; and in their fitful radiance those solemn countenances looked almost ghost-like.

But notwithstanding the divers petty annoyances, those good people listened eagerly to the learned harangue of that acknowledged leader in the bravest assaults on the kingdom of Satan.

The bold speaker had gone on triumphantly for some time, and succeeded in working up the fears as well as the pious zeal of his auditors to a wonderful pitch, when, all of a sudden, as the gust blew open the eastern door, their ears were assailed by an accumulation of such unearthly sounds as they never heard before; and they absolutely started from their seats. It seemed as if a prodigious band, composed of all the high-keyed instruments that had been invented since the world began, had begun to play, without any regard to tune or time. The conclusion that a legion of remorseless devils had arrived, was adopted with one accord, and those worthies who would have gone forth unflinchingly to meet any earthly foe, stood trembling with fright. And was there not reason for their apprehensions — reason in the facts that he who was then addressing them was the most determined foe of all the dark powers, and that now, probably, a desperate attempt was to be made to extinguish him? The horses neighed and twitched at their bridles, and a straying bull ran bellowing down the street as if the prime minister of evil himself were in pursuit.

The invaders, whoever they were, seemed approaching; and after the first paroxysm of terror was over, a general rush was made to escape from the house, no one appearing to dream that within those sacred walls they were most safe from all assailants from the nether world. Pell-mell they rushed from the doors; and even the windows had to yield to the eagerness of some. In an astonishingly short space the house was cleared. And it seemed as if some flew into the air and others sank into the earth, so quickly was the whole neighborhood evacuated. And there stood the Old Tunnel, solitary and alone, the winds whistling among the rafters and sporting with the feeble tallow-dips like cats playing with expiring mice. But the unearthly noises continued to distract the air. And in a short time another terror was added. Guns were heard, in quick succession. True, this gave the thing a little more of a natural and christian aspect; but when once safely housed, few thought of venturing abroad till morning should reveal the position of affairs.

The next day surely did bring a revelation; and a rather comical one it was. It came through Ephraim Rand and Obed Mansfield, two of the most alert sportsmen in the place. They had a splendid lot of wild geese for sale. And the solution of the mystery made some of the good people hang their heads as low, in shame, as did the Windham folk on the occasion of the frog invasion.

The solution was simply this: An immense flock of wild geese had been overtaken by the sleety storm, which so obstructed their flight that they did not arrive here at the seashore till night had set in. The ice had so accumulated upon their wings that they saw the hazard of putting out over the sea. Being forced to alight, they seemed to think it as well to have a jolly time, and so began with exercising their voices. They had taken possession of a field in the vicinity of the meeting house, and while adjusting their plans for the night seemed to grow more and more excited. Their unearthly trumpetings soon caught the practiced ears of Ephraim and Obed, who, seizing their guns, speedily made merchandize of a goodly number.

We gather the following account of a most extraordinary occurrence, alleged to have taken place at the Old Tunnel, on a Sunday afternoon, in June, 1687, from some notes on the blank leaves of a manuscript sermon.

There was a very promising and deeply pious young man in the town, named Daniel Graves. He was much respected, in particular, for the good influence he exercised over the young men with whom he associated. His death took place in a very sudden and awful manner, in the early part of the month just named. Being at work in his father's field, when a violent shower came up, he sought shelter under a tree. But hardly had he reached the shelter when a terrific electrical discharge occurred, shattering the tree, and killing him instantly. This startling dispensation was the occasion of the preaching of the sermon from the blank leaves of which our account is derived. We presume the discourse was by Mr. Shepard, though that fact does not distinctly appear. The funeral took place on a Friday, and on the following Sunday a very large concourse gathered to hear the sermon. And all felt so great an interest in the deceased, and his mourning parents, for he was an only child, that they attended on the services with softened hearts, and minds open to receive the good influences that might arise from a recounting of his virtues.

A long, solemn prayer had been made, the Scriptures read, and the last couplet of the hymn lined off. Then, just as the minister was making ready to rise from the bench in the pulpit, to name his text, before the astonished gaze of the whole congregation, the deceased young man appeared, standing erect in the pulpit. With a pale and serious countenance he carefully surveyed the assembly. Then he took the Bible, opened it, and placed the mark against a particular text.. Having done this, he again cast his eyes over the congregation, till he met the gaze of a blooming little girl of some twelve summers, the daughter of a neighboring farmer. It was her gentle hand that laid the flowers on his coffin, on the day of his burial, and her gentle heart that almost broke when she saw the sods placed upon his grave. Bestowing an earnest and tender look upon her he slowly raised his hand, and in the act of beckoning, vanished away.

The choir were paralized, and could not finish their strain. The young girl fainted, and others present were greatly moved. The minister, however, and one or two others, appear to have seen nothing of the apparition. And having seen nothing, the godly man was so amazed at the proceedings that he called loudly upon old Deacon Newhall, for an explanation. Many voices volunteered to give the desired information. And when it was given, he seemed at first inclined to doubt the good faith of their senses. But before such a cloud of witnesses, his incredulity gave way, and was succeeded by an astonishment that quite equalled theirs.

After a few minutes of silence, they became sufficiently calm to allow of the services being proceeded with. On turning to the Bible, the minister found the mark at the very passage which he had chosen for his text, though he felt certain that he had not opened the book. It will not be wondered at that this occurrence produced a profound sensation. Various explanatory theories were proposed; but we do not learn that any particular one was fixed upon, in the popular mind, as sufficient. Of course, a great portion of the people could never be persuaded that it was not a genuine ultramundane appearance; an appearance full as inexplicable as that of the phantom ship at New Haven, which had created such a sensation throughout New England, many years before. And to the savans of this day, who so well understand the mysteries of atmospheric refraction, we imagine, it will furnish a much more inexplicable phenomenon. It is not in our power to furnish any explanation that would be more satisfactory than what would occur to the intelligent reader. We simply give what comes to us as fact, and cannot hold ourselves responsible for what conclusions it may lead to.

But this narration would be incomplete did we omit to add a few words regarding the little maiden to whom we have already briefly alluded. She was, in very early childhood, much in the habit of running across the field to the house of Mr. Graves, where she was always welcome, to amuse herself in the garden or within doors. Daniel would meet her with a smile, and was ever ready to aid her in the pursuit of happiness, even through her own childish ways. But, above all, as soon as her opening mind had gathered sufficient strength, he loved to instill into it the most useful instruction. Often would he sit by her, on the green sward, and in a familiar way, without catechism or story book, lead her to a lively contemplation of the beautiful and pure. She became tenderly attached to him; would often run to take his hand on the way to meeting; and never seemed so happy as when nestling close beside him in the sanctuary. She was a rare little maid; possessing extraordinary quickness of perception, and a fascination of manner, quite remarkable.

We shall not attempt to describe, in detail, the effect of the spectral appearance upon her. The impression was deep, but not unpleasant. She loved to talk about it, and never seemed to doubt that the beckoning was intended to apprise her of an early death. But it created no fear; seeming only to inspire her with more and more zeal to profit by the good instruction she had received from the departed dear one. She often declared to her friends, with an assurance solemn and affecting, that she should soon follow him to a better land. And so it turned out. When the brown leaves of autumn began to fall, she was laid in her little churchyard bed, beside her beloved friend.

Is it not pleasant and profitable to linger in these sacred precincts — to listen to the earnest voice and stately periods of the godly preacher — to scan the grave countenances of the old, the bright and healthful faces of the young — to hearken to the prolonged strains of sacred song? But in this last named portion of the service, to be sure, there was a little awkwardness, arising from the necessity of lining off the words, in couplets. Yet the music was performed by voices as sweet as are ever now heard in any of the multitude of pretentious "churches" that cluster around the consecrated site on which for so many years the Old Tunnel stood, in solitary grandeur; and performed, too, in as exact concord and as perfect time. What if the unsanctified music of the organ never echoed within those walls? The worshipers there believed it just as well to employ their own voices in uttering praise as to use machinery. What if the fanciful tunes of modern days did not greet their ears? They were content to march sedately along their heavenward way, to strains as measured as the ocean swell, instead of hopping and skipping along under the enchantments of ebon minstrelsy.

We have a sort of fugitive hope that we may, at some future time, again visit this endeared shrine. And perhaps we may be left to resume the pen and bring before the reader certain instructive scenes and characters pertaining to later times. What a pregnant history is embodied in the period stretching on from 1700 to 1800, and thence for another quarter of a century, to the time when the favored spot which had so long known the motherly structure, began to know it no more? But we would by no means be understood as promulgating a determination to inflict on the innocent and unsuspicious community another volume, as such an inconsiderate course might induce some compassionate friend to try the restraining power of bonds. Good intentions, it is true, may mitigate the gravity of an offence. But it is difficult to overlook some follies.

And we must withdraw from those hallowed courts wherein so many devout souls were strengthened and sustained by the spiritual bread and wine; those hallowed courts wherein, for generation after generation, gathered maturity as manly and true, youth as beautiful and pure, as ever bowed down in the most gorgeous temple on earth.

And where are all those who went up thither during the period of which we speak? The old, have for scores of years lain beneath the sod. The young men and maidens, loved, wedded, became parents, grew gray, and departed in the great procession. The infants, who irreverently screamed as the baptismal water was sprinkled upon them, also became old men and women and passed away. The consecrated structure itself became hoary with age, shattered and unfashionable, and long since disappeared.

We have said that the Old Tunnel was, for generations, the gathering place of the most unalloyed of puritanical stamp. And we need not repeat that it is with unfeigned diffidence that we speak of their characteristics and opinions and of the position they chose to occupy.

It is difficult for a writer to treat to any extent of the Old Settlers without sometimes appearing to be inconsistent with himself. The difficulty is in the subject. There is so much to praise, and intimately connected with it so much of at least a questionable character, that the reader cannot be expected at all times fully to distinguish the stand point from which a given view may have been taken.

All know how easy it is to find fault, and how prone most of us are to magnify the failings rather than the virtues of others. Indeed, there seems to be much less capacity required in distinguishing evil than good. And where we find twenty who can at once discern every blemish in another, we do not find three who can as readily perceive the good points. A readiness to judge of others does not involve a presumption of superiority, as one may be vastly inferior to another and yet entertain a very just conception of him. And besides, every man has some point in which he is superior to other men.

In speaking of the early settlers, no one will deny that they possessed characteristics as cold and cheerless as the northeast wind that howled over their granite hills. But they also possessed characteristics bright and beautiful as the sunshine upon the blooming hills. The very earliest of the Puritan settlers in New England, with exceptions, were more liberal in their views than those of the succeeding generation. The first, were reared in England, many of them in the bosom of the established church, and by association with minds of different orders and discipline, naturally had many of their sterner points polished down; while those born and educated here, had little opportunity for circulating with those of other views, and naturally inclined tenaciously to their training.

It was an anomalous age that gave birth to the colonization of New England. The history of the world presents no other point like it. The elements which ultimately formed into those systems of polity which in our day shed such lustre upon the name of England, upon our own nation, upon every community of the same lineage, were still in their incipient stage of action, though long before had the premonitory pulsations been felt. The weighty pall of ignorance, superstition and servility, which had spread over the island realm from the early feudal days, had become gradually illuminated by the progress of a reformed religion and the gushing out of a flood of light through the art of printing. The popular masses were not now identified with the clods of the earth; the lordly path was not hedged with bowed vassals. A more commanding but still not clearly defined conception of individual worth and responsibility, of true liberty, was acting like leaven and working the mass into that state where some master hand could mold it to the loftiest purposes.

But no age is without some traits of greatness and goodness, for man at no time and in no place is entirely devoid of the sacred principles on which they rest. There was greatness in the feudal times. Some leading principles that marked the castellated grandeur of that period have come down like stalking giants to us, leaving their footprints on every intervening age, and commanding the reverence of the wise and good in the most refined period that the world has seen.

The Elizabethan was an age in travail with great events, and itself one of undefinable greatness; an age of extremes; as it were, of noonday and midnight; with no softening of dawn or twilight. There was a keen perception of the rights of man, of the value of the human soul; and a vigorous determination to trample on those rights, to enslave that soul. It was an age of bigotry and blood; of high conception and chivalric deed. It was the age in which Puritanism began its work.

No mirror, as we have before remarked, can more faithfully delineate the character of a people than their laws. Laws are the offspring of circumstances, and through them the genius, spirit and condition of a nation are manifested. And many of the lofty principles recognised in the jurisprudence of that age will hold sway so long as law is required to regulate the conduct of men. Take them from our own worthily extolled web of justice, and some of the brightest threads will be gone.

The swaddling-clothes of Puritanism were of black. The fiery eyeballs of persecution glared upon the infant's smileless countenance. And pitfalls and sharp rocks were in the path of the tottering feet. The reformers were at first sneeringly called Puritans, because they were striving to purify the English church of certain rites and dogmas, unscriptural, as they to them appeared, which were of papal parentage and which Elizabeth had retained probably from the servile desire to avoid a rancorous opposition from the many powerful Catholics still in her dominions. The bosom of the church soon became too thorny a pillow for their repose; for whatever sins that church may have to repent of, the petting of recreant children is surely not one of them.

Reforms are usually better than reformers; and if we could only have the former without the latter the world would be all the better for it. Reformers are apt to press hotly and uncompromisingly towards an end, regardless of the damage that may be done collaterally. The Puritans afford no exception; at least in marked instances. They adhered to their system, rough-hewn and forbidding in many of its features, with a tenacity strangely unyielding and a zeal not always generous, not always enlightened or discreet. Nor were they backward, as opportunity offered, in carrying the war into the enemy's territory. Their influence began to be felt, their inroads to be feared. Theories new and of overwhelming moment began to agitate the non-hereditary ranks. And the ruling powers, clerical and lay, had certain fearful glimpses forward to a time when the swelling surges might in one general destruction involve the great ecclesiastic and regal fabrics.

Sincerity and zeal are not proof of justice and truth, though often worthy of respect. Martyrdom itself is not evidence of merit in the cause for which it is suffered. But whatever may be our views, or whatever may have been theirs, on the great matter of christian truth and man's duty, we cannot recur to the trials and sacrifices, the perseverance and strong faith of the New England fathers, without sentiments of high respect, of reverence, of awe. And some examples of such exalted character present themselves, as make us proud to tread the earth they trod.

Behold the godly Eliot. See him take his dark way into the wilderness, to seek out and gather together the straying red men that he may break to them the bread of life. For many days together we see him on his lonely way among the snows of winter, hungry and chilled, at night seeking the shelter of some hollow tree or overhanging rock, and wringing the water from his garments lest through the cold, dark hours they freeze upon his limbs. And when the inhospitable chiefs bid him quit their domains, he boldly declares to them that he is on his Master's business,— a Master who is mightier than they — and will not desist. I will not leave you, he says; I will pray for you; I will preach to you; I will convert you. He kept his word. He suffered, wept and wrestled for them. He gave them the word of life in their own tongue. He persevered, and won their respect, their confidence and love. And there rose up a brawny phalanx, the breath of whose grateful praise will play upon his brow in the upper Paradise, sweetly as their own beloved south wind plays upon the weary hunter's brow.

Who does not follow with reverential steps the course of Roger Williams, whose history embodies such a commentary on the contrarieties of puritan character. See him take his devious way into the country of the Narragansetts, beyond the colonial jurisdiction, banished from those still dear companions whose hearts he had often cheered in their labors and trials; from those firesides where childhood had rejoiced in his smiles, where age had been made glad by his heavenly love and sympathy. Banished — by whom, and for what? By his own compeers, by those with whom and for whom he had labored and suffered, because, conscience-urged, he had disseminated views of God's truth and man's duty, lofty indeed, but differing from theirs. And see the great work that he performed in the savage country to which he bent his steps. From the little band that followed, and the awe-struck natives, he formed a church. And God's praise never ascended in more acceptable strains than were thence borne upward by the wintry wind. And then was reared in that inhospitable wilderness, a political fabric, based on far broader conceptions of human liberty and right, than had vivified other portions of this wakening land.

Who, without a thrill, can contemplate the character and course of Hugh Peters — a character and course full of incongruities, yet noble and commanding. See him, in youthful vigor, moving by his fervid eloquence audiences of thousands of the denizens of London;

then stealthily following the fleeing pilgrims to Holland, cheering them by his counsels, aiding them by his means.

Pass over a brief space, and behold him on the margin of Wenham Pond, addressing the assembled children of the shadowy land. There stands he in the full strength of manhood, upon the forest studded declivity, the beautiful lake stretching out before him, rejoicing in the summer sunlight, and bearing upon its unruffled bosom the fairy-like Indian barks. The gray old oak and flaunting pine lave their roots in the renovating waters, and the unscared birds gambol among the foliage. And who are they, surrounding the pale brother from the far-off land of the rising sun, and listening to his story of wonders. They are a band of strayed brothers. The strong armed forest father is there; the young hunter from the chase; the warrior from the battle ground. And there the white eagle plume waves over the dusky brow of the forest maid.

And again, behold him in the little rustic sanctuary of the Third Plantation, by his tempestuous eloquence arousing the hearts of the desponding settlers.

See him again in Old England, pleading with zeal ardent and unquenchable for the rights of the suffering colonists and making his influence felt at the very heart of the nation. Behold him a master spirit riding on the stormy waves of the Commonwealth, exemplifying again, in his own course, some of the contrarieties of the age; taking the field with the parliamentary hosts; praying ardently and fighting valiantly under the same banner. "Verily," says Cromwell, "I think he that prays best will fight best." An expressive commentary on the spirit of the age.

Where shall we look again for him? On the sledge, seated on his own coffin, in the mournful procession, approaching the fatal block, to meet his destiny as a regicide; and to meet it, too, with the resignation and nerve of exalted christian heroism.

And, lastly, see his blood-smeared and ghastly head with sightless eyes yawning from a parapet of London Bridge, the object of scorn and indignity to the rude multitude.

The singularly dark views of human nature taken by many of the old clergy were perhaps to some extent engendered by the spirit of the times and the cloudy circumstances by which they were so frequently surrounded. Often did they seem to labor to render the Christian's path thorny, his race melancholy. Their minds were deeply exercised on the great and glorious truths of God's word, but the dark side was kept in view. They appeared not to realise that with justice and dread, God himself had mingled mercy and love. They pondered on the terrors and pains of hell, rather than the joys and bliss of heaven. The rocky cliffs that frowned above the surges that lashed these wild shores, and the hills that towered above the shadowy plains, were so many Sinais, from which were constantly issuing the lightnings of Jehovah's wrath, the thunders of his law. In cold and gloomy strains their hallelujahs reverberated among the dim vales, and their austere bearing and harsh speech were fitted rather to chill than cheer the warm of heart.

Yet it was not so with all. There were many free souls glowing in the warm atmosphere of the brighter promises; joyous souls, quickened by the sweet inspirations of mercy and love; true christian souls, shedding all around the most blessed influences of our holy faith.

There are many still backward in awarding the praise justly due to the early settlers. They look at isolated facts and blemishes, and from them argue that no real or at least intended good could have proceeded from such people. And when the undeniable and substantial blessings are forced into recognition, they turn to discover their origin elsewhere.

Many enlightened minds, who have little sympathy with the dark and cold features of the old theology, believing that something brighter and more heart-attracting would have accomplished still more, are yet ready to do reverence to those worthy fathers for the great benefits that they undeniably did secure for all generations that were to succeed them on this soil.

The early settlers so intimately blended the secular with the ecclesiastical character, that we are, without doubt, constantly liable to mistake the motive or principle from which this or that result flowed. A community may possess vast political sagacity and yet cling to a very poor religious faith; or it may possess the loftiest conceptions of christian truth, and yet act upon false principles of worldly wisdom. And when they are endowed in a large measure with both worldly wisdom and christian grace, it is not easy to analyze their economy.

This intermingling of the secular with the ecclesiastical is shown in the fact to which we have before alluded, that no one was eligible to office unless he were a regular church member. This may be viewed by some as savoring of the darkness from which they had professedly just fled. All history testifies that in a union of church and state, pure religion is most liable to suffer. And hence any tendency to such union is worthy of being guarded against. In this enlightened age and country, however, there is probably little real danger, though the cry of wolf must needs at all times be more or less distinctly heard. But the object of the requisition alluded to admits of more than one explanation. Perhaps they could devise no better way by which to keep the churches full. And we cannot divest ourselves of the conviction that if at this day it should be determined that none but church members could be office holders, there would be such a rush into the sacred folds as no revival since the great day of Pentecost has produced.

www.ingramcontent.com/pod-product-compliance
Lightning Source LLC
Chambersburg PA
CBHW030422300426
44112CB00009B/808